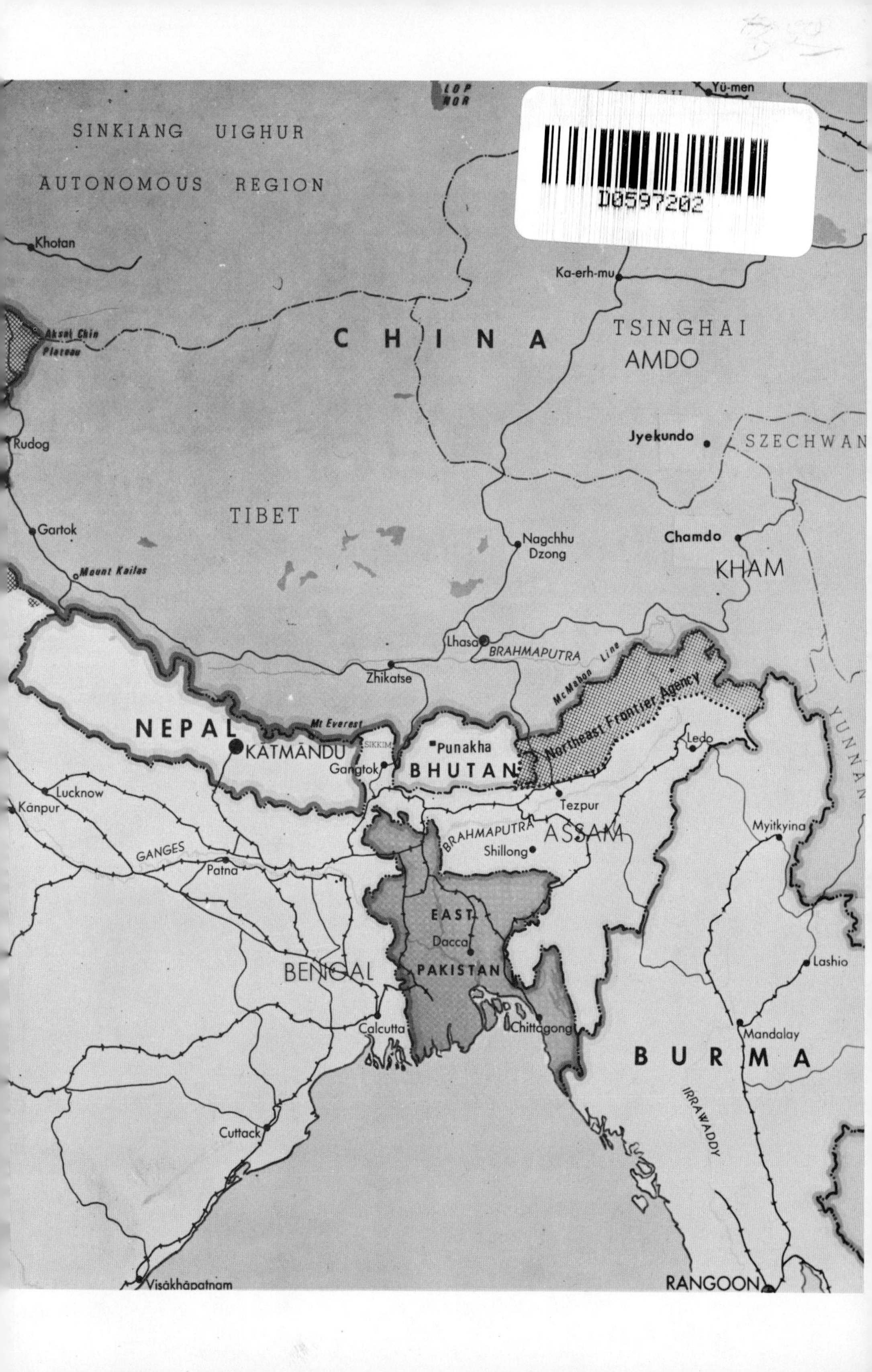

SINKIANG UIGHUR
AUTONOMOUS REGION
LOP NOR
Yü-men
Khotan
Aksai Chin Plateau
CHINA
TSINGHAI
AMDO
Ka-erh-mu
Rudog
Jyekundo
SZECHWAN
TIBET
Gartok
Mount Kailas
Nagchhu Dzong
Chamdo
KHAM
Lhasa
BRAHMAPUTRA
McMahon Line
Zhikatse
Northeast Frontier Agency
Mt Everest
NEPAL
KĀTMĀNDU
SIKKIM
Gangtok
Punakha
BHUTAN
Ledo
YUNNAN
Lucknow
Kānpur
Tezpur
BRAHMAPUTRA
ASSAM
Shillong
Myitkyina
GANGES
Patna
EAST
Dacca
PAKISTAN
BENGAL
Lashio
Calcutta
Chittagong
Mandalay
BURMA
IRRAWADDY
Cuttack
Visākhāpatnam
RANGOON

A HISTORY OF SINO-INDIAN RELATIONS

A HISTORY OF SINO-INDIAN RELATIONS

HOSTILE CO-EXISTENCE

John Rowland

pseudoname for John Waller
deputy CIA station chief, New Delhi: 1955–57,
Station chief, 1968 —
Kenneth Conboy, CIA's Secret War in Tibet, p. 234.

D. VAN NOSTRAND COMPANY, INC.
Princeton, New Jersey
Toronto *London*

1967

Van Nostrand Regional Offices: *New York, Chicago, San Francisco*

D. Van Nostrand Company, Ltd., *London*

D. Van Nostrand Company (Canada), Ltd., *Toronto*

Published simultaneously in Canada by
D. Van Nostrand Company (Canada), Ltd.

Library of Congress Catalog Card No. 66-29857

PRINTED IN THE UNITED STATES OF AMERICA

FOR BARBARA

CONTENTS

	INTRODUCTION	ix
1	*Manchus and Mongols*	1
2	*Back Door to China*	12
3	*The Great Game*	25
4	*McMahon Draws a Line*	41
5	*The Year of the Iron Tiger*	51
6	*Not a Needle or Thread*	62
7	*Enter Panch Sheela*	76
8	*The Bandung Spirit*	91
9	*Cold War Comes to India*	104
10	*Exit Panch Sheela*	117
11	*Cold War at the Conference Table*	133
12	*Nepal: India's Lost Buffer*	144
13	*The Pamir Knot: Crossroad of Crises*	156
14	*A Time of Reckoning*	166
15	*Marx, Malthus and the Middle Kingdom*	174
16	*Pakistan: India's Troublesome Flank*	188
17	*Road to Reality*	207
	NOTES	219
	BIBLIOGRAPHY	231
	INDEX	239

INTRODUCTION

There are few places more critical to peace yet less well known than the Himalayan boundary regions which separate India from Communist China. The tensions which keep these two countries on the edge of conflict are as dangerous as they are inevitable, not only because they bear directly on the future direction of Asia but because they are part of the potentially even more significant problem of Chinese-Soviet rivalry. Chinese actions toward India provide a critical index of the extent to which Peking is willing to risk nuclear war in its drive to extend Chinese power in order to fulfill an imagined destiny. For this reason the history of hostile co-existence which underlies Sino-Indian relations is worth exposing to view.

Implicit in the long record of India-China contact are geopolitical reasons for Communist China's present hostility toward India. Unfortunately, however, some of the realities of border policy were lost sight of by independent India's political philosophers, who sought new formulas more consistent with their urgent desire for world peace and Asian solidarity. China's true intentions and the reasons behind them could not, therefore, become fully recognized until the Tibetan revolt in 1959, when the flight to India of the Dalai Lama provoked Peking to come out from behind its façade of friendship and reveal an openly threatening attitude toward its southern neighbor.

If Red China's intentions and motivations were not at first clear, India can blame Peking for its added deceit in camouflaging them with peaceful pretension. India naturally wanted to believe that China was sincere in subscribing to Nehru's *Panch Sheela*, the five principles of peaceful co-existence. India also wanted to believe that its 1954 pact with China on the status of Tibet, which established these principles, was sufficient statement of policy toward China. Nehru could not rely on physical containment; this had been possible for Britain but was impossible for militarily weak, independent India. Nor could Nehru depend on collective defense arrangements without doing violence to the concept of non-alignment which he symbolized. With the options thus limited, India followed a policy of moral containment until Peking's own actions revealed this policy's inadequacy. Through events and necessity there evolved a new policy of containment which involved both Soviet and Western aid and a modified stand on non-alignment as required in the interests of national defense. Whether this policy will work in the long run depends on many factors—not least of which is the ability of India and Pakistan to resolve their festering dispute over Kashmir, or the continuing strong United States and Soviet stake in the safety of India.

Any case study of Chinese aggression must take into consideration certain fundamental drives and constants which have characterized China's history and have led inexorably to its present position. India-China relations emerge as a geopolitical rondo, the basic theme of which is the inevitability of conflict at points where the countries come into contact. It is for this reason that Tibet and the Himalayan border region—from Assam to the Pamirs—are important today.

Tibet may not be the sacred center of the universe which the early Aryan tribes of India believed it to be, but it is the political junction of Asia's three largest land powers—China, India, and the Soviet Union. It is also Asia's ideological watershed dividing democratic South Asia from totalitarian China. The Tibetan plateau has traditionally served as a no-man's-land between antagonists, while the great Himalayan range has served as a rampart to guard India's approaches. Tibet is thus the stage on which the historical drama of China-India relations has been enacted.

The drama begins to an overture of Buddhist scriptures hailing the eightfold path of right beliefs and serving as siren song to the Chinese far beyond. Lord Buddha's teachings—an appropriate forerunner of Nehru's fivefold doctrine of *Panch Sheela*—filtered through the Himalayan passes to blend with a primitive Tibetan cult of magic to become Lamaism. However much this philosophy was premised on peace, its sectarianism and corruption led to serious internal political unrest which made Tibet vulnerable to predatory moves of its Mongol and Chinese neighbors. In one early effort to impose peaceful co-existence on Tibet, China's armies in the eighth century erected a stone pillar in the center of Lhasa on which was inscribed an agreement to hold as sacred "the happiness of neighbors" and to avoid "fighting as between enemies." This monument still stands to mock the subjugated Tibetans.

Against a backdrop of local politico-religious intrigues the first act of China-India relations was climaxed by the invasion of Lhasa by Chinese Emperor K'ang Hsi in 1720. Successive Mongol invasions of Tibet had made China aware of the vulnerability of its borderlands. Provoked by fear that Mongol control of Lamaism's See would be the first step toward the unification of the Mongols, the Manchu Emperor installed in the Potala a puppet claimant to the throne of the Seventh Dalai Lama, establishing at the same time China's first significant claim to Tibet.

Act Two: Enter India! Plans of the British East India Company to explore Tibet as a commercial market and find an open back door to China died with the Third Panchen Lama at the court of the Manchus. Whether British Governor Hastings' would-be ally, the Panchen, died of smallpox or was murdered by his Chinese hosts to prevent the British from using him to get a foothold in Tibet is not clear. But his death permitted China to strengthen its position in Lhasa. British ambitions in Tibet were thwarted for another century.

Act Three: Enter Russia! Imperial Russian expansion eastward inevitably collided with Manchu expansion westward and provoked boundary tensions which still affect Sino-Soviet relations. While a stronger Russia was able to impose its will by a series of treaties in the nineteenth century, the Chinese people's concept of greater China has never been abandoned, and today the Russian treaties are attacked by Peking as the products of imperial aggression. Agents of the Czar also probed southward into the Pamirs, where they engaged the British in a game of imperial intrigue during the last part of the nineteenth century. By 1904 suspected Russian influence over the Dalai Lama prompted the British to invade Lhasa and in this way avoid what Lord Curzon described as an eventual "Russian Dominion of Asia." Great Britain was, however, unwilling to overextend itself in Tibet and for more far-ranging reasons of policy found a basis for compromise with the Czar. By an agreement signed in 1907 both rivals agreed to a neutral buffer belt separating the two empires, which extended from Persia to Tibet.

The vast and inhospitable Tibetan plateau provided an ideal buffer for India's northern frontier. This was reinforced by an inner line of defense in the form of a belt of Himalayan dependencies flanked by separately administered security zones. Russia, too, saw Tibet as an essential buffer with which to protect the outer reaches of its empire, and Sinkiang, on Tibet's northern border, as a potential inner line of defense corresponding to Britain's Himalayan barrier. The formula of Chinese suzerainty but not sovereignty in Tibet suited the purposes of both England and Russia. It provided a legal Chinese presence and thus avoided the dangers that would result from a vacuum; yet it deprived Peking of any legal excuse to annex Tibet whenever it became strong enough to do so. General Kuropatkin, while Russian Governor of Turkestan, expressed the Russian fears in 1916 when he said, "The future danger of Russia from this empire of 400 million [China] is beyond all doubt." Britain, also farsighted enough to anticipate a resurgent China, pressed for an agreement on Tibet which would define a clear boundary between Tibet and Assam and establish a secondary buffer zone called "Inner Tibet" between Tibet proper and China. But the declining Chinese—ever conscious of their heritage and destiny—refused to ratify such efforts to deprive them of sovereignty over Tibet. The disintegration of the Chinese Empire and the long humiliation of Japanese occupation before and during World War II temporarily eliminated China as a power in Asia. But never did the Chinese lose their fundamental conviction that they would ultimately dominate Asia, nor sign away what they conceived to be their legal basis for domination.

The departure of British power from the subcontinent and the rise of a new China under Communism were the basic factors in a new situation following World War II. As Nehru put it: "We stand at the crest of change, looking at it, and a tremendous drama is unravelling before our eyes. But we are not mere onlookers, we are actors in this drama."

With Nehru playing the lead, Act Four began with the Red Chinese invasion of Tibet in 1950. India's leader was in one way faced with the same problem which faced Britain a half-century earlier: could another power be allowed to control Tibet? Of course, in the first situation Curzon, then Viceroy of India, had the power to eliminate the incipient Russian threat, while Nehru fifty years later did not have the strength to prevent a Chinese military invasion of Tibet, already underway. While *de facto* accommodation thus had to be made with superior force, it was a significant mistake of principle for India to accede formally to China's absorption of

Tibet. Even an enfeebled China had in 1914 refused to ratify Britain's formula for Tibet when the power position was reversed. The real tragedy, however, was that Nehru saw fit to use the 1954 treaty with China on Tibet to enunciate *Panch Sheela*. The Indian Praja Socialist opposition press phrased it well at the time: "We think the Prime Minister need not have gone out of his way to give China a kind of moral certificate in regard to the action in Tibet. . . . we think there should be some way for big nations to acquire friendship and create a 'peace area' without extinguishing the independence of a small nation that might have the misfortune of lying between them." The significance was that while China used its basic ideology, revolutionary Communism, to complement and rationalize its geopolitical need to secure Tibet (Tibetan serfs were "liberated" from "reactionary" landlords), India's new ideology of *Panch Sheela* was at cross-purposes to its historical need to refuse recognition of Chinese sovereignty in Tibet.

Act Five, the present, requires a bewildering change of scenery. Tibet, which has been absorbed by China, no longer exists as a buffer protecting India. Symptomatic of its advancing position, China now covets the south slope of the Himalayas—a logical consequence of its obsession with territorial security. Despite India's dynamic role since independence as a champion of non-alignment, China paranoiacally persists in branding India a "running dog" of Great Britain and the United States and thus sees the Himalayas as a point of confrontation with the West.

Three disputes—those between the Soviet Union and China, India and China, India and Pakistan—become interlocked in the Kashmir-Pamir knot region at the western extremity of the Himalayas. Stretching northward from the trijunction of Kashmir, China and the USSR is the disputed Sinkiang-Soviet border, where Sino-Soviet tensions simmer. In Kashmir itself India and Pakistan face each other uneasily across a cease-fire line after fighting a brief but bloody war in September 1965. A conference sponsored in Tashkent by the USSR in January 1966 brought the two antagonists to reaffirm the cease-fire line established two decades ago by the United Nations but in the process created new tensions between China and the Soviet Union, whose opposing Kashmir positions reflect their conflict on the India-China border issue. A vitally needed military supply road leading from Tibet to Western Sinkiang across the disputed Aksai Chin plateau in northern Ladakh holds the key to China's border dispute with India. Here India and Chinese patrols still snipe at each other as a reminder that more significant hostilities could break out with relatively little provocation. Western-initiated anti-Communist collective defense systems—the Southeast Asia Treaty Organization (SEATO) and the Central Treaty Organization (CENTO)—founder in a morass of political complexities as their linchpin, Pakistan, draws closer to Communist China.

With China's occupation of Tibet and the extension of a military road network southward to the Himalayas, the buffer zone has shifted to the Himalayan border states, where China now competes with India for primacy. But seen from New Delhi this area is no substitute for the Tibetan plateau, whose vast distances and impossible terrain for so long barred the way to India. As seen through Peking's eyes the relationship between India and the Soviet Union is distressingly reminiscent of Britain's co-existence with Russia in Central Asia in 1907. In both cases China was isolated. Moreover, the breakdown of the buffer system places Communist China and the Soviet Union in dangerous proximity along the tension-ridden border of Sinkiang, where subversion and ethnic hostilities characterize the disharmony of these one-time allies.

Reduced to its essentials, this confused matrix of intertwined tensions—all manifestations of conflict bred of proximity—can be blamed on the disappearance of a buffer system no longer possible in a modern world of rapid communications. The basic theme of the rondo reappears. What has changed is the scope and potential consequences of tension in South and Central Asia. The flowering of China's first atomic mushroom on a remote Sinkiang testing range on October 16, 1964 was an event long dreaded by Western, Soviet and uncommitted leaders alike. Operational perfection of Peking's nuclear war machine may possibly generate increasing Chinese bellicosity. Perhaps equally dangerous is China's population explosion, which neither Marxist planning nor renewed efforts toward birth control seems able to prevent. There may be ugly logic in the fact that Red China has made faster progress in the art of annihilating life than in preventing it. Also dangerous is the ideological weaponry implicit in Peking's role as champion of revolution and enemy of peaceful co-existence. Heretical modifications of the gospel according to Marx—enunciated by Khrushchev in February 1956 at the 20th Congress of the Soviet Communist Party—provided China with an opportunity to contest for leadership of international

Communism on the issue of doctrinal fidelity and gave it an issue with which to attract revolutionaries of all kinds. Peking's doctrine was described in September 1965 by Defense Minister Lin Piao as a master strategy to encircle North America and Europe by Africa, Asia and Latin America—the so-called revolutionary rural areas of the world. This is Peking's bid to gain political strength from the colored and underdeveloped peoples of the world who comprise the majority and to exploit their economic frustrations and racial sensitivity. Implicit in this plan is Chinese-inspired unrest and instability in Asia and Africa for decades to come.

To what extent Communist China is prepared to risk major nuclear war in fomenting wars of liberation and violent revolution is a critical question. Certainly China's actions more than its words will give clues to the answer. In its border dispute with India, which reached one climax in 1962 and another in 1965, China has tended to prove doctrine by action. Less obvious indices of China's attitude toward aggression can be found in political and subversive actions in the supposedly irredentist border regions of Ladakh, Nepal, Sikkim, Bhutan and the Northeast Frontier Agency of India, which Peking's propaganda once described as the "five fingers" of the Tibet "palm." Also important is the strong pro-Chinese faction of India's Bengal Communist Party, which represents significant subversion in India's most important province. This penetration of India itself recalls Mao Tse-tung's dictum, "The way to world conquest lies through Havana, Accra and Calcutta."

Future developments in Sino-Indian relations must reveal further indications of China's intentions, and for this reason they must be watched carefully. But while awaiting the developments of the future, it should be helpful to examine the lessons of the past. The curtain of history is raised for the first act in a drama which began a long time ago. The scene is Tibet, where China and India first met and where they have known each other the longest.

CHAPTER 1

MANCHUS AND MONGOLS

The first of the many prophecies was that Tartars of Lower Tartary would become masters of Thibet. Secondly, that the country would be invaded by Tartars of Upper Tartary. Thirdly, that the latter would sack and ruin the land and send all the spoils to their own country. Fourthly, that they would murder many religious Lamas, destroy monasteries and convents, profane temples and commit other horrors. Fifthly, that the King would be killed with his whole family. Sixthly and lastly, that China would attack, defeat the tyrannical usurpers and conquer the Kingdom.

Tibet's book of Lungh-ten, the prophecies of Urgyen

The earliest Aryans believed the world to be a lotus floating on an ocean. A dimly perceived form of Asia was the only world they knew. In the center, touching the heavens, was a magnificent eruption of snowclad peaks encircling like a flower the heart of the blossom which they called Meru. It is this 15,000-foot plateau which in modern times has been known as Tibet.

From Tibet flow the great rivers of Asia like an enormous network of veins. The waters of the Ganges, Brahmaputra, Indus, Salween, Mekong, Yellow and Yangtse all rise in the icy passes of greater Tibet and run for thousands of miles until they escape into the seas. The Tibetan plateau—cradled between the Himalayas to the south, the Karakorum Range to the west and the Kunlun Range to the north—covers an area nearly twice the size of France. The vast wastes and jagged outcroppings form a moonscape of indescribable desolation where Hindu gods, Buddhist saints and assorted demons left over from a more ancient time mingle in the bewildering pantheon of Lamaism.

The Tibetan people believe their progenitors to have been an ogress named Dras-rin-mo and a giant monkey named Hulumandju. Tibetan folklore tells how the virgin ogress became lost in a Himalayan pass close to the border of India. Near the point of despair, she was rescued by the monkey who, "with great demonstrations of joy," wooed her with wild fruits. Ippolito Desideri, an eighteenth-century Jesuit scholar and missionary in Lhasa, wrote delicately that "this strange pair became so friendly that she bore him several sons."[1] Only with time did the race finally evolve as human. This legend of a simian Adam and sinful Eve, set in a Himalayan Garden of Eden, is an ingenious synthesis of Genesis and Darwin.

Thanks to their land's natural ramparts, forbidding deserts and rarified atmosphere, the Tibetan descendants of Dras-rin-mo and Hulumandju have to some extent been spared unwelcome trespassers. The peoples of the several lotus petals have historically found Tibet neither a convenient crossroads for trade nor a viable invasion route through which to attack each other. The world's highest plateau has been a natural barrier or, to use the geopolitical jargon, a "buffer land." In the main it has been a successful buffer insofar as it kept apart the historically antagonistic empires of Tartary, China and India, but this role has been a trying one. Tibet has had to cushion many shocks of aggression, and for varying periods of time—including the present—it has suffered the humiliation of foreign occupation. Yet in the past it has always been able to throw off its conquerors and ultimately reassert its independence because of its hub position. No one neighbor, however covetous, could in the past indefinitely hold Tibet in the face of another neighbor's opposition.

Tibet became a nation in the seventh century through the tribal conquests and diplomacy of Song-tsen Gampo, a remarkable chieftain from Ladakh (now part of Kashmir) who is credited with having introduced many elements of Indian culture. Although he entered into diplomatic negotiations with China in A.D. 634, friendly relations with that neighbor foundered when his request for the T'ang Emperor's daughter, Princess Wen-ch'eng, was rudely denied.[2] History has known no more ardent suitor than Song-tsen Gampo. Under his banner Tibet invaded western China and after seven years of campaigning forced the Emperor to relinquish his daughter.

The Tibetan leader's prize was a woman who was to have nearly as much impact on the land as her husband. She shared honors in the royal household with another wife—a Nepalese princess. This was a surprisingly successful example of marital co-existence. Both wives in fact collaborated in converting their mutual husband to Buddhism. While this philosophy had filtered into Tibet nearly two hundred years earlier, it did not gain significant momentum until Song-tsen's rule. His Chinese queen not only encouraged the importation of Buddhist scriptures from India, but she provided the impetus for the development of a written Tibetan language based on Indian script with which to propagate the faith. She also encouraged the establishment of monasteries where a clergy could be trained.

From her astrological studies the Queen had learned that Tibet was "like a female demon lying on her back"—probably a variation of the story of Tibet's Eve, Dras-rin-mo. For this reason she directed that the monasteries be built astride hilltops, which she imagined to be the demon's arms and legs, so that the ogress could be contained.[3]

Tibet's age of greatness was the ninth century. Under the warrior king, Ti-song De-tsen, it became one of the great powers of Asia. Northern India, Baltistan, Gilgit and Kashgar all fell to Ti-song De-tsen's armies, and even China was forced to pay tribute. Tibetan chronicles define the ninth-century empire as having common borders "with the Chinese King of Astrology, the Indian King of Religion and the Persian King of Wealth."[4]

Ti-song De-tsen's most significant contribution, however, was religious, not military. Recognizing the progressive degeneration of Buddhism in his realm, he set about to purify and invigorate it. He was particularly influenced by an Indian Tantric Buddhist teacher whom he invited to Tibet, Padma Sambhava—or Urgyen, as he was known by Tibetans. The lives and transmigrations of Urgyen as recorded in Tibetan scriptures are closely modeled on the life of Lord Buddha.[5]

According to one account of Urgyen's coming, he imperiously announced upon arrival: "O King of mountains and snow, O nobles of famine and dearth, submit ye all to my power, miserable offspring of wild monkeys." Pointing to heaven he then shouted "Hui!" whereupon "black clouds obscured the sky, thunder resounded in the mountains, vivid flashes of lightning and a fearful tempest broke over the terrified people." The King dismounted and humbled himself before the new Messiah, who was "seated on a magnificent throne."[6]

Actually Urgyen contributed more to Buddhism's corruption than to its purification. Perhaps recognizing the strong addiction of the Tibetans to black magic, he incorporated in his doctrine much of the sorcery of the primitive "Bon" religion which predated Buddhism. It is this blend which has come to be known as Lamaism. He emphasized the union of spiritual and material forces, symbolically representing them as the sexual union of god and goddess. The sexuality of Urgyen's teachings appealed to the Tibetan monks and stimulated a trend of increasing licentiousness within the monasteries of the Urgyenist sect, known popularly as the Red Hat sect.

Urgyen is also remembered as something of an oracle. The Jesuit Desideri, who in 1716 studied Urgyen's scriptures, was astonished by his powers of prophecy. The first prediction which was to prove unerringly accurate warned that Tartar (i.e., Mongol) invaders would conquer Tibet.

The West knew virtually nothing about Tibetan civilization when in 1245 Pope Innocent IV sent Friar John of Plano Carpini as his emissary to the court of the Mongol Kuyuk Khan, who was then considered "the most imminent danger to the Church of God." What Carpini learned about Tibet was for the most part vague and inaccurate. He reported, for example, that the Tibetans "have a most astonishing or rather horrible custom, for when anyone's father is about to give up the ghost, all the relatives meet together and they eat him."[7] In 1253 William of Rubruck, a Franciscan monk, also visited the Mongol court and contended that some of the tribesmen of Tibet were once in the habit of eating their dead parents "so that for piety's sake they should not give their parents any other sepulchre than their bowels."[8]

Marco Polo reported briefly on Tibet, although he only skirted its northern fringes. He described the country as part of the Mongol realm. It is known that Genghiz Khan conquered the high plateau in 1206 and again in 1226–1227. Recognizing the need for a civilizing force in his empire, Genghiz's grandson Kublai Khan turned to Lamaism, becoming a convert in 1270.[9] The Great Khan recognized the political advantages of a religious link with Tibet.

Kublai Khan invited the Head Lama of the large and influential Sakya monastery near Lhasa to his court and later declared him ruler of Tibet. Thus began a dynasty of Sakya priest-kings in Tibet who, in varying degrees, drew support from the Mongols. The relationship was more that of patron-priest than suzerain-vassal in the political sense. Kublai's armies never penetrated deep into Tibet nor was any effort made to administer it. Any suzerainty he assumed was more theoretical than real. In fact, the ecclesiastical influence of the Tibetan Sakya Lamas in Mongolia was far more important than Mongol political influence in Tibet at that time.

The Urgyenist sect or Red Hats became progressively more corrupt. The priesthood abandoned celibacy and certain monasteries reveled in sexual orgies which made mockery of the faith they represented. Doctrinally the Red Hats became lost in the worship of a confusing assortment of goddesses and demons.

Conditions were again ripe for a reformer to appear when onto the scene strode Tsong Khapa, whose name when literally translated means "the man from the land of onions." Tsong Khapa launched the *Gelugpa* reform, more commonly known as the Yellow Hat movement because of the yellow miters which the reformist monks wore to distinguish themselves from the supposedly debauched Red Hat monks. New monasteries were opened in which the purified doctrine was studied.

The Yellow Hats found patrons and protectors among Mongol chieftains to the north. The fourth reincarnation of Tsong Khapa, a lama named Sonam Gyatso, enjoyed the patronage of Altan Khan, a Mongol chieftain, and was declared by him to be the *Dalai Lama Vajradhara* or "The All-embracing Lama—the Holder of the Thunderbolt." This title was posthumously awarded also to his two predecessors, believed to have been his pre-incarnations; thus Sonam Gyatso entered history as the Third Dalai Lama.

It was the Fifth Dalai Lama who finally broke the power of the Red Hat sect during the middle of the 17th century. The Great Fifth, as he is now known in Tibet, allied himself with Gushi Khan, Chief of the Oelot Mongols of "Lower Tartary"—the Koko Nor region in northeast Tibet. With the encouragement of the Fifth Dalai, Gushi Khan marched the Oelots into Tibet. This caused another of Urgyen's remarkable prophecies to come true since he had written that "the Tartars of Lower Tartary would become masters of Tibet."[10]

The Great Fifth is remembered for many things, including the founding of the office of "Panchen Lama." The Panchen in successive reincarnations thereafter exercised ecclesiastical power over an area west of Lhasa from his throne in the Tashilhunpo monastery near Shigatse. The Fifth Dalai Lama selected his beloved teacher (and posthumously, his teacher's three predecessor incarnations) as Panchen. The Great Fifth must also have credit for building the Potala—thereafter the traditional See of the Dalai Lama and famous landmark of Lhasa.

In 1652 the Dalai Lama traveled to Peking to visit the first Manchu Emperor of China—an act of diplomacy and good neighborliness which the Chinese have since twisted to allege China's domination of Tibet. In fact, it was not until the rule of the second Manchu Emperor, K'ang Hsi, that China exerted any meaningful power over Tibet. The Manchu ruler, not yet confident of his own power, would scarcely have dared assume a suzerain stance toward Tibet and risk provoking the Oelot and other Mongol tribes which were backing the Fifth Dalai Lama.[11]

The Great Fifth succeeded in restoring ecclesiastical power in Tibet. Only after he died was authority restored to the lay monarchy—the institution used by the Mongol proconsuls to exercise power in Tibet. There is some question as to the exact time of death because Sangye Gyatso, his Grand Vizier (and possibly his bastard son), went to great lengths to conceal it for several years. By the time it became known that the Fifth Dalai was no longer alive, Sangye Gyatso had firmly established himself as Regent. This deceit so infuriated the Chinese Emperor that he began plotting with the Mongols against the Vizier.

In 1705 Latsang Khan, a Qosot Mongol prince who had commanded the Grand Vizier's forces, seized the government in a military *coup d'etat.* Latsang however, was able to consolidate his power only with the strong support of Emperor K'ang Hsi. This was the first beginning of meaningful Chinese political influence in Tibet.

K'ang Hsi reasoned that a Qosot Mongol ally in Tibet would provide a buffer against the hostile Dzungar Mongols from the area now known as Sinkiang who by then were seriously menacing the western reaches of his empire. Manchu supremacy in China was relatively safe so long as Tibet remained a friendly neighbor or at least a neutral buffer. If Lhasa, however, were to fall under Dzungar domination and if Tibet were absorbed into a greater Mongolia united by common religion, Manchu rule would be gravely jeopardized. Latsang needed Manchu support not only to ward off the predatory Dzungars but to defend his secular throne against Yellow Hat conspiracies aimed at restoring ecclesiastical power.

The Sixth Dalai Lama was the key to serious discontent, which seethed within the Yellow Hat monasteries and brought them into conspiratorial contact with the Dzungar and Oelot Mongol tribes to the northwest. A witness to the intrigues in Lhasa and faithful chronicler of them was Ippolito Desideri, whose sympathies were clearly with Latsang Khan. The pious Jesuit priest described the Sixth Dalai as a profligate playboy who drank, gambled and generally behaved so badly that "no girl or married woman or good looking person of either sex was safe from his unbridled licentiousness." Less harsh critics describe him as a boy of exceptional intelligence and talent. He was certainly Tibet's greatest poet.[12]

Dissolute as he was, the Lama was loved by the Tibetan people and provided a potential rallying point for any uprising. Latsang Khan recognized the danger and formed a plan to eliminate him. In 1707 the Qosot Khan sent the doomed Lama on a journey to China—allegedly for ceremonial purposes but actually to dispose of him. The Tartar escort stopped in Li-tang short of the Chinese border to carry out its sinister design. In a poignant scene before his death the Dalai Lama asked trusted members of his entourage to tell the Tibetan people not to weep—that he would be reborn on the borders of China near the spot of his execution and here they should search for him. The Dalai's death near Li-tang curiously fulfilled the first part of a prediction which he had earlier committed to verse:

> It is not far that I shall roam,
> Lend me your wings, white crane;
> I go no further than Li-tang,
> And thence return again.[13]

His return also came true as prophesied, but before the Dalai could be reborn near Li-tang, Latsang Khan arbitrarily selected a twenty-five-year old monk—possibly his own natural son—to be a puppet Dalai. This enraged the orthodox Tibetans, particularly the Yellow Hat clergy, who refused to recognize the illegal selection. Even Emperor K'ang Hsi, on whose favor Qosot Mongol rule depended, thought Latsang had gone too far. The Manchu Emperor delayed recognition of the new Dalai and, having become thoroughly alarmed at such political blundering, assigned to Lhasa a high-ranking Chinese "adviser." The latter shrewdly extracted tribute from Latsang as the price for Chinese protection, and it is this act which China believes provides a basis for claiming suzerainty over Tibet. Although Tibetans, with justice on their side, would later claim that the acts of an alien and imposed Mongol king cannot be considered binding on the Tibetan nation, the Chinese henceforward refused to concede that Tibet was wholly independent of Peking.

Finding themselves unable alone to resist Latsang's authority, the disgruntled Yellow Hat monks began plotting seriously with the Dzungar and Oelot Mongols, whose leader was Tse-wang Rabden. This chieftain raised two armies—one of which he commanded personally—and prepared to invade China. The objective of the first army was to regain the child Seventh Dalai Lama and block the Chinese Emperor from sending reinforcements to Latsang. Rabden's ultimate and very ambitious goal was to conquer all of China and seize the throne from the Manchus. First, however, Tibet had to be wrested from Latsang, and this was the task of the second army—a 6,000-man expeditionary force of combined Mongols and Tibetans led by a warrior monk, Tsering Dundup.

The invasion of China failed completely. Not only was Tse-wang Rabden unable to "liberate" the child Dalai from the Chinese, but his Dzungar-Oelot force was severely mauled by the Emperor's forces. News of this took a long time to reach Tibet. In the meantime, Tsering Dundup—following the original strategy—spread the word among the Yellow Hats that his approaching army was accompanied by the true Seventh Dalai.

On December 1, 1717 the invading force attacked Lhasa from four directions. This signaled a mass uprising of the Yellow Hat monks within Lhasa. According to pre-laid plans ladders were let down from Lhasa's walls, enabling the attackers to scale the ramparts more quickly. The northern and eastern gates of the city were thrown open by secret sympathizers at a precisely agreed-upon time. By daylight the Dzungars were masters of Lhasa. Tsering Dundup's troops reveled in orgies of looting which nearly stripped the city of its sacred relics and treasures.[14]

The ravages of the Mongols were terrifying, but no less so were the excesses of their confederate Yellow Hat monks. No longer restrained by Latsang, the Yellow Hats savagely set upon their Red Hat rivals, massacring all they could find and destroying their monasteries.

The Potala, more heavily fortified than the rest of the city, was held until the end by Latsang and a handful of loyal defenders. But on the third day of fighting it too was stormed. The Mongol king escaped through a secret passage just ahead of his pursuers only to be cut down as he tried to flee the town. This marked the end of the Qosot Mongol dynasty in Tibet and fulfilled with startling accuracy still another prophecy of Urgyen's.

Urgyen had written that Tibet would be invaded by Tartars of Upper Tartary which was, in fact, the home of the Dzungar Mongols. He added that the Tartars would sack the land and send home the spoils. Moreover, he predicted that they would kill lamas, desecrate monasteries and commit many other atrocities. He capped his prophecy with the specific detail that the king and his family would be slain.[15]

The Oelot-Dzungar invasion was exactly what the Chinese Emperor had feared. It represented a dangerous step toward unification of the Mongols. Rabden's abortive invasion of China by way of Siling was only a tactical feint in support of the invasion of Tibet, but the Emperor knew that the Mongol's ultimate goal was seizure of his own throne. With Latsang dead and Tibet secured, an important buffer against the Mongols was lost, and achievement of the Dzungar goal was now possible.

On the plea of the threatened Latsang Khan, a Chinese army had begun the long and arduous march toward Tibet before Lhasa fell to the Dzungars. The Emperor, who still had custody of the Seventh Dalai Lama and knew that Tsering Dundup had thus been unable to produce him in Lhasa as promised, estimated that disillusionment with the new Mongol masters must be rising in Lhasa.

Chinese troops by forced march crossed the great desert to Dam, just north of Lhasa. In preparation for a final attack on Lhasa, the Chinese made the tactical blunder of digging in behind a hastily built stone fort. This was to be their grave. The Chinese delay at Dam gave the Dzungar troops time to prepare an attack. Weakened by the long march, the Chinese were unable to break out of their fortifications and found themselves surrounded and imprisoned by a strong body of Dzungar troops. The wretched Chinese, denied provisions, first ate their pack animals. When this source of food was exhausted, they ate the bodies of less hardy comrades as the latter succumbed to starvation. Finally, after enduring a month's siege, the survivors surrendered only to be massacred to the last man as they filed out of the fort. This was an unbearable humiliation for the Emperor, who vowed he would repay the Mongols.

While many of his ministers were strongly opposed to risking a new campaign in Tibet, which would be enormously expensive and difficult to sustain, K'ang Hsi was determined to crush the Mongols. He knew that unless he could defeat them they would rapidly become strong enough to threaten his empire. Thus he raised a second expeditionary force. This time he paid well to attract the best mercenaries of the empire. He particularly sought Mongol mercenaries who were a match for the fierce Dzungars defending Lhasa.

The second expedition, launched in 1720, was commanded by the Emperor's fourteenth son. The main force was this time sent by way of Tachienlu—a more populated route on which the army could live off the land. With the Chinese army rode the young Dalai Lama—the Emperor's trump card.

The campaign was shrewdly advertised as a holy war. Tibetans along the invasion route were invited to join the crusade under the banners of the true Dalai Lama and to drive from their land the alien Dzungar Mongol rulers. This strategy worked. As the grand army marched toward Lhasa, the Tibetans turned out by the thousands to welcome their Dalai. Many monks willingly joined the Chinese force, while others who lagged behind were prodded to join.

The huge invading army arrived at the outskirts of Lhasa, where it confronted a weakened garrison of only 4,000 Dzungars who knew that they could expect no reinforcements. Sensibly the city should have bowed to superior force and surrendered to the Emperor's son; but unintimidated, the defenders took the offensive and sprang a surprise attack.[16] The hard core of the Chinese attacking force was held in reserve, waiting until Dzungar energies had been spent. On the fourth night of battle the Chinese mounted a flanking attack which crushed the Dzungars.[17] This victory is of considerable historic significance to the Chinese since it provided the first real basis for their claim to Tibet.

But all this had been written. Urgyen had foreseen it and had entered it in the record nearly a thousand years before. He had unerringly prophesied that the Chinese would attack and defeat the Mongols from Upper Tartary who had usurped the throne of Tibet.[18]

By invading Lhasa, Emperor K'ang Hsi had not only secured

China's flank and established a foothold in Tibet, but he had gained an important lever of influence over the Mongols. This holy city was a religious See for the Mongolian tribes just as much as it was for Tibetans. The patron-priest formula which had for long kept these two peoples in a unique alliance would now keep Tibet a vassal of the Chinese Emperor instead.

CHAPTER 2

BACKDOOR TO CHINA

The objections I have made against an expedition into Bhutan hold good with respect to Nepal and Lhasa for this sole reason: communications cannot be kept open and, should our troops march into these countries, they must consider all communication with the low country out of the question.

George Bogle, leader of the first English mission to Tibet, 1774–75

Following their invasion of Lhasa in 1720 the Manchu rulers experimented with various approaches to the problem of controlling Tibet. One of the most practical ways was to prevent the investiture of succeeding Dalai Lamas—by murder if necessary. Thus, for more than a century after the Manchu invasion Tibet was ruled by regents who were responsive to China.

As the Dalai Lama's power eroded under the regency system, the Panchen Lama assumed greater importance throughout the country. One outstanding Panchen, Lobsang Paldan Yeshi, at length dared to defy Peking. But this was because he had made contact with a new empire fast rising in India to the south—an empire of British merchants.

The way had been opened for British power in South Asia on the last day of the sixteenth century, when Queen Elizabeth affixed her seal and signature to a royal charter establishing the East India Company. Eight years later the Company's flagship Hector dropped anchor off Surat on the west coast of India. Its captain, William Hawkins, rowed ashore on August 24, 1608 to become the first Englishman to reach the Moghul realm. Thus began an imperial adventure which would make England great and have a profound effect on the course of history. But Hawkins was concerned with trade, not empire—with money, not glory. Even more immediately he was concerned about his own skin. Portuguese traders who had preceded him did not welcome English rivalry and harassed him at every turn. As Hawkins recounted, "I could not peep out of doors for fear of the Portugals who in troops lay lurking in the byways . . . to murder me."[1]

Despite Portuguese hostility and intrigues Hawkins made his way to the fabled Moghul court at Agra, south of Delhi, where he petitioned Emperor Jehangir for license to trade. Jehangir was friendly at first, but he denied permission to trade. Having succeeded in poisoning the Emperor's mind against Hawkins, the Portuguese had won the first round against the English.

Clinging tenaciously to its beachhead at Surat, the Company somehow survived despite intense Portuguese hostility. But not until 1615, when a Portuguese naval squadron was routed off Surat by British men-of-war, was the Company safe. Hereafter, free from any serious rivalry, the traders prospered. New trading depots were opened throughout India, and England's merchant knights grew rich. Clive's victory at the Battle of Plassey near Calcutta in 1757 secured Bengal for the Company and marked the real beginning of British power in India.

It was inevitable that the Company would dream of riches beyond the great Himalayan barrier on the north. Since Herodotus' time tales of limitless treasures of gold had reached India from Tibet. Every river which cascaded from the high Tibetan plateau had washed down gold-flecked sand to excite the coastal dwellers of its delta. The corporate imagination of the East India Company conjured up an El Dorado which could be had for the taking. The Company was intrigued by reports received as early as 1644, describing Tibet as an unlimited source of borax. English merchants traded heavily in this commodity, buying it in India from native traders, who brought it in driblets out of Tibet, and selling it in the world market on a near monopoly. The English were also, of course, interested in new markets for their manufactured goods.

In March 1768 the Company's Court of Directors, meeting in London, went on record with a recommendation that Tibet and West China soon be investigated as outlets for English cloth goods. Samuel Turner, a Company officer who was later to lead one of the earliest missions to Tibet, summed it up: "The continuity of Tibet to the western frontier of China . . . suggested also a possibility of establishing by degrees an immediate intercourse with that empire through the intervention of a person so revered as the [Panchen] Lama and by a route not obviously liable to the same suspicions as those with which Chinese policy had . . . of a foreign access by sea."[2] Perhaps Tibet could be a back door to China.

In 1771 the Directors raised the idea of exploring the Himalayan principality of Bhutan, north of Bengal, and the Assam Valley, as well as Tibet, with an eye to developing new markets. But it took Warren Hastings—a highly controversial, visionary Governor of Bengal—to carry out this policy. By 1774 he was prepared to probe into Tibet. This sort of adventure appealed to Hastings. He was a man of action and a man of will. Moreover, he found a long-sought excuse when he received unexpectedly a letter in March of that year from Lobsang Paldan Yeshe, the Third Panchen Lama of Tibet—or Teshoo Lama, as he was then more commonly known.*

In a most conciliatory and ingenuous style the Panchen asked Hastings to cease hostilities with the Rajah of Bhutan. The trouble to which he referred had begun when Bhutanese raiders in 1772 had kidnapped the Maharajah of Cooch Behar, a vassal of Tibet who ruled over a small princely state wedged between Bengal and Bhutan. The kidnapping had provoked Hastings to send a punitive expedition into Bhutan. Outfought by Company troops, the Rajah of Bhutan sought protection from the Panchen Lama, who was his suzerain, and the latter took the unprecedented step of writing Hastings.[3]

The Englishman interpreted the Panchen's letter—the first communication to pass between a Tibetan leader and the English—as an overture for relations. He notified the Company that he had replied to the Panchen, proposing a treaty of amity and commerce between Bengal and Tibet.[4]

Hastings selected as his emmissary to Tibet, George Bogle—a twenty-eight-year-old Scotsman in the Company, who was smart, personable and well grounded in affairs of Bengal and Bhutan. It is indicative of the Governor's confidence in Bogle—or perhaps in his judgment of men—that he gave his young ambassador wide powers. Once over the Himalayan passes Bogle would be on his own. There could be no reliance on communications with Calcutta. Hastings'

* Lobsang Paldan Yeshe is customarily known as the Third Panchen Lama, but this formula for numbering does not take into consideration three predecessors to the actual first Panchen Lama, who were awarded the title posthumously.

letter of instructions stated broadly: "The design of your mission is to open a mutual and equal communication of trade between the inhabitants of Bhutan [Tibet]* and Bengal, and you will be guided by your own judgment in using such means of negotiations as may be most likely to effect this purpose."[5]

Bogle had an intelligence mission as well; the interests of trade and empire could not even then be completely separated. He was to report on the "road between the borders of Bengal and the city of Lhasa, the customs of the country and the communications between Lhasa and its neighbors."[6] The latter obviously and particularly included China, but Bogle was also instructed to inquire about the countries which lay between Lhasa and Siberia. Hastings farsightedly recognized the strategic implications of Tibet's hub position vis-à-vis India, China and Russia, even though he did not yet have precise enough geographical data with which to refine these implications.

Bogle set out from Calcutta on his mission in May 1774. He was accompanied by Alexander Hamilton, a surgeon of the East India Company, and Purangir, an emissary sent by the Panchen Lama to guide them. As the party passed through Bhutan, it was intercepted by a messenger from the Panchen Lama asking Bogle to postpone his entrance into Tibet. The Panchen's letter explained to Bogle that Emperor Ch'ien Lung of China had decreed that no "Moghul, Indian, Pathan or Englishman" should be admitted to Tibet without royal authority; therefore, Bogle must await permission from Peking. After an appeal delivered by Purangir, the Panchen waived his objections without further reference to China. Only later did Bogle discover that the trouble had been in Lhasa—not Peking. The Panchen ultimately confided in Bogle that the Regent of the child Dalai Lama in Lhasa had been the obstruction to his mission. This puppet of the Chinese had warned that the English objective was to conquer Tibet.

The Panchen Lama did not accept the Chinese stricture and had the political sense to recognize that the English could provide a counterbalance to Manchu power. He overruled Lhasa and received Bogle at a temporary camp site near the southern Tibetan city of Shigatse. This was the first official contact between Britain and Tibet.

* Tibet was then sometimes referred to as Bhutan, despite the fact that there was a distinct principality which bore that name.

Upon meeting, the two men must have found it difficult to conceal their mutual curiosity. Bogle described the Panchen Lama as a man about forty years old, "of low stature and, though not corpulent, rather inclined to be fat; his arms as white as those of a European; . . . his whiskers never above a month long. He was open, frank, generous, and extremely good humored."[7]

Almost immediately the Panchen apologized for his Bhutanese vassal—criticizing him for his unnecessary attack on Cooch Behar. He told Bogle that he had always disapproved of the Rajah of Bhutan's capture of the Cooch Behar prince and the war with the *Fringies.** The Panchen complained that the Bhutan Rajah considered himself "powerful in arms and would not listen to advice."[8]

As their friendship grew, the Panchen Lama confided to Bogle that the Regent—contrary to his advice—had encouraged Bhutan to war on Cooch Behar. Because the Regent's judgment was patently wrong, the Panchen had felt strong enough to override him and receive the English emissary. Convinced that Hastings had acted in good faith by withdrawing from Bhutan and certain that the chances for lasting peace would be greatly improved if Bogle were graciously received, the Lama had disregarded Lhasa. In effect, he told the Regent to leave relations with the British to him.

With much pomp and ceremony Bogle and Hamilton were received at Tashilhunpo—the Panchen Lama's See near Shigatse.[9] Talks with the Panchen Lama began auspiciously and in a spirit of conciliation. The Lama conceded that the Fringies were "a fair and just people." Bengal, he explained, was a place very close to him since he had lived there during two previous incarnations. Of course, trade was the principal topic of official discussions. The Panchen was completely positive on this score. After being assured by Bogle that Bengal was no longer under Moslem control and that Buddhist traders from Tibet would be well treated there, the Panchen indicated that he would be willing to open his borders for trade and had in fact "written to Lhasa on the subject of . . . a free commercial communication between his country and Bengal."

Bogle sensed it would not be that simple and wrote back to Hastings that—despite the Panchen's zeal—he "did not much like the thoughts of referring . . . to Lhasa." Bogle explained: "I had

* Tibetan expression for "English."

reason to think the Ministers had entertained no favorable idea of me and my commission."[10] His pessimism was entirely justified. Although the Regent sent two emissaries from Lhasa to talk with Bogle, it was clear in the end that they would make no trade agreement. Pleading the need to gain the Emperor's permission, the Lhasa emissaries refused to act. Bogle wrote that "the Chinese would freely open the whole of Tibet but the Tibetans themselves are terribly secretive."[11]

The Panchen Lama seemed genuinely sorry that he could not accommodate the British request for trade rights. As Bogle was leaving Tibet, the Panchen said apologetically and with astonishing candor, "You know what difficulties I had to struggle with—the jealousy of the [Regent] . . . and the people of Lhasa! Even now they are uneasy at my having kept you so long."[12]

Bogle did not accomplish what he set out to do. Trade relations were not established, nor was he able to convince the Lhasan authorities that British intentions were entirely peaceful. Yet his mission was on balance a success. He gained for England the confidence and friendship of the Panchen Lama, who was to prove a strong champion of the Company's interests. This young officer of the Company had been a worthy ambassador. He genuinely liked the Panchen Lama; not unnaturally this sentiment was reciprocated. Bogle had bridged a wide cultural gap to find an enduring personal relationship which gained for England and the Company a valuable friend. Bogle's parting emotions can be sensed in a valedictory letter in which he wrote: "Farewell, ye honest and simple people. May ye long enjoy the happiness which is denied to more polished nations; and while they are engaged in the endless pursuits of avarice and ambition, defended by your barren mountains, may ye continue to live in peace and contentment, and know no wants but those of nature."[13]

This first embassy to Tibet was also immensely useful for the information Bogle was able to bring back. His detailed observations revealed the great importance of Tibet in the continental trade of Asia. He found that Tibet produced gold, musk, yak-tails, wool and salt which Tibetans exchanged for cloth goods, leather and luxury goods.

Most of the trade with China was along the caravan route via Sining. Usually the caravans were so-called tribute missions, but they nevertheless constituted a form of organized trade. The Dalai Lama and the Panchen Lama would send to the Emperor rich "tribute" cargoes of ceremonial scarves, holy relics, amber rosaries, bronze Buddha images and incense. In exchange, the Emperor would send the Lamas presents of satin, silver goods and gold trinkets, which in many cases exceeded the value of the Tibetan trains. This was commerce as the word is understood today. In fact, the retinue of the tribute caravans included Indian trading pilgrims called *gosains*, who waxed rich and influential on their lucrative trade. Whatever its ceremonial origins, tribute had little political meaning in Tibet by the eighteenth century.

Hasting's intuition had told him that Russia—however far from Lhasa—posed a danger not to be ignored. His intuition was reinforced by Bogle's intelligence, which revealed that significant trade between Tibet and Russia did exist. This trade was for the most part conducted by Kalmuks from Eastern Turkestan and Buriat Mongols from Siberia. In yearly caravans they brought furs, Russian hides, yak-tails and fresh-water pearls, which they exchanged for cloth, amber, spices and gold. The Panchen Lama questioned Bogle closely about the Empress of Russia. His interest in her was apparently aroused by stories which filtered through to Lhasa telling of Russia-China boundary quarrels. Bogle sensed that the Lama was, even then, genuinely concerned about the possibility of a clash between Asia's two expanding empires as they veered closer to each other in Central Asia.

Bogle's strategic insight into the Himalayan and trans-Himalayan region proved to be amazingly accurate. British Himalayan policy was for many years consistent with his conclusions, and it must be assumed that his recommendations to Hastings indeed influenced the early shaping of British policy. These recommendations have no less pertinence for India today. For example, Bogle had this to say about Tibet and the border states:

> Attempting [to take possession of Bhutan] by force will never [be an] answer. The difficulties are unsurmountable, at least without a force and expense much greater than the object is worth. . . . The objections I have made against an expedition into Bhutan hold good with respect to Nepal and Lhasa for this sole reason: . . . communications cannot be kept open and should our troops march into these countries they must consider all communication with the low country out of the question till they return.[14]

Communications were then and are now the key to control of the Himalayan states and the Tibetan plateau. This was equally true for the Chinese, whose routes and supply lines to Tibet were much longer and more hazardous than those from India. This was why Communist China in mid-twentieth century first built roads before it attempted to consolidate its control over the Tibetan plateau and then extended its road network southward to the Himalayas as a requirement for ultimate control of Nepal, Sikkim and Bhutan.

The threat of a new empire rising in India to challenge Imperial China in Asia was ominous enough to the Manchus. But for emissaries of this empire to visit the court of the Panchen Lama and negotiate behind the backs of the Chinese proconsuls in Lhasa was to give immediacy to the threat. If Tibet were to fall under the Company's influence, the Manchu Empire would be flanked by two "barbarians"—the British as well as the Russians. Emperor Ch'ien Lung found this worrisome. He could do little about the British, but he could at least try to bring the Panchen to heel.

Ch'ien Lung sent repeated messages inviting the Panchen Lama to Peking during the years 1777 and 1778. With one or another unconvincing reason the Panchen declined them all. Perhaps he realized that in Peking he would be vulnerable to Chinese pressures. He may even have feared for his life at the hands of the Emperor. Or perhaps he was genuinely apprehensive about the smallpox epidemic which raged through China.

Once again the Emperor invited the Panchen Lama in a letter written in 1779. The message—flattering in tone—described elaborate plans which were being made to celebrate the Emperor's seventieth birthday and implored the Panchen to attend the ceremonies. The Panchen could no longer refuse; when he finally did accept, however, it was with great reluctance. He confided to a few friends that an inner instinct warned him that he would never return.

Filled with this foreboding the Panchen Lama set forth on his epic visit to China in July 1779. Five thousand troops were his escort as he marched regally through Tibet. This journey was a rare spectacle, which brought crowds of his countrymen to pay homage as he swept by. Whenever he paused, a platform caparisoned with rich brocades and deep cushions was erected. Enthroned above his people the Panchen sat patiently, his right foot extended and unshod so that the faithful could touch it with their foreheads as they filed by.

The Tibetans met heavy autumn snows in the Koko Nor region of north Tibet, which forced them to bivouac for the winter at Kumbun, birthplace of Song-tsen Gampo, who introduced Buddhism into Tibet and who is believed by Tibetans to be reincarnated in the body of the Panchen Lama. Here Purangir, faithful agent of the Company, caught up with the party on a mission for Hastings.

Hastings had arranged a plan for Bogle to go to Canton by sea in the naive hope that a trade agreement with Tibet could be worked out with the Emperor of China. Purangir was to solicit the Panchen's approval of the plan, then meet Bogle in Canton and escort him to Peking. Taking advantage of his friendship with the Panchen Lama, Bogle hoped also to take up with the Emperor the matter of debts owed by Chinese merchants to English sea traders. Heretofore the English had been unable to gain access to Peking and the Emperor's court to redress their grievances. Bogle believed that by riding in on the Panchen's coattails he could perhaps at least gain a royal hearing. If satisfaction could not be obtained on the spot, he hoped to set up some permanent channel of communications to the Emperor through which complaints could be heard and adjudicated.

As the Panchen Lama neared the Emperor's summer palace at Jehol, the receptions became more numerous and progressively more elaborate. At one place His Holiness was met by the Emperor's first son riding at the head of 10,000 royal troops.

On August 25, 1780 the Panchen Lama finally reached the summer palace. Purangir's description of the Emperor's meeting with his guest at Jehol[15] belies latter-day Chinese allegations that the Tibetan Lama humbled himself before the Emperor. As had been the case when the Great Fifth Dalai Lama visited the Manchu court, the Panchen Lama was not required to kowtow or otherwise signify vassalage to the Emperor. Ch'ien Lung met him forty paces from the throne and "immediately stretching forth his hand and taking hold of the Lama's, led him towards the throne where after many salutations and expressions of affection . . . the Lama was seated by the Emperor upon the uppermost cushion with himself on his right hand." Purangir added, "Much conversation ensued."

It was on the fourth day of meetings that the Panchen Lama raised the matter of his relationship with the English. He told the Emperor: "In the country of Hindostan [India], which lies on the borders of my country, there resides a great prince or ruler for whom I have the greatest friendship. I wish you should know and regard him also; and if you will write him a letter of friendship and receive his in return it will afford me great pleasure as I wish you should be known to each other and that a friendly communication should in future subsist between you."

The Emperor's reply, although polite, betrayed his concern. He asked suspiciously about "the extent of the country" ruled over by this prince and "the number of his forces," and interrogated Purangir on other details. His replies were cautious, but we can assume they did nothing to dispel Ch'ien Lung's fear that the British Empire in Asia would rival his own and eventually absorb Tibet into its realm. Purangir, for example, reported that Mr. Hastings was Governor of Hindostan and "the extent of the country he governed was not near equal to that of China but superior to any other he knew and that the troops of that country [numbered] upwards of three *Lakhs* [300,000] of horsemen."

In the autumn the Emperor returned to Peking from Jehol accompanied by his holy guest. Here the Panchen Lama once again raised with the Emperor the matter of the British. When questioned afterward by the Company, Purangir claimed that the Emperor assured the Lama that he joined "most heartily with him in what he wished as it would give him much pleasure to know and correspond with the Governor of Hindostan." Ch'ien Lung promised, moreover, to "cause a letter to be immediately written to the Governor in such terms as the Lama would dictate." One can guess that either Purangir exaggerated the sincerity of the Emperor's response or the response was made simply in an effort to be polite. Chinese records include no mention of this conversation, but then it is unlikely that they would. Naturally, the Emperor would not want the Panchen Lama's views a matter of permanent record, and it is unlikely that he seriously considered corresponding with a British trading company. It is difficult to believe that the Panchen Lama would have been naive enough to think that he could bring the Chinese Emperor to endorse his close relations with the British.

More likely the Panchen Lama raised the matter to impress upon the Emperor that the British could be protectors of Tibet should China attempt to interfere with Tibet's autonomy. This was in all probability a political maneuver—part of the Panchen Lama's strategy of playing the Chinese off against the British. It would have been interesting to see whether the Emperor allowed Bogle to join them in Peking. He probably would have found excuses to exclude him since to do otherwise would be tantamount to condoning close Tibetan-English ties. The matter never came to a test, however; the Panchen Lama suddenly sickened and died.

Purangir recalled that the stricken Lama had ". . . complained of a violent headache and in less than an hour more he was seized with a most violent fever which continued very severe until about the same hour the next day when his disorder was discovered to be the small pox."

The Panchen Lama took a turn for the worse on the fourth day of his illness and expired "as he sat at prayers between two large pillows, resting his back against the wall." His death was widely believed to have been caused by the Emperor. Tibetans historically distrust Chinese motives when a Grand Lama is invited to Peking. They assume that the Chinese will impose their will on him or, failing this, dispose of him on the assumption that his next incarnation will prove more malleable. It was natural, therefore, that a large body of opinion in Tibet was convinced that the Panchen Lama was murdered in Peking. Great significance was attached to the sudden flight of the Panchen Lama's brother to Nepal, which was interpreted as an impulsive effort to escape from a Chinese plot against the Lama's entire family.[16]

Whether or not the Emperor was guilty of the Panchen's death, he certainly gained by it. Power in Tibet reverted to the Dalai Lama in Lhasa and was held in escrow for him by the Regent, who was under the Chinese *Ambans'* watchful eyes. The Regent, long a puppet of the Chinese, strongly opposed relations between Tibet and the British and could be relied upon to follow Peking's dictates.

Bogle died in India within a few months of the Panchen's death. Hastings' Tibet policy had rested heavily on the relationship between Bogle and the Panchen Lama. With their passing went the Company's best chances for trade with Tibet. Although Hastings sent another mission to Tashilhunpo in 1783 under Lieutenant Samuel Turner, the new incarnation of the Panchen Lama was still a child, and his Regent gave Turner no encouragement whatsoever.

The complete collapse of Hastings' "forward policy" came not long after he was relieved as Governor General. Lord Charles Cornwallis, who replaced him, stumbled badly on Himalayan policy. Through ineptitude he lost even the goodwill which Hastings had gained. A series of petty disputes over currency and trade had touched off a Gurkha invasion of Tibet from Nepal in 1788, causing the child Panchen's Regent at Tashilhunpo to turn to the Company for help. In a pathetic letter to the Governor General the Regent confided that if British help were not forthcoming he must accept Chinese military assistance. This he did not want since he knew that the Manchus would use the Gurkha invasion as an excuse to tighten Peking's hold on Tibet. The letter concluded with a plea that the Governor General keep his letter most secret since its contents, if known to the Chinese, "would bring ruin and destruction upon him."[17] Cornwallis responded tardily and unimaginatively, claiming that the Company could not afford the cost of war against Nepal, had no reason to attack Nepal and did not want to offend the Chinese Emperor lest it disrupt the Company's sea trade with China.

The commander to whom the Emperor had first entrusted Tibet's defense actually bought off the Gurkhas with promises of tribute rather than risking battle with them. This act of cowardice was kept secret from Peking as long as it could be, but when the promised tribute payment to the Gurkhas was not forthcoming the skeleton clattered from its closet. The Gurkhas, who felt cheated, erupted again in 1791, this time sacking the Panchen Lama's treasure-laden monastery at Tashilhunpo. Furious with the cowardly commander who had deceived him, the Emperor sent under forced march a large and remarkably effective army which routed the Gurkhas in a brilliantly conducted campaign over icy passes during the winter of 1792.

While his troops retreated from Tibet in disorder, the desperate Gurkha Rajah of Nepal tried to mend his fences with the British. He hastily signed a trade pact which the Company had long been seeking, hoping thereby to qualify for defense assistance. But having already angered the Emperor and failed the Tibetans, Cornwallis now refused to help the beleaguered Nepalese, thus alienating victor and vanquished alike. Ignoring reality altogether, Cornwallis despatched Captain William Kirkpatrick to Kathmandu to attempt mediation. Cornwallis' offer of mediation was unfortunately too late to help Nepal and was resented by the Chinese, whose victory entitled Peking to impose terms on Nepal. Arriving months after the war was over, Kirkpatrick only served to excite further the Emperor's suspicion that the British had secretly backed the Gurkhas in their ill-fated adventure in Tibet.

Whatever faint hopes for Tibetan trade which the Company had clung to were now vanished. As predicted by the Panchen's Regent, the Chinese tightened their grip on Tibet. The Dalai and Panchen Lamas were forbidden to exercise power independently of the Chinese *Ambans*. The latter, moreover, were empowered to select puppets of their choosing as Lamas. It was the intention of the Emperor to absorb Tibet into the Manchu empire and deny it any of its traditional attributes of autonomy. To impress this upon the Tibetans a tablet describing the new terms of Chinese control was erected in September 1793 in front of the *Jo-kang*, Lhasa's holiest place of worship. Tibet was now truly a "forbidden land."

CHAPTER 3

THE GREAT GAME

I assert with confidence—what I do not think any of her own statesmen would deny—that her [*Russia's*] *ultimate ambition is the dominion of Asia.*

Lord Curzon,
Viceroy of India,
1898–1905

More than a century passed before the British again made a serious attempt to penetrate Tibet. When the attempt was finally made, it involved other stakes than commerce. For the spreading power of Imperial Russia not only threatened British interests in India but endangered the balance of power in the Orient.

Although the Russian Empire had been expanding for four hundred years, it had been confined to the heartland of the Eurasian continent. This expansion had not troubled the British, but when in the nineteenth century Russia pushed southward toward Britain's empire and threatened to upset power equilibrium in the East it became of vital concern.

Russia began to extend its rule modestly toward the end of the fourteenth century after the Mongol tide had begun to recede from its highwater mark of conquest. By the middle of the sixteenth century the Khanates of Kazan and Astrakhan had fallen to the Russians. A century later found the Russians on the banks of the Amur River in Siberia, where they skirmished with advance units of the Chinese. A line between Russia and China, awarding the entire Amur Basin to the Manchu Emperor, K'ang Hsi, was finally drawn by the Treaty of Nerchinsk in 1689. While this agreement remained in force for nearly two centuries, it did not contain Russia's eastward expansion indefinitely.

Russia was able to extract from China the left bank of the Argun and Amur rivers in Siberia by the Treaty of Aigun, signed in 1858. Two years later by the Treaty of Peking the Manchus relinquished to Russia the land between the right banks of the Ussuri and lower Amur rivers and the Pacific Ocean. This permitted Russia to build Vladivostock and from this base extend its influence along the northern Pacific coast.

The 1860 treaty and the supplementary protocol of Tarbagatai, signed in 1864, took advantage of the declining Manchu power to realign China's western boundary in Russia's favor. In 1881, by the terms of the Treaty of St. Petersburg (or Treaty of Ili, as it is sometimes known), China regained part of the rich and strategic Ili Valley leading into western Sinkiang, which had earlier been lost through Russian pressure. But this treaty and subsequent refinements agreed to in 1882, 1883 and 1884, which tended to be disadvantageous to China, are among the protocols which Peking has recently attacked as imperialist-imposed, "unequal" treaties, and which it uses today as a basis to insist on a redefinition of its Central Asian boundary with the Soviet Union.

Russia's *Drang nach Osten* was entirely natural. A sense of Great Russian nationalism overlay a deeper, more instinctive drive to control the Asian hordes which had once conquered the Russian people. Moreover, in the nineteenth century exploration and imperial conquest were the trend in the Western world. While other European powers scrambled for empire in Africa and along the ocean fringes of Asia, Russia pressed eastward into Central Asia to fulfill its version of "manifest destiny." Cossack horsemen, like adventurers and pioneers everywhere, were irresistably drawn to the next prize over the horizon—then on to the next. Expansion bred expansion. Tashkent was taken in 1864, Samarkand in 1868, Bokhara in 1869, Khokand in 1876, Merve in 1884 and Pendjdeh in 1885. By 1895 the Russians had reached the Pamirs, overlooking the Indian subcontinent.

This was the time of the "Great Game," a name invented by Indian Army officer Captain Arthur Conolly to describe British-Russian political fencing in Central Asia. Conolly forfeited his own life for the Game when he was beheaded in Bokhara while on a secret mission for the government of India. Long-range reconnaissance and espionage of this kind served as probing antennae of two empires which veered perilously close to each other as the nineteenth century came to a close.

By the end of the nineteenth century there had developed in Russia a cult of *Vostochniki*, or "Easterners," who believed that it was Russia's mission to conquer continental Asia. Russian orientalists such as General M. N. Prjevalskii helped popularize the concept of Central Asian unity with Russia. V. P. Vasil'ev, one of Russia's leading oriental scholars, said in 1883 that Russians advanced toward the East as liberators of peoples oppressed by the "tyranny of internecine strife and impotency" and had a sacred duty toward the "oppressed."[1]

In 1890 the Russian philosopher Vladimir Solov'ev stated that Russia must advance eastward to defend Europe against the "yellow power." In the same year Crown Prince Nicholas toured the Far East, dramatizing Russia's increased interest in it. He was accompanied by the influential Prince Ukhtomskii, whose colonial philosophy had concluded that "people of various races feel drawn to us and are ours by blood, tradition and by ideas. . . . This great and mysterious Orient is ready to become ours."

It had been Ukhtomskii who, when war broke out with Japan in 1904, rashly predicted that Russia would defeat Japan and then conquer China. He also theorized that "the English would intervene and Russia would have to drive the English out of India."[2] These were strong words, particularly since they were spoken by a man who served as the Crown Prince's mentor on Far Eastern affairs. Nicholas' adoption of an aggressive policy toward Asia after he became Czar can probably be traced in some measure to Ukhtomskii's influence. Also influential was Witte, Russia's Minister of Finance, who promoted the construction of the Trans-Siberian Railway as a means of encouraging industry and marketing Western Siberia's grain production. Both men had visions of a Russian empire in Asia, although Witte viewed it more from an economic point of view. He saw in a Far Eastern rail network a means to compete commercially with England in China.

Russia's contacts with Tibet had initially been through the Mongols, many of whom were Lamaists. Certain Mongol tribes referred to the distant Czar as *Tsagan Khan*—"Chieftain of the White Horde." Catherine the Great had initiated a correspondence with the Mongolian Grand Lama of Urga betraying her more than casual interest in Mongolia.[3] In 1783 Turner saw at Tashilhunpo a Russian Orthodox Bible given to the Panchen Lama by Jebtson Dampa Hutkhtu, the Mongolian Grand Lama, who had received it originally from the Russian Empress. This strangely unsuitable gift for one lama to give another was accompanied by a request for advice on how to meet Catherine's increasingly aggressive moves toward Mongolia. In Peking, Russia was viewed as another foreign barbarian, whose domination of the Mongols posed a threat in Central Asia more formidable than that of the British traders in India and along the coast. The British Empire in India was still separated from China by the Himalayas and the endless wastes of Tibet, but the Russian "White Horde" inexorably advanced toward the Chinese across the flat steppes of Central Asia.

The Mongol concept of Tsagan Khan has an ancient parallel in Tibetan mythology. It was prophesied that Song-tsen Gampo, founder of Tibet's religion, would one day be reincarnated as a mighty prince and conquer the world in the name of Buddhism. The prediction specified that the seat of the new empire would bear the name Chang Shambhala and would be located three thousand miles northwest of Lord Buddha's birthplace in northern India. There were other clues as well which suggested Russia as the seat of the new empire.[4] At least, such an interpretation of the legend was found useful by a most mysterious Buriat Mongol lama who sought to promote Russian policy in Lhasa. This extraordinary agent of the Czar—known by various names and aliases but most accurately as Aguan Dorjiev—was the most effective player of them all in the Great Game which swirled around Tibet at the turn of the century. He had a disturbing effect on the Central Asian balance of power and set in motion a series of moves and countermoves which would ultimately provoke the British to march on Lhasa.

As tutor and confidant of the Dalai Lama, Dorjiev gained enormous influence in Lhasa and was able to convince many Tibetans that Czar Nicholas II was, in fact, the great Prince of Buddhism who ruled from Chang Shambhala. Dorjiev was author of a pamphlet intended to prove that Chang Shambhala means "Russia" and that the Czar is a worthy reincarnation of the venerable founder of Buddhism.[5]

Lord Curzon, Viceroy of India, was at first not inclined to take the Buriat lama seriously. London became suspicious of Dorjiev only when Hardinge, then British Chargé d'Affaires in St. Petersburg, clipped and sent to the Foreign Office an article in the October 15, 1900 issue of the *Journal de Saint Petersbourg* which described this mystery-monk's audience with the Czar at Livadia Palace in Yalta. Hardinge's report added, "I have not been able, so far, to procure any precise information with regard to this person or to the missions on which he is supposed to have come to Russia." Since, however, Dorjiev had been described as a representative of the Dalai Lama and was rumored to have brought a letter to the Czar from His Holiness, Hardinge's report aroused deep suspicion in both London and Calcutta.

Curzon fitted the news of Dorjiev neatly into his favorite thesis that Russia's "ultimate ambition is the dominion of Asia." The Viceroy had personally toured Central Asia. He had taken note of Russian General Skobeleff's ringing promise that the Czar's Empire would "organize masses of Asiatic cavalry and . . . hurl them into India." Even if a Russian invasion of India seemed remote, the presence of Russian troop concentrations in Central Asia tied down comparable British forces in India. This was awkward at a time when the "thin red line" was stretched to the limit against the Boers in Africa. Also the British *Raj* could not allow its subjects in India to see nearby a power comparable to British power. The Great Mutiny of 1857 was still recent enough so that England could not take for granted the loyalty of the "natives."

One of Curzon's first acts as Viceroy was to bring under his personal control the vulnerable borderlands. He reasoned, for example, that China's Sinkiang dependency north of Ladakh and Tibet would eventually fall to Russia. The latter had already stationed in Kashgaria, Sinkiang a consul general guarded by an impressive Cossack escort. Moreover, there was much talk of a new Russian rail line which would extend to Eastern Sinkiang and make an invasion of that area logistically feasible. The Viceroy feared that after Sinkiang, Tibet would be next. If Tibet came under Russian influence, India would be exposed and vulnerable along its entire 2,500-mile northern boundary.

Sir John Ardagh, who had been Director of British Military Intelligence in 1896, argued for fixing a definite boundary in the Pamirs far enough forward to prevent Russian expansion into Turkestan and Hunza. He felt that the Sino-Japanese War had revealed serious Chinese weakness and that the consequences of this would be eventual Russian annexation of Kashgaria. Ardagh was convinced that "Russia, as in the past, will endeavor to push her boundary as far south as she can for political reasons even if no real military advantage is sought."[6] Adding substance to this view was the disturbing knowledge that in 1888 and again in 1890 Russian missions had visited the Mir of Hunza in his tiny principality northwest of Kashmir. The Czar's envoys reputedly had dangled before him enticing offers of aid. Curzon supported Ardagh's views mainly because the Russians had established a threatening military outpost in the Taghdumbash-Pamir area north of Hunza. In 1899 Curzon as Viceroy pressed strongly for support of the Mir, saying, "If we do not stand by the Hunza men in a case when right is so obviously on their side, we shall give the impression that Russia has only to threaten in order to carry the day."[7]

In March 1899 the British government proposed to Peking that China recognize Hunza's claims to the western end of the Taghdumbash area in return for which the British would agree to negotiate a firm boundary in the Aksai Chin area where Ladakh, Tibet and Sinkiang come together. So anxious were the British to clear up this festering dispute in Taghdumbash which made Hunza vulnerable to Russian intrigues that they probably would have made major territorial concessions to the Chinese in Aksai Chin had the latter accepted the British offer to negotiate. London would probably have conceded to the Chinese most of the arid Aksai Chin plateau, which is today the crux of India's northwest boundary dispute with China. The Chinese would not agree, however, and missed an opportunity never again to be offered by the British. With this perspective, it is not surprising that Curzon began to view Dorjiev's activities as having an important part in Russia's master plan for Asia.

Well primed in St. Petersburg with a line calculated to appeal to the Dalai Lama, Dorjiev argued that China was too weak to protect Tibet from the British and might, in fact, give the country to the British as a sop. English infidels would then occupy Lhasa and usurp the rule of lama priests. The Buriat extolled Russia as a powerful military nation which could protect Tibet. Hinting that Czar Nicholas II had embraced Buddhism, he pointed out that the classic patron-priest relationship would give the Dalai Lama ecclesiastical power over all of the Russian Empire.

Dorjiev also brought a letter to the Dalai Lama from the Czar inviting His Holiness to send an envoy to Russia for further discussions. Swayed by Dorjiev's influence, the Dalai Lama, without notifying the Tibetan National Council, impulsively sent to St. Petersburg an ornate cushion to serve as his throne while he talked to the great White Lama. Tibet's Prime Minister intervened, however, and made it clear to the Dalai Lama that he had overstepped the bounds of his authority by making plans to visit Russia. He also reminded the Dalai that the National Council was not yet convinced that Tibet needed Russian protection.

Dissuaded from going to Russia, the Dalai Lama sent instead a mission consisting of eight senior statesmen headed by Dorjiev, whom he accorded the rank of plenipotentiary. The group made its way secretly across India under the very nose of the British and boarded a ship for Russia. By June 1901 Dorjiev was back in Russia, much to the consternation of Curzon. The June 25, 1901 edition of the newspaper *Odessa Novosti* reported that the city of Odessa would welcome that day an "extraordinary mission from the Dalai Lama which was proceeding to St. Petersburg with diplomatic instructions of importance." The article added that Dorjiev, leader of the mission, "had letters from the Dalai Lama which would raise the matter of a permanent Tibetan mission in St. Petersburg for the maintenance of good relations with Russia."

The British government instructed its Ambassador in St. Petersburg, Sir Charles Scott, to protest. Count Lamsdorff, Russian Foreign Minister, dismissed as "ridiculous" and "utterly unfounded" stories that the Tibetan group had a diplomatic role, and compared the Tibetan mission to similar missions sent by the Pope to the faithful around the world. This was too much for the British to accept. Scott was instructed to inform Lamsdorff that "Her Majesty's Government would naturally not regard with indifference any proceedings that might have a tendency to alter or disturb the existing status in Tibet."[8]

Evidence has since come to light that Lamsdorff was not fully aware of the Palace's dealings with Dorjiev and may not have approved of what he did know. The Dorjiev affair had the earmarks of a Palace adventure. Certainly it was the kind of undertaking which would appeal to Nicholas II, who had a somewhat romantic and mystical nature. Sir Cecil Spring Rice, later British Ambassador to the United States, wrote Sir Charles Hardinge about the atmosphere in St. Petersburg: "I expect that the Emperor is immensely pleased by the compliments lavished on him by the Dalai

Lama. . . . He likes being called the 'Step-son of Heaven' and the '169th Incarnation.'" Sir Cecil was of the following opinion: "The real reason [for the Emperor's Tibetan aspirations] is the idea which he has fixed in his mind that if he assumes . . . the right to act as temporal protector of the chief center of the Buddhist faith, he will become the moral chief of the continent of Asia."[9]

When Dorjiev returned to Lhasa in December 1901, he allegedly presented two Russian proposals to the Potala. One called for stationing in Lhasa a prince of the Russian royal house as ambassador. The other—more serious—suggested that Russia and Tibet conclude an agreement requiring Russia to come to Tibet's rescue in the event of attack by the British. The Dalai Lama was very much in favor of concluding such a treaty; Dorjiev had done his job well. But, as could be expected, the Chinese *Amban* in Lhasa opposed it, calling the mere idea of a treaty with Russia "treason to His Imperial Master, the Emperor of China."[10]

The Government of India did not at that time know what was really going on in Lhasa. A little intelligence leaked out to British frontier officers in Darjeeling and Kalimpong. But it was mainly unreliable hearsay from native travelers; and by the time this type of news reached India it was hopelessly out of date. The most alarming version of the report on the secret treaty came from Peking when Sir Ernest Satow, British Minister, reported that Russia had undertaken to guarantee the tottering Chinese Empire, in return for which Tibet would become a protectorate of Russia.[11]

Satow's report had an air of plausibility. The Manchu—or Ch'ing—dynasty was rapidly disintegrating. Japan had defeated China in a brief war in 1895. The Boxer Rebellion of 1900 provided an occasion for Russian troops to occupy Peking as part of the international rescue mission. Russia—not yet at war with Japan—had penetrated deeply into Manchuria and Western Turkestan. The Pamirs were under the Czar's control, and it was generally accepted that Chinese Turkestan and Mongolia would probably be next. China was in no position to resist Russian expansion. Moreover, it needed the Czar's protection against Japan, which posed a serious and immediate threat. Russia, for its part, would find an understanding with China useful because of a similar imminent threat from Japan.

However plausible this reasoning may have appeared, the rumor of a Sino-Russian accord could not be established as fact, and both Peking and St. Petersburg vigorously denied the reports. Denials, however, did little to allay the fears and suspicions of Great Britain. Curzon himself asserted that he was a firm believer in the existence of a secret understanding—if not a secret treaty—between Russia and China about Tibet.

What made reports of Russian success in Lhasa all the more difficult for Curzon to bear was his own painfully obvious lack of success. While Dorjiev was being received at court in St. Petersburg, Curzon's efforts to communicate with the Dalai Lama were being rebuffed. Not only had the Dalai Lama refused to admit British traders under the terms of treaties signed previously with the Chinese—supposedly Tibet's suzerain—but he refused even to have the matter discussed. It was now obvious to Curzon that there were influences at work in Lhasa specifically hostile to the British. Clearly Dorjiev was at the heart of the trouble.

Russian players in the Great Game seemed to be outscoring British players. Landon, the London *Times* correspondent who later accompanied the first British mission to Tibet, observed, "What the Russians did in allowing Dorjiev to represent them unofficially in Lhasa we should have been glad to be able to do and it is a deplorable thing that the millions of northern Buddhists under our sway do not produce men of the capacity which is exhibited by a Dorjiev." Landon added, "Such quick-witted adventurers are often the most effective screen which can be interposed between two advancing nationalities so long, of course, as they are officially recognized by neither."[12]

Not having a Dorjiev, all that was left to Curzon was direct action. On June 26, 1902 he sent a representative named White to Giagong in Sikkim to reassert British rights to the territory which had been previously seized by the Tibetans. This threat of force succeeded, and the Tibetans retreated behind the line recognized by the British. Just as it had not honored the Chefoo Convention of 1876 in which China permitted Britain to trade in Tibet, Lhasa protested the validity of the 1890 convention between India and China which had defined the Sikkim border with Tibet, claiming that the Tibetan government had never signed it. But White's mission at least provoked a response from the Chinese *Amban* in Lhasa, who promised to produce a high-level Tibetan to begin negotiations.

Curzon—correctly as it turned out—had little faith that the Tibetans would ever get down to negotiations. His patience was threadbare. Believing that the root of the difficulties with Tibet was

Russian influence in Lhasa, the Viceroy still saw force as the only solution. On January 8, 1903 he proposed to London that a mission with armed escort be sent to Lhasa and there settle once and for all India's relationship with Tibet.

London was reluctant to indulge Curzon in his forward policy. White's mission had already provoked Russian protests. Any move deep into Tibet could be expected to bring a stronger reaction from St. Petersburg. As a compromise, the Viceroy was given authority to send a mission to Khamba Dzong, the nearest inhabited place inside Tibetan territory easily reached from Giagong. Curzon chose as leader Major Francis Younghusband, an officer of the India service who had already made a brilliant record along the frontier. His escort would consist of two hundred rifles, calculated to make his negotiating voice more convincing. The plan called for Younghusband to meet in Khamba Dzong with a high-level emmissary of the Dalai Lama and a representative from China. It was hoped that firm agreement on trade and boundary matters could finally be reached with the Tibetans at this meeting. But if agreement proved impossible, Curzon would have convincing evidence that Lhasa had no intention of abiding by British-Chinese agreements. The real significance of this would be the confirmation that Tibet had fallen under serious Russian influence.

The Khamba Dzong mission failed since an adequately ranking Tibetan negotiator never appeared. Smarting under this indignity, Curzon grasped at every shred of evidence which supported his stand that Tibet must be brought to heel by armed invasion. Younghusband, no less aggressive than Curzon, obliged the Viceroy by sending back all sorts of intelligence which supported the forward policy.

Curzon's force of will and tenacity more than anything else was responsible for finally wearing down London's resistance. In October 1903 Younghusband was authorized to advance into Tibet as far as Gyantse. The Secretary of State for Indian Affairs telegraphed further instructions on November 6, specifying that the permission to proceed "should not be allowed to lead to occupation or to permanent intervention in Tibetan affairs" since the sole purpose of the mission was to "obtain satisfaction."[13] Prime Minister Balfour's Conservative government—wobbly and unsure of itself—was proceeding warily lest it risk censure for an adventurous policy in Tibet.

The mission's escort was augmented by nearly three thousand men under Brigadier J. Macdonald. Younghusband—recalled to the summer capital in Simla for final orders—was frank in acknowledging his bewilderment at the instructions which he received. Obtaining "satisfaction" for real and imagined insults against the Indian government seemed like a strange purpose for a military expedition when at issue were important matters of trade rights which the British had been seeking since 1873. Younghusband saw little difference between his objective and that of Warren Hastings a century before. It was "to put our intercourse with the Tibetans on proper terms."[14] This would require a permanent mission. Younghusband and Curzon, of course, both understood that the real issue was British primacy in an area essential to the security of India. Imperial Russia could not be allowed to enter the vacuum which was being created by the disintegration of the Manchu Empire. But Curzon was not overly concerned by London's strange rationale. At least he had authority to act; events would let him have his way.

After one brief engagement with Tibetan border troops and another clash along the way, Younghusband's force reached Gyantse in April 1904. The Tibetans, however, were no more willing to negotiate here than at Khamba Dzong. To the contrary, they attacked the British on May 5.

London—already more deeply involved in Tibet than it wanted to be—now had no alternative but to order the mission to advance on Lhasa. The British column moved quickly to Tibet's capital, meeting only minor opposition along the way. On August 2 Younghusband came within sight of the Potala and saw the goal which had so long eluded Englishmen. Soon after entering Lhasa he learned that the Dalai Lama and Dorjiev had fled northward to Urga, Mongolia, where they became political refugees under the protection of the High Lama of Mongolia. The Grand Lama was also accompanied by his Chief Magician, whose magic now failed but who could at least find some satisfaction in the accuracy of an earlier prophesy which promised that the "Year of the Wood Dragon" (1904 by Western calendars) would bring disaster to Tibet.

Curzon had been withdrawn from India in the midst of the expedition to Lhasa. This removed the architect of the forward policy and its staunchest defender. The cautious Balfour government—overwhelmed by the results of a policy which it had backed into—wanted to withdraw from Tibet as soon as possible. Especially worrisome to Whitehall was the treaty Younghusband had negotiated with the defeated Tibetans, which in two respects deviated from his instructions. One clause specified that the British were to occupy the Chumbi Valley until the indemnity had been paid—a period of seventy-five years. Another clause appended to the treaty enabled the British to send a representative to Lhasa "to consult with high Chinese and Tibetan officials on such commercial matters of importance as he has found impossible to settle at Gyantse." London wanted neither to occupy Tibet nor place an agent in Lhasa and had earlier gone on record to this effect in correspondence with the Government of India. Younghusband's dissenting views on these points were well known. Both he and Curzon had argued that there should be a British resident posted permanently in Lhasa.

It is a measure of Younghusband's convictions that he exceeded his instructions in negotiating a treaty which, if left to stand, would have made Tibet a virtual vassal of England. Although there was something grand about Younghusband's march to Lhasa, he treated the political aspects of his mission in a most cavalier fashion. His actions cannot be condoned even in the light of history, and London certainly did not forgive him at the time. He was to some extent made scapegoat for a Tibet policy which had never been popular and had in fact become acutely embarassing as Great Britain sought agreement with Russia. Nevertheless, he must bear a fair share of blame for allowing a myopic view of the Tibetan problem to enable him to conclude a solemn agreement which could never be carried out.

The stationing of a British representative in Lhasa would imply political aims and would thus be unnecessarily provocative to St. Petersburg, with whom London was then trying to reach an *entente cordiale*. The other disturbing fact was that Younghusband had negotiated directly with the Tibetans—pointedly excluding the Chinese *Amban*. This could be interpreted to mean that Tibet and Britain no longer recognized China's suzerain role and, further, that Britain had assumed the position of suzerain in China's place. This not only added to Russia's uneasiness but outraged Peking as well. London knew that China's legal presence in Tibet was valuable to prevent a vacuum which the Russians might find inviting. Clearly a new agreement had to be reached with Peking to rectify the situation.

On April 27, 1906, after eighteen months of negotiations, Great Britain reached agreement with China on Tibet. Younghusband's Anglo-Tibetan Convention of 1904 was endorsed by China only after important modifications had been made. Peking had wanted Great Britain to recognize full Chinese sovereignty over Tibet. This, of course, was rejected as being inconsistent with Tibet's buffer role, but the British did agree to preserve Chinese suzerainty and give up any privileged position secured by Younghusband's agreement.

London stabilized Russian relations in Central Asia by the Anglo-Russian Convention of 1907. This important treaty settled competing interests of the two countries in Persia, Afghanistan and Tibet. Both countries agreed not to station representatives in Lhasa and to negotiate with Tibet only through China. Tibet, in short, would henceforward serve as a buffer between India and Russia. With their traditional disregard for Chinese suzerainty and with perhaps more foresight than the British, the Tibetans refused to sign either the Anglo-Chinese Convention of 1906 or the Anglo-Russian Convention of 1907. Nevertheless, the latter agreement ended whatever hopes the Dalai Lama had for Russian support. The Great Game may have officially ended when Younghusband marched into Lhasa, but the 1907 treaty provided the real framework for a period of British-Russian co-existence in Asia.

Curzon left India before Younghusband's mission was completed, and with him went an era. Curzon had a concept of empire which fitted the Victorian period that was ending. Curzon at the height of his influence is said to have forbidden the singing of "Onward Christian Soldiers" in the churches of India on the grounds that this hymn contained the subversive lines, "Crowns and thorns may perish, Kingdoms rise and wane." But this did not prevent his own crown from perishing nor his kingdom from waning. This controversial Viceroy's forward policy made sense in the context of its time, but times were changing. Moreover, Curzon had been wrong and London right in one critical respect; Tibet could never appropriately be a British vassal.

Lord Curzon's Tibet policy, which culminated in the Younghusband expedition and the flight of the Thirteenth Dalai Lama, has been accused of providing China with an opportunity and excuse to reassert power which heretofore had been only a "constitutional fiction"—to use Curzon's own words. On the other side of the argument, Balfour's government has been blamed for permitting

China to regain its position of power in Tibet by insisting on a new treaty which re-established Chinese primacy. If Curzon could defend himself, he would doubtless argue that London's diplomacy, by undoing what he had accomplished, was to blame. Lord Morley, Secretary of State for India, did believe that Chinese control of Tibet was tolerable so long as the border states of Nepal, Sikkim and Bhutan remained firmly under British control, but the forward-policy adherents argued that abandonment of Tibet to China—even if militarily endurable—set a bad precedent. Seeing British weakness in Tibet, could China, when strong again, resist the temptation to move against the border areas?

Yet it is understandable that London at the turn of the century sought to use Chinese influence as a counterbalance against Russian power—amply demonstrated to be the more dangerous of the two. The formula which the British were groping for in the early twentieth century was an autonomous Tibet, subject to a weak Chinese suzerain and guaranteed by a British-Russian treaty. This formula denied Tibet to Russia, provided a buffer for the Indian Empire and enabled India to trade freely with Lhasa.

In refusing to sanction the terms for Tibet which Curzon and Younghusband favored, London could have justified its action by the need to reach accommodation with Russia so that both empires could co-exist peacefully from Persia to the Pamirs. But even without this consideration it would have been folly to push the boundaries of British rule northward beyond the Himalayas and across the Tibetan plateau to the borders of China. As Bogle had wisely said many years before, "Communications cannot be kept open. . . ." Even if the required British forces had been available, they could never have been supported in far-off Tibet garrisons. Moreover, for Britain to man a common frontier with China was to invite conflict in an area where China had the advantage.

The British had traditionally viewed Tibet as a lucrative extension of the subcontinent market, but its trade value could never be worth the cost of policing what would surely prove to be a hostile Tibetan population. The Indian subcontinent, for all its diversity in language, race, color, religion and culture, is a geographic entity with natural boundaries—the seas and the mountains. It had been under British rule for 150 years, so there existed common services, a common constitution and a government with more continuity than had ever existed before. Tibetans, however, are not part of the subcontinent any more than they are part of China. They have always considered themselves separate and independent despite temporary foreign incursions and fluctuating Chinese suzerainty. The British in 1906 could only have ruled with force—more force than could be spared in view of far-flung imperial commitments.

While the Tibetan plateau was a buffer in the sense that it was a political no-man's-land, India's defense was doubly assured by a system of border states or frontier zones under British influence. The Northwest Frontier Province, the princely states of Kashmir, Bhutan and Sikkim, and the Kingdom of Nepal were turrets astride the Karakorum and Himalayan battlements.

Imperial Russia similarly needed a buffer belt, and this was provided in Northern Persia, Afghanistan and Tibet by the 1907 Anglo-Russian Convention. Like Great Britain, Russia also needed an inner defense line. The emirates and khanates of Turkmanistan and Turkestan, Sinkiang and Outer Mongolia thus figured in St. Petersburg's strategic planning.

If Curzon can be accused of cherishing outdated dreams of expanded empire, Nicholas can similarly be criticized for harboring fantasies which led him to grasp at the key to Lamaist power in greater Tibet and Mongolia. Dorjiev and Younghusband in very different ways were themselves skillful players of the Great Game. It was their masters who were guilty of bad judgment. While the instincts of Whitehall rescued England at the eleventh hour from Curzon's zeal and were able to keep empire doctrine intact, the instincts of the Russian Foreign Office—of Lamsdorff specifically—were not strong enough to check the adventures of the political dilettante Nicholas. Thus the Dorjiev operation, once revealed, had to be played to its logical but foredoomed end.

China's frontier policy has had the advantages of long-established tradition and consistency. The Great Wall defines the limits of the Middle Kingdom—the citadel of the Empire. While blessed with power—or the "mandate from heaven"—successive dynasties have pushed China's frontiers deep into the inner Asian borderlands of Manchuria, Mongolia, Sinkiang and Tibet. During the ebb phase of dynasty the frontiers have contracted as the tribes and vassals reasserted their independence from the Han Middle Kingdom. These phases of the cycle may have determined China's *de facto* boundary lines. But never are the Chinese in any doubt that the real boundary is still the point of greatest thrust during earlier periods of expansion.

In 1907 the Manchu dynasty had nearly reached the end of its life cycle. Chinese power in Lhasa had been more nominal than real for decades. By the end of the century Peking's inability to defend Lhasa—from either Russian intrigues or British invasion—was proof of Manchu impotence. But the Emperor would make one last effort in Tibet before the "divine mandate" was, at least for a time, withdrawn. Even in dying, the sinking regime was perhaps conscious of its obligation to some still unknown future dynasty, and the Emperor extremely reluctant to accept an outer limit of the Heavenly Empire in the subcontinent.

CHAPTER 4

McMAHON DRAWS A LINE

Well authenticated records—both Chinese and Tibetan including the China-Tibet treaty of 822 AD *and the Chinese maps of the Tang dynasty—indicate historic Tibetan frontiers such as are shown by the red line on the skeleton map which I now lay upon the table.*

Sir Henry McMahon, February 17, 1914 at the Simla Conference

The genesis of the "McMahon Line," India's Assam boundary, is a story of Great Britain's efforts to limit Chinese authority in Tibet and to commit the Chinese to accept the Himalayan crest—India's vital rampart of defense—rather than the Himalayan southern base as the northeast boundary between India and Tibet. The drawing of this line represents a vital phase in Chinese-Indian relations. China's Communist dynasty fifty years later would reap the benefit of its predecessor's stubbornness and sense of greater Chinese destiny in refusing to accept Britain's formula. Independent India, inheritor of Britain's Indian empire, would suffer the consequences.

The events which led to a tripartite meeting of India, China and Tibet in India's summer capital of Simla in 1913 on the status of Tibet began with the flight of the Dalai Lama from Lhasa to Mongolia in 1904 to escape Younghusband's troops. British forces had chased the Lama from the Potala into ignominious exile, and British diplomacy had foiled his scheme with Dorjiev by concluding the Anglo-Russian Convention of 1907. The Dalai was an exile, whose return to Lhasa required Chinese cooperation. Although under the Emperor's control, Tibet's God-King was not without some bargaining power. The Chinese, who had seen how difficult it was to control Tibet without him, thus found it in their interest as well as his to reach an accommodation, and the Dalai was allowed to return. Before leaving Peking the God-King also made his peace with the British. He sent word to King Edward VII through His Majesty's Minister in Peking that it was his "sincere desire that peace and friendship should exist between the two neighboring countries."[1]

The Dalai returned to the Potala in December 1909. Despite earlier promises made to him, it soon became apparent that the Chinese would be content with nothing less than total absorption of Tibet. An expeditionary force under General Chao Erh-feng moved against Tibet. "Butcher Chao"—as he is still remembered by the Tibetans—brutally subjugated eastern Tibet and made preparations to march on Lhasa. Having so recently fled the capital to avoid Younghusband's invading army, the unfortunate Dalai now found himself forced to appeal to the British to stop Chao Erh-feng. It was too late, however; an advance column of two thousand Chinese troops under General Chung Ying entered Lhasa in February 1910.

Peking had put a price on the head of each of the Tibetan ministers, and it was clear that they intended to force the Dalai Lama himself to serve under duress as puppet to Chao's occupation army. Rather than to endure this, the Dalai decided again to flee—this time to the protection of the British. A pitiful force of Tibetan soldiers fought a rear-guard action while the God-King and his entourage made good their escape to Sikkim on horseback.[2]

The Chinese made no effort to conceal their intentions. Chao Erh-feng had drawn up a new administrative blueprint creating an enlarged province of Sikang and incorporating in it much of eastern Tibet. Direct Chinese jurisdiction would, in fact, have extended to within sixty miles of Lhasa if this plan had been carried out. Other ominous clues to Peking's intentions were attempts in 1910 to press old claims to Nepal, Bhutan and Assam Himalaya. Provoked by official Chinese announcements describing these areas as being in vassalage to China, London warned Peking in strongest terms that any attempt to make good these false allegations would be resisted.

Chinese designs on the Himalayan foothills of Assam were underscored by the dispatch of troops to seize Poyul—a town just north of Abor tribal territory along the Tsangpo-Brahmaputra River. More serious were reports that Chao's agents had convoked a meeting of Mishmi tribal headmen and elicited from them expressions of allegiance to Peking.

Such evidence of Chinese pressure in Assam Himalaya—India's northeast frontier with Tibet—made the British extremely uneasy. If the Assam hills were to fall under Peking's control, the rich Assam Valley itself would no longer be tenable. London was cautious, however. British coastal trade with China was flourishing and could not be jeopardized. Moreover, London did not want to provide St. Petersburg with any excuse to revise or disregard the recently concluded 1907 convention. Thus, despite repeated warnings from the government of India regarding Chinese moves toward Assam, London found itself in a dilemma which made retaliation difficult.

The hill tribes of Assam had always been troublesome. East of Towang the Himalayan foothills are inhabited by aborigines—the Akas, Daflas, Apo, Manis, Miris, Abors and Mishmis. There was no governmental structure—no tribal federation—with which the British could negotiate. Each forest village served only an autonomous headman. The Assam kings traditionally used petty bribery to keep the hill tribes from raiding into the valley; thus when the British acquired Assam in 1826 as a result of the First Burmese War, they simply continued the same system. Military occupation or civil administration in the usual sense of the word would not only have appeared difficult but, until Chao Erh-feng's campaign, unnecessary.

Another approach to the hill tribe problem was to create a buffer zone which would reduce contact—and consequently friction—between the civilized valley dwellers and the primitive hill tribes. The Bengal Eastern Frontier Regulation of 1873 described an "inner line" running eastward along the foothills from the Bhutan boundary. North of this line travel and residence were strictly controlled. Delimiting the northern boundary of the buffer zone was an "outer line." North of the outer line were the tribal areas of Assam Himalaya which the British in 1910 considered part of their sphere of influence and responsibility even though they were not formally administered by the government of India.

It was British policy to leave the tribes alone. As long as tribes existed in a free state and there appeared to be no question of rival foreign influences on them, the British saw no reason to disturb the existing situation. British tea and lumber interests in Assam eyed the forested Himalayan foothills with undisguised interest and government of India officials longed to explore in depth this uncharted, primitive area. But official policy—clearly enunciated in the

Government of India Act of 1858—forbade occupation and discouraged exploration. The act specified that the revenues of India could not be used to defray the expenses of any military operation carried on beyond the external frontiers. Since for purposes of this act the external frontier was to be the outer line, there could be no question of British military protection for business ventures or exploration in the tribal areas of the Assam foothills. Moreover, the political reaction in Great Britain against Younghusband's expedition to Lhasa had caused the new Liberal government of Campbell-Bannerman to steer clear of any moves in the Assam hills which could be interpreted as a return to a forward policy.

Noel Williamson, Assistant Political Officer at Sadiya, Assam, proposed in 1911, however, to travel up the Dihang extension of the Brahmaputra toward Tibet into Abor tribal country, to investigate reports that the Chinese were pushing into this territory. On March 6 of that year the provincial government of East Bengal and Assam recommended to the Viceroy that Williamson be permitted to make this trip on the somewhat thin justification that he "arrange with the hillmen for the payment of poll tax for land cultivation."[3] The Government of India replied by telegram on March 22, asking specifically whether Williamson intended to cross the outer line. This was followed up with another telegram on March 23 which "assumed" that it would not be necessary for him to go beyond the line. Calcutta knew its men well and clearly had its wind up about Williamson, so once more he was queried. None of the messages reached him, however, because he had set out from Sadiya on March 4—long before Calcutta had had a chance to reply to the first message sent by the Governor of East Bengal! This was "initiative" in the Younghusband tradition.

Late in March Williamson was in the vicinity of the village of Kebang, whose inhabitants had become frightened by tales that the English party was the vanguard of a British punitive mission. A band of Kebang Abor warriors, later estimated at more than one hundred, tracked the Englishmen, and first found Williamson's companion, Dr. Gregorson, at an encampment called Panggi, where he had been left by Williamson to tend some sick porters. The frenzied Abors fell on the helpless doctor and cut him down with their swords. The tribesmen, now blooded, continued after Williamson, whom they overtook at a village called Komsing, north of Kebang.

While talking with village elders, Williamson noticed that four armed Kebang men had joined the circle. Uneasy at their obvious surliness he asked the headman, "What are these men from Kebang doing in Komsing?" At this moment one of the warriors flourished his long knife, and on signal the Kebang warriors fell on Williamson and hacked him to death. Most of his porters were also slaughtered on the spot, although a few managed to escape through the dense forest and make their way back to Sadiya, where they reported the massacre.[4]

It is ironic that only by death was Williamson able to accomplish what he had sought to do in life—bring the Assam Himalayan tribal areas under firm British control. His tragic death provided an excuse to send a military campaign into the Assam hill tribe areas, including those infiltrated by the Chinese. Major General Hamilton Bower in 1911 led the Abor Expedition, which was meant to demonstrate control and pre-empt administration of the Himalayan southern slopes before the Chinese could do so.

Chao Erh-feng had occupied Lhasa, but he had not completely subjugated Tibet. Active resistance to the Chinese continued in the southeast, while in Lhasa the people passively resisted the Chinese in every way they could. The Panchen Lama, whom the Chinese had wanted to head the government in the place of the Dalai, refused to do so. The Tibet National Assembly adopted a sullen and sometimes hostile attitude toward the alien occupation force. From exile in India the Dalai Lama did what he could on a diplomatic level to help his country. He pleaded for British help against the Chinese. He even secretly solicited Russian aid, only to suffer the humiliation of having his one-time "protector"—now bound by the Anglo-Russian 1907 Convention—reject his plea through official British channels.

Peking ultimately realized that it could not rule Tibet without the God-King unless they deployed a tremendously large army of occupation—a lesson which the Chinese would remember for forty years, when they would next seize an opportunity to occupy Tibet. But before China could reach an arrangement with the Dalai Lama, the Emperor and the Manchu dynasty were swept away by the Chinese Revolution. The upheaval, which began in 1911 and made China a republic, was felt almost immediately in Tibet. The Chinese garrison in Lhasa mutinied and broke up into unrully mobs, which foraged through the countryside, looting as they went. With a vengeance bred of hatred and long frustration, Tibetans rose against the disorganized Chinese and slaughtered thousands of them before the British intervened to rescue survivors. By January 1913, the Dalai Lama was able to return safely to Lhasa and reassert his authority.

The most meaningful bond between the Manchus and the Dalai Lamas had been the patron-priest relationship. This cord of religion had been snapped when a secular republic came into being. Tibetans no longer felt any tie with China. The Chinese concept of empire, to the contrary, was not religiously based, and in April 1912 the new Republic proclaimed that Tibet, Mongolia and Sinkiang were equivalent to provinces of China and thus integral parts of the Chinese state.

By no stretch of the imagination could Tibetans recognize the new President of China, Yuan Shih-kai, as a successor to their Manchu patron. While they may have traditionally recognized that some suzerain authority was vested in the Emperor, they never recognized the suzerainty of the Chinese state. This distinction provided Tibet with its best case for independence. It is significant that Dorjiev, who understood Tibetan psychology, had felt it necessary to disguise Nicholas II with the robes of a "White Lama" before attempting to project him in the patron's role.

The Dalai Lama declared Tibet's independence by publicly refusing to acknowledge that he drew his authority from China's recognition of him. With perhaps more symbolic than actual significance, Dorjiev was welcomed back to Lhasa. But his presence understandably gave rise to speculation that Outer Mongolia had concluded a secret pact with Tibet and—coming on the heels of Russian moves in Mongolia*—this disturbed both the Chinese and the British. It also resulted in new urgency to settle Tibet's status and boundaries once and for all.

Neither the Chinese Republic's policy of considering Tibet a province nor the Dalai Lama's rejection of Chinese suzerainty suited the British. London found useful Peking's "suzerain" role since it provided China with some legal primacy yet deprived it of effective control. Its legal presence prevented a vacuum which Britain still feared might be filled by Russia.

Chao Erh-feng's campaign, particularly his probes into Assam,

* The Russo-Mongolian Agreement of October 12, 1912 made Outer Mongolia a virtual protectorate of Russia.

had made clear the dangers of an ambiguous status for Tibet. In August 1912 London proposed to the new Republic that Tibet's status be negotiated on the basis of the situation which had existed before Younghusband's mission. After much reluctance the Chinese agreed not only to negotiate Tibet's status with the British but to accept a representative of Lhasa as co-equal plenipotentiary in the negotiations. The inclusion of such a representative was, in fact, an important part of Britain's diplomatic plan. It was calculated that Tibet's full participation in the negotiations would constitute evidence of autonomy, thereby adding substance to whatever agreement on Tibet was finally reached.

The Simla conference began in India's picturesque summer capital in October 1913. The host and British delegate was Sir Henry McMahon, Secretary to the Government of India and an impressive Victorian, who officially assumed the role of "mediator" between the other two participants. This pose was adopted in part for tactical reasons, but it was also meant to circumvent the prohibition against direct negotiations with Tibet contained in the Anglo-Russian Convention of 1907. The Tibetan delegate was Lon-chen Shatra,* a Chief Minister in Lhasa. The Chinese were represented by Ivan Chen, who fought stubbornly for China's position but seemed, nonetheless, genuinely committed to reaching a settlement based on compromise. Contrary to later Chinese claims, China was not forced to attend Simla nor did Chen's performance in any way suggest that he was negotiating under duress.

The main point of contention during the six months of negotiations was the boundary between China and Tibet. The area which is ethnically Tibetan has always extended further than the area under Lhasa's political control. Perhaps influenced by the new Mongolian pattern—in which Outer Mongolia became an autonomous buffer responsive to Russia, while Inner Mongolia remained a province of China—McMahon proposed that an Outer and an Inner Tibet be created. Outer Tibet—or that area traditionally under Lhasa's control—would be master of its own internal affairs and could thus serve as a buffer between India and China. Inner Tibet—an integral part of China—would serve as a buffer between Lhasa's Tibet and Russian-dominated Outer Mongolia. From British India's point of view this formula offered protection from both Russia and

* Lon-chen is a Tibetan title meaning "Chief Minister."

China and recognized at the same time that the farthest reaches of ethnic Tibet could not practically be controlled from Lhasa.

McMahon was an enthusiastic believer in the buffer concept. He equated "frontier" with "buffer" and defined each as a tract of neutral territory separating two potentially antagonistic neighbors. A "boundary" to McMahon was a specific line, either delimited by precise map description or demarcated by ground surveys.[5] He believed that it was the frontier, buffer zone which had greatest importance and considered a boundary line of considerably lesser significance—particularly when it ran through uninhabitable mountain or desert terrain. Yet it was the inability of China and Tibet to agree on a boundary between Inner and Outer Tibet that prevented China from ratifying the Simla Convention.

In the light of the current China-India boundary dispute it is significant that the India-Tibet boundary itself, proposed at Simla, did not cause the difficulty. This line, known since as the McMahon Line, runs along the crest of the Himalayan watershed in India's northeastern frontier area. By this delimitation McMahon sought to make Assam Himalaya secure and remove any ambiguity about India's sovereignty over the tribal areas on the mountain's southern slope.

China raised no objection to McMahon's formula at Simla in 1914 or in the several years following the conference during which Britain still hoped for Peking's acceptance of the convention. But in 1960, during boundary discussions with India, the Communist Chinese negotiators denied that the Tibet-Indian boundary question had ever been formally raised at Simla. They alleged that the subject had been discussed only "secretly," behind the back of their delegate.

The record, however, does not bear out this accusation. In 1914 McMahon insisted that the political status of Tibet could not be meaningfully discussed until the limits of the country were defined. When Ivan Chen explained that he was not yet authorized to join in boundary discussions, McMahon suggested that to save time he discuss it with the Tibetan delegate.[6] Chen did not raise any objection to this proposal, and bilateral discussions were held between January 15 and January 31, 1914 in the midst of the Simla Convention. An exchange of letters between the British and Tibetan representatives on March 24 and March 25, documenting the results of

A rare 17th century engraving of the Potala as it appeared in mid-17th century before the Great Fifth Dalai Lama began construction of the palace in Lhasa that still stands today.

(*Above*) Emperor K'ang Hsi—the first Emperor to establish an important Chinese claim to Tibet. (Chinese painting reproduced in *Jehol, City of Emperors,* by Sven Hedin, 1933.)

(*Left*) Aguan Dorjiev, agent of the Czar in Tibet. (From *Tibet, Past and Present,* by Sir Charles Bell, 1924.)

Palace of Punakka in Bootan. (Engraving from *An Account of an Embassy to the Court of the Tashoo Lama in Tibet,* by Samuel Turner, 1800.)

The Dalai Lama delivering a sermon at the Buddha Jyanti ceremonies in Calcutta during his 1956 visit to India.

High in the Himalayas the Dalai Lama rests with a squad of loyal Khamba tribesmen in his flight from the Red Chinese in March, 1959. (Wide World Photos.)

these discussions, constitutes the Anglo-Tibetan Boundary Agreement of 1914.

Even before this, on February 17, McMahon had tabled a statement with an explanatory map describing the boundaries of Tibet. In doing this he said: "Well authenticated records, both Chinese and Tibetan including the China-Tibet treaty of 822 A.D. and the Chinese maps of the Tang dynasty, indicate historic Tibetan frontiers such as are shown by the red line on the skeleton map which I now lay upon the table."[7] This same map was attached to the draft Simla Convention. Thus to a significant extent Chen was concerned with the India-Tibet boundary question at Simla, regardless of any subsequent claims to the contrary. Since Chen initialed the Convention—Article 9 of which makes specific reference to Tibet's boundaries and refers to the map attachment showing the McMahon line in red—it is unreasonable for China now to allege that the India-Tibet boundary was not taken up at Simla.[8]

On July 3, 1914 the Simla Convention was signed by Britain and Tibet. The Chinese government refused to be a party to it even though Chen had initialed the draft agreement—a step which usually connotes informal acceptance. Subsequent but unsuccessful efforts were made to gain Peking's adherence to the Convention.

Peking's main reason for rejecting the Simla Convention stems from China's basic and traditional unwillingness to relinquish rights to territory which it considers to be eternally part of the "celestial" realm. It is likely that the idea of negotiating on equal terms with a country which it considered to be a vassal prejudiced China against any reasonable solution from the start. Yet by a series of other bilateral agreements negotiated by Tibet, and because Tibet's participation in the Simla conference was at least tolerated by China, Tibet's right to "settle her own relations with India"[9] has, in fact, been recognized by China, as pointed out by India in 1961.

The door was left open in the event China chose later to accept the Simla agreement. But Republican Peking's attitude remained consistent with constant and historical Han assumptions which consider "retreat" a phenomenon of weakness and "advance" an inevitable consequence of regained strength. China would not sign away what it assumed it could regain at a later date. As a result there was never again an opportunity to resolve the status of Tibet and establish its boundaries to the satisfaction of all parties.

Following the Simla conference China's energies were first devoted to building a modern and viable state. External threats intruded, however, and the new Republic floundered. A Tibetan monk from the Chumbi Valley prophesied in 1922, "This is the time for the Lower Horpas [Japanese] to rise to the position of a Great Power."[10] A decade later Japan invaded Manchuria and plunged China into a marathon war of survival which was finally won only in the context of Japan's total defeat in World War II. China, the "sick man of Asia," was easy prey for Japan, whose imperial ambition included at a minimum all of East Asia, Australasia, and the Western Pacific.

World War II left Tibet relatively untouched. Except for a reconnaissance mission to Lhasa by Tolstoi and Dolan—U.S. army officers investigating the feasibility of an alternate overland route by which the Allies could supply China—Tibet was completely bypassed by the combatants. Yet, even before Japan attacked China and well before World War II, a new storm was gathering which would be infinitely more significant for Asia. With astonishing foresight and political acumen the Thirteenth Dalai Lama saw its implications for Tibet before he died in 1931. In his will, drawn up a few months before his death, the Dalai Lama told his people, "The present is the time of the five kinds of degeneration in all countries.* In the worst class is the . . . red people."[11]

The God-King was referring specifically to Communists, whom he knew had gained control of Russia and had, as he wrote, "taken away all the sacred objects from the monasteries in Mongolia." The anti-religiousness of Communism deeply distressed the aging Lama, and he solemnly warned his people: "Unless we can guard our own country, it will happen that the Dalai Lama and the Panchen Lama, the Father and the Son, the Holder of the Faith, the glorious Rebirth will be broken down and left without a name."[12]

How accurate his warning was!

* War, calamities of nature, etc.

CHAPTER 5

THE YEAR OF THE IRON TIGER

We understand that the United Nations have decided to stop aggression whenever it takes place.

From a government of Tibet telegram to the Secretary General of the United Nations in 1950, protesting Chinese Communist aggression

1950 was a year of crisis in Asia. It was the year the Korean War began and the year France faced defeat in its exhausting war in Indo-China. South Asia was troubled by problems which were less only by comparison. A revolt against the ruling "Rana" aristocracy focused momentary attention on the remote Himalayan kingdom of Nepal. India's relations with Pakistan were still tense in the wake of partition, and emotions on both sides ran high as the United Nations Security Council examined the Kashmir dispute. Communist insurrection wracked Hyderabad State in Central India, while linguistic, religious and sectional antagonisms less dramatically tore at newly independent India's fragile unity.

In Tibet, where the calendar designates the years by combining the names of an element with the name of an animal, 1950 was the "Year of the Iron Tiger." For Tibetans it was a cataclysmic year—more ferocious even than its name suggested. On August 15 the shocks of the fifth worst earthquake in recorded history caused several mountains in Tibet to shift and villages to be buried.

Robert Ford, a British radio operator under contract to the Tibet government in the eastern border town of Chamdo, described an eerie red glow on the horizon accompanied by shattering earth tremors which brought Tibetan villagers streaming in terror from their crumbling homes.[1] Other eyewitness reports gradually filtered through to the rest of the world and told of landslides which filled valleys and blocked rivers. It was reported in the Calcutta *Statesman* on August 16 that the epicenter of the earthquake was a point in the Eastern Himalayas about fifty miles from the northeast border of Assam. The article added that "holiday crowds in Calcutta celebrating Independence Day ran for shelter as the city rocked," and the severity of the shocks was such that at the Alipore meteorological office the pen of one of the seismographs was thrown completely off the recording drum.

Tibet's tragedy was compounded when the Tsangpo River—father of the mighty Brahmaputra—fought its way out of a prison of earth created by the quake and rampaged wildly through Assam, washing out two thousand villages as it went. The important center of Sadiya in Assam was inundated, while thousands were made homeless in the area surrounding Jorhat. Landslides had forced the Tsangpo to find a new bed—in some places many miles from the old.

Then, recalling the warnings sounded by the Thirteenth Dalai Lama in his last will and testament, the greatest catastrophy of all befell Tibet. Red armies struck on October 7, 1950. More than 30,000 troops of Communist China's so-called People's Liberation Army invaded eastern Tibet. Another force struck western Tibet, crossing Indian soil in the Aksai Chin corner of Ladakh.[2] This latter thrust, which went unnoticed for several years, is significant because it was Communist China's first violation of independent Indian territory and because the Red forces traveled a route which later was the site of a secretly constructed Chinese trunk road.

The main attack was aimed at the town of Chamdo, whose defenses crumbled on October 19. Ngapo Ngawang Jigme, the Commissioner General of Kham Province, who commanded three thousand Tibetan defenders, fled as the Chinese approached but was quickly intercepted by advance columns and forced to surrender the province to the invaders. It was at this time that Ngabo was persuaded to shift his personal loyalties to the Communists, and he thereafter became prominent as Peking's most important collaborator. Soon after the fall of Chamdo, Chinese forces secured control of the Chamdo-Lhasa road and prepared to march on Lhasa itself.

The invasion of Tibet had been loudly heralded by China's propaganda machine, which tried on one hand to weaken Tibet's will to resist and on the other to intimidate the Government of India and prevent it from opposing China's act. India was accused of crimes of aggression and expansion which Communist China itself intended to commit; cause was purposely confused with effect in such a way as to reverse blame. The new Indian nation was challenged by Peking to prove its independence by repudiating the British-India policy toward Tibet and relinquishing residual rights in Lhasa inherited from the British *Raj*. According to Communist propaganda, India—"a running dog of the Anglo-American imperialists"—was the aggressor. Typical of Peking's anti-Indian propaganda diatribes during this period was an accusation that "the American Government and the reactionary clique of the Indian Government were conspiring in an imperialistic expansion into the Chinese Province of Tibet."[3]

The Chinese also claimed "proof" of India-British collusion in a fanciful story which they embroidered to account for the murder of Geda, a high-ranking lama or "Living Buddha," who had been sent back to Tibet for the purpose of negotiating an unopposed occupation of eastern Tibet. Peking charged that this envoy—documented as Vice-Chairman of the Sikang Provisional Government—was captured by the Tibetan army on orders of "the British special agent, Ford." It was alleged that he had then been fed poison, after which "his stomach and head began to ache, his mouth exuded yellow saliva, his nostrils bled and leaked gore and his limbs were numbed." He died the follow day, while "his entire body turned black and the skin fell away at the touch of one's hand."[4]

Robert Ford had maintained communications at Chamdo for the Tibetan government when the Chinese invaded. After his capture by the People's Liberation Army he was brutally interrogated in an effort to force him to confess that he had murdered Geda and had been the instrument of secret British collaboration with Tibet. The real details of Geda's death are obscure, but if he was killed by Tibetans, it is certain that his executioners felt it justified. Geda was a collaborator who had sold out to the Chinese many years before. According to the December 1950 issue of the Communist magazine *People's China*, he had "helped the Chinese Red Army during the Long March in 1935" and more recently had "supported the People's Liberation Army when Kangting was liberated."

Doctrine as well as propaganda is an important weapon for Communism. Propaganda must serve doctrine and doctrine must justify the act. Doctrine may, of course, be interpreted or it may evolve, providing it is made to do so with enough grace and ingenuity to maintain a semblance of consistency, but it must not be obviously ignored or violated. Applicable to Tibet was the Communist line on "nationalities and minorities." The Tibet issue struck close to the heart of Peking's most dangerous problem—Han dominance over the many ethnic minorities in China.

Stalin had established basic Communist doctrine on the nationality and minority question and had specifically defined a "nationality" eligible for full national independence. In 1913 he wrote: "A nation is an historically evolved, stable community of language, territory, economic life and psychological make up, manifested in a community of culture."[5]

The Chinese People's Republic avoided the problem in its own case by denying that its minorities fulfilled the requirements established in Stalin's doctrine. Spotting a convenient loophole, Peking exploited Stalin's words, describing nationalism as being either "progressive" or "reactionary." Burhan, Red China's doctrinal expert, declared, "Any national movement which seeks separation from the Chinese People's Republic for independence will be reactionary since, objectively considered, it would undermine the interests of the various races . . . and thus work to the advantage of imperialism."[6] Tibet was portrayed as a clearly reactionary, national minority which according to this interpretation of Stalin, had to be "liberated" and kept safe within the People's Republic.

An early statement by Peking on this subject is contained in the Constitution of the Chinese Soviet Republic, drawn up in Kiangsi under Mao Tse-tung's leadership on November 7, 1931. It recognizes "the rights of self-determination of the national minorities in China, their right to complete separation from China and the formation of an independent state." It specifies that "all Mongolians, Tibetans, Miao, Yao, Koreans and others living in the territory of China shall enjoy the full right of self-determination."[7]

Unhappily for the Tibetans, Chinese minority doctrine shifted away from Stalin's statement and for that matter from China's own Kiangsi Constitution. Following an announcement by the Chinese government on January 1, 1950 that the "liberation" of Tibet was one of the main tasks of the People's Liberation Army, the Nationalities Affairs Committee met in Peking to discuss the Tibet question. Vice-Chairman Chu Teh directed the meeting and reiterated his government's determination to "free" the Tibetan people. He explained the newest interpretation of the minority and nationality policy as laid down in the government's Common Program. This document, which had been adopted by the People's Political Consultative Conference in September 1949 and first applied to the Tibetan case, specifies that "All nationalities . . . have equal rights and duties" and declares all nationalities to be equal in status.[8]

It was the practical, not the theoretical, which interested the Tibetans. As seen through their eyes China was simply guilty of aggression. The threatening tone of Peking's propaganda, particularly as contained in repeated announcements promising that Tibet would soon be "liberated," was the only doctrine with meaning for Tibet. The Lhasa National Assembly, convening in extraordinary session, recognized the need to seek outside help and made preparations to send friendly delegations to those countries which could reasonably be expected to come to its rescue. Special envoys were prepared to plead Tibet's cause in the capitals of India, Nepal, Great Britain and the United States. Peking took note of this by accusing the delegations of being "traitorous." It warned that any nation receiving a "friendly delegation" from Lhasa would be considered hostile to the People's Republic of China.

In May 1950 K. M. Panikkar, India's new Ambassador to China, was determined to reach a peaceful settlement of the Tibet issue. He recalled in his book *In Two Chinas; Memoirs of a Diplomat* that he was "fairly optimistic about working out an area of cooperation by eliminating causes of misunderstanding." He also claimed that Nehru "in general" agreed with his convictions that the British-Indian policy of claiming special political interest in Tibet could not be continued by independent India.[9] It was thus unlikely that India at this particular moment wished to court Peking's displeasure or risk its new approach to China by receiving a Tibetan delegation which had assumed a sovereign posture; and undoubtedly Peking's threat influenced New Delhi's decision.

Hope was fast running out for Tibet, and in Lhasa it was becoming clear that if any autonomy were to be retained it would have to be the result of direct negotiations with Peking. Finding no alternative course, Tibet succumbed to Communist pressure and agreed to sending a mission to negotiate agreement on their future relationship.

Lhasa had wanted the talks held on neutral ground—specifically in Hong Kong where Chinese pressure would be less. But the mission delegates were held up in India en route to Hong Kong because British authorities procrastinated in issuing visas to them. They perhaps did not want Crown territory to be involved in any settlement in which the Tibetan delegation's mandate to negotiate or the propriety of its negotiating at all were in doubt. Since there were bound to be elements of duress implicit in the negotiations, the British were also understandably hesitant to provide good offices for an agreement which would not have world acceptance.

Talks began in New Delhi with the newly arrived Chinese Ambassador to India in September 1950, but almost immediately the Chinese insisted that they be moved to Peking. At first the unhappy Tibetans agreed since Peking's propaganda was threatening, but new reports of Red troop movements toward the capital caused the government to stop its delegation in transit to Peking. Tibet was willing to negotiate an honorable settlement but was not yet willing to negotiate as puppets of a Chinese-controlled regime in Lhasa.

New Delhi reacted officially to Chinese military action in Tibet on October 21 when Indian Ambassador Panikkar was instructed to present the Chinese with an *aide memoire* of concern. The approach was most revealing; India appealed mainly to China's self-interest rather than showing concern for its own well-established rights in Tibet. The note stressed that India's interest was "only to see that the admission of the People's Government to the U.N. is not again postponed."[10] It ignored entirely the rights of the Tibetans as well as the principle of self-determination which India had always proclaimed. The need for a peaceful solution was emphasized in terms of Chinese self-interest, not in terms of the principle of world peace which India professed to hold as the main pillar of its foreign policy.

On October 26 another Indian note pled for a peaceful approach to the Tibet problem and urged China to cease hostilities lest the Tibetan delegation feel that it was negotiation under duress. Still there was no reference to the rights of the Tibetans nor to the fact that Chinese action represented an affront and danger to India. During an interview with a Reuters correspondent in Kashmir on October 30, Nehru made a curious effort to excuse China's actions by blaming the Soviet Union for misguiding China with inaccurate intelligence. In this connection Nehru recalled recent Moscow releases which alleged that Anglo-American intrigues in Tibet were aimed at bringing Tibet into an anti-Communist bloc. He wondered whether China might not have thus been influenced in its decision to move into Tibet.

While Nehru was attributing Chinese sins to Soviet misadvice, Peking, with considerably more candor, presented its own case in a note to India. The communication dated October 30, 1950 stated bluntly: "The Central People's Government of the People Republic of China would like to make it clear Tibet is an integral part of Chinese territory and the problem of Tibet is entirely a domestic problem of China." New Delhi's argument that Peking's actions in Tibet jeopardized China's admission to the U.N. was dismissed as irrelevant, which indeed it was. The note also linked India with the forces of imperialism whose Tibetan intrigues made Chinese occupation of Tibet necessary.[11]

New Delhi realized it must take a stronger line, and on October 31, for the first time in this crisis, it officially recognized that India's interests were at stake. This was a move toward realism, though its tardy introduction perhaps prejudiced the case. It was acknowledged in a note to Peking that Tibetan rights should have been considered. From a legalistic point of view it is significant that the word "suzerainty" was used to describe China's relationship with Tibet. This suggests that India at this date still held to the British position on Tibet. It is also significant that in Chinese translations of the Indian note "suzerainty" was replaced by the word "sovereignty"[12] which more accurately described Peking's allegation that Tibet forms part of China.

New Delhi's note also claimed definite commercial and communication rights in Tibet—rights inherited from the British. Here again the Indian Government revealed that to the degree it was sure of its own position it followed the former British-Indian approach despite Panikkar's statement attributing to Nehru the view that British-Indian special interests should be repudiated.[13] The note doubtless meant to convey to the Chinese government that the latter had no right to abrogate unilaterally a long-standing agreement which had the force of custom as well as law; but because most of the rights referred to had been the fruits of British imperialism, this passage probably only strengthened Peking's conviction that India still fronted for the British Empire.

What about the rights of the Tibetans? Later during a parliamentary debate Nehru conveyed his opinion that "according to any principles, the last voice in regard to Tibet should be the voice of the people of Tibet and nobody else."[14] This of course was not to be the case, but Lhasa still had hope on November 7 when it protested to the United Nations and charged the Chinese with open aggression.

On the advice of India (which was unwilling to sponsor Tibet's case before the United Nations) Tibet cabled a direct appeal to the Secretary-General, saying plaintively, "We understand that the United Nations have decided to stop aggression whenever it takes place." The appeal included the accurate but futile assertion that "Tibetans feel that racially, culturally and geographically they are far apart from the Chinese." It was also pointed out that even if the Chinese found the reactions of the Tibetans unacceptable, there were "other civilized methods by which they could ascertain the views of the people of Tibet," and "should the issue be purely juridical, they are open to seek redress in an international court of law."[15]

El Salvador requested that Tibet's complaint be included as an agenda item, and it was distributed by the Secretary-General on November 24 as an official note. On the same day a Chinese Communist delegation, which had been invited to the U.N. to present a complaint against alleged U.S. aggression in the Taiwan area, presented their credentials to the U.N. The presence of the delegation headed by General Wu Hsueh ch'uan* gave the U.N. a discreet opportunity to negotiate informally with China on the issue of Chinese participation in the Korean war, but it distracted attention from the Tibetan problem. Tibet became very much a side issue.

The first official indication of India's position had been revealed by Mr. N. Gopalaswami Ayyangar, Railway Minister and member of the Foreign Affairs Sub-committee of the Indian Cabinet. Presiding over the *Indian News Chronicle* foreign policy forum in New Delhi, he had said, "We are prepared to support Tibet's case to the extent that China should have solved this question by peaceful means."[16] During the discussion in the General Committee of the U.N. General Assembly the Indian representative, Jam Saheb of Nawanagar, supported a proposal earlier introduced by the U.K. representative, Mr. Kenneth Younger, that the Committee should defer decision on

* General Wu Hsueh ch'uan, a USSR-educated and Russian-speaking Chinese officer, is a member of the Chinese Communist Party Central Committee.

El Salvador's request until a better idea could be formed of the possibilities of a peaceful settlement. Malik, the USSR delegate, agreed with the United Kingdom proposal but added that Tibet affairs were the exclusive concern of the Chinese government. Nationalist China expressed shock at the Communist Chinese militant approach and the fact that it endangered peace in Asia, but Taiwan made very clear that Tibet had been part of China for seven hundred years. (This, of course, was simply the traditional Han instinct reasserting itself.) Perhaps because of the Indian and British attitude, the Steering Committee voted to postpone consideration of the El Salvador item on the grounds that China and Tibet were seeking a bilateral solution to their disagreement.[17]

Tibet protested the postponement and reiterated that it would accept any decision which the U.N. would render. There was in fact no further negotiating with the Chinese. The Tibetan delegation, having been stopped in India and told not to proceed, had not even reached China. The Dalai Lama had instead appointed a three-man delegation to present his country's appeal directly to the U.N. The group had reached India on its journey to Lake Success by the time the Steering Committee had taken its action.

This was Tibet's first lesson in postwar international politics. The lesson was still pertinent nine years later when Communist China administered the *coup de grace* to Tibet and the Dalai Lama again appealed to the U.N.—this time from his place of refuge in Mussoorie, India. In 1950 sympathy from the non-Communist world was abundant, but the willingness and ability of the free world to support its convictions with tangible acts of assistance were very limited. The Tibetan people felt they had been let down by India and the U.N. They could not easily grasp why the U.N. was unable to censure Communist China and at least marshal world opinion behind their cause. It was very difficult to understand why the U.N., which was at war with the Chinese–supported forces in North Korea, could not apply the same standards of aggression to the Tibet case.

World attention was indeed focused on the war in Korea to the exclusion of lesser crises. It is likely that China timed its invasion of Tibet to coincide with this event. India was genuinely concerned about the threat to peace posed by China's role in the war and, in its first major debut as honest broker for peace between East and West, India believed it important to retain Communist China's confidence. Yet Peking—far from appreciating India's forebearance on the Tibetan question—continued to criticize New Delhi's role. India's U.N. delegate, Krishna Menon—presumably reflecting the official attitude—was moved to comment, "They [the Chinese] appear to be very angry with us but we must not be angry with them."[18]

On November 16 Communist China reaffirmed its position in a note to the Government of India. Chinese policy was reiterated: "The Central People's Government of the Republic of China . . . has repeatedly made it clear that Tibet is an integral part of Chinese territory. . . . The Chinese People's Liberation Army must enter Tibet, liberate the Tibetan people, and defend the frontiers of China. This is a firm policy."[19] The note also clarified Peking's definition of regional autonomy: "According to the provisions of the Common Program . . . the regional autonomy granted by the Chinese Government to the national minorities inside the country is an autonomy within the confines of Chinese sovereignty." Peking had strayed far from Stalin's original doctrine of minorities. The conscientiousness with which Peking provided itself with a new doctrinal basis for its actions was certainly motivated by the threat which the regional autonomy thesis presented to China in the handling of several other national minority groups. Clearly more than just Tibet was concerned.

Finally, to justify its aggression, India was linked with "imperialist aggressors" who were interfering with China's domestic affairs. Peking deeply regretted that "the Indian Government has regarded a domestic problem of the Chinese Government—the exercise of its sovereign rights in Tibet—as an international dispute calculated to increase the present deplorable tension in the world." It was piously contended that "the entry into Tibet of the Chinese People's Liberation Army is an important measure to maintain Chinese independence, to prevent war and to defend world peace."

The entry of 200,000 Chinese troops into Korea ten days after this note was sent could, by the same logic, also be justified as an important measure to "prevent war and defend world peace!" When Nehru discussed the Tibetan situation in Parliament on December 6, he strangely made no mention of China's entry into the Korean War. He simply summarized India's position on Tibet, saying that India was "interested in Tibet's maintaining her autonomy which she had had for the last forty years at least." He did not challenge

China's suzerainty over Tibet but insisted that India "did lay considerable stress on the autonomy of Tibet."[20] It is significant that this latter quotation appeared in the official record of parliamentary debates but was dropped from the text in another publication—also official—entitled *Jawaharlal Nehru Speeches, 1949–1953.*[21] The obvious implication is that by January—three months before the conclusion of the Sino-Indian Agreement on Tibet—the Indian government did not want to lay stress on the "autonomy of Tibet."

Nehru concluded his remarks in Parliament with an expression of hope that the government of China would "even now try to settle the matter peacefully."[22] Nehru had gone as far as he was willing to go. It was not far enough to help Tibet, which had to rely on its own efforts to appease the iron tiger which held it tight.

CHAPTER 6

NOT A NEEDLE OR THREAD

Some day we must pay the . . . Tibetans for the provisions we were obliged to take from them.

Mao Tse-tung to Edgar Snow, *Red Star Over China*

The Red Chinese invaders knew that the Fourteenth Dalai Lama was the key to control in Tibet. Every other formula for control tried in the past had simply reinforced Peking's conclusion that effective suzerain authority depended on some cooperation by the Dalai Lama. The Chinese had tried to bypass the Dalai by substituting for him the authority of the Panchen Lama or by ruling directly through Chinese military power, but neither of these methods had worked. Only when some viable relationship had been established between the Chinese patron and the Tibetan God-King or his regent were they able to make their suzerain authority felt in any meaningful manner.

Rather than risk the investiture of a Dalai Lama who might prove intractable, the Chinese for many years encouraged rule by a regent even if it meant arranging for the child Dalai to be murdered before he came of age. A regent, lacking divine authority and public worship, was infinitely easier to manipulate. Pure military force such as that wielded by Chao Erh-feng could accomplish short-range objectives, but so long as a large army could not be easily moved and supplied, military rule in the face of a rebellious Tibetan population was out of the question.

In 1950 Chinese Communist strategy based on centuries of experience required an accommodation with the Dalai Lama so that Tibet could be controlled and administered through the existing monastic structure without the need for an enormous military presence.

Peking planned, nevertheless, successive measures of tighter control which would finally permit direct rule and total absorption of the country. But before direct rule could be achieved, roads and airfields had to be constructed so than an army of occupation large enough to enforce it could be supported. Simultaneously the Panchen Lama's authority and power had to be increased so that he could be used as a counterweight to the Dalai in the critical interim period before the Red army could take over.

The Chinese plan also called for large-scale programs to indoctrinate and educate Tibetan youths—to wean them from Lamaism so that the Dalai Lama's influence on the new generation would be lessened. Then to insure a docile population Peking planned to dilute the population by mass importation of Chinese laborers and farmers.

In an effort to reach the Dalai Lama and gain his cooperation the invaders made a clumsy effort to subvert his eldest brother, Thubten Jigme Norbu. As Chief Lama of Kumbun Monastery in northern Tibet, Norbu was readily accessible to the Chinese; and when the invasion began he was immediately taken into custody and subjected to severe pressure. Either through innate arrogance or colossal insensitivity the approach to Norbu was astonishingly crude. Political commissars bombarded him with Communist propaganda. They described to him their plan to absorb and communize Tibet and dangled before him the prize of the governorship of Tibet if he could successfully bring his brother into camp.

Norbu rejected these overtures and was incensed by their implications. As the Chinese approach became more threatening he realized that he would probably be held hostage and used as a lever to force the Dalai Lama to accept Chinese demands. Reasoning also that his brother would be better served if warned of the Chinese plan, Norbu feigned willingness to cooperate. He agreed to travel to Lhasa and attempt to persuade his brother to welcome Chinese troops as liberators of Tibet.[1]

Traveling with two other lamas from Kumbun, Norbu reached Lhasa on December 8, 1950, where he warned the Dalai Lama against permitting Chinese forces to enter the capital. The God-King convened his chief advisers to discuss this problem. It was clear from the efforts made to subvert Norbu that the Dalai figured prominently in Peking's strategy to control Tibet. They recognized that the only way that the Dalai Lama's flexibility of action could be assured was for him to leave Lhasa and seek refuge in a safe area where easy flight to Indian sanctuary would be possible.

The Chinese had requested an early response to their terms conveyed by Norbu. According to these terms the Tibetans were to send a negotiating delegation to China overland through Kham Province. This route was specified because the delegation which had been sent earlier was held up in India. Although the earlier delegation to Peking was originally stopped on orders from Lhasa, the Chinese persisted in believing that the Indian government was influencing them to procrastinate.* The Tibetan National Assembly deliberated and agreed that a new mission would be sent via Kham as specified but not until the Dalai Lama and his family were safely located near the Indian border. On the morning of December 18, His Holiness reluctantly left Lhasa for Yatung in the Chumbi Valley near Sikkim where he could wait in safety. He was Tibet's only trump card in its negotiations for existence.

The Dalai Lama was then only sixteen years old—by tradition two years too young to assume power from the Regent. But the National Assembly, on advice from state oracles and lamas, hastily staged the investiture ceremony in November so as to provide Tibet in this hour of national emergency with a ruling pontiff. This would deprive the Chinese of any opportunity to bypass the God-King or replace him with the Panchen Lama in their efforts to gain political control. The investiture would also serve to unite the country in crisis and minimize the importance of any factionalism within the government.

Tibetans were also haunted by the prophecy that the line of Dalai Lamas would end with the Thirteenth. If two years were allowed to pass before the Fourteenth was enthroned, this worrisome prediction might well come true. Only by moving up the investiture and holding it before the Dalai left Lhasa could such a catastrophe be averted. The British Tibet scholar, Sir Charles Bell, had dismissed this prophecy as a fabrication of some mischievous

* This belief was clearly reflected in the Chinese notes to India and, for that matter, the Government of India's note of October 31 was not drafted in such a way as to persuade the Chinese to believe otherwise. The note stated: "In view of these developments the Indian Government are no longer in a position *to advise the Tibetan delegation* to proceed to Peking unless the Chinese think it fit to order their troops to hold their advance into Tibet [italics mine].[2]

monks of the Tengyeling Monastery in Lhasa who for political reasons wanted to discredit the Thirteenth Dalai Lama.[3] Yet the events of 1950 must have seemed to Tibetans as an unhappy fulfillment of this persistent prediction, and it is understandable that the National Assembly was moved to take the precedent-breaking step of enthroning the Dalai at so young an age.

The wheel of life ever turns. As he had done in his Thirteenth reincarnation, the Dalai Lama sought sanctuary from Chinese invaders in the shadow of India. This time China's traditional expansionist stimulus had been revitalized by the doctrine of Communism but the centrifugal force generated was essentially the same as that which had thrust Chao Erh-feng's troops into Lhasa in 1911. The Dalai this time did not actually cross into India. Sixteen days after his departure from Lhasa he set up headquarters on Tibetan soil in Yatung within easy reach of India should negotiations with Peking break down. He took with him part of the Tibetan treasury and deposited it safely in Sikkim and sent his brother, Norbu, on to Calcutta to make advance preparations for establishing a government in exile should this prove necessary.[4]

The Lhasa bureaucracy was left practically intact, and the two Prime ministers, Lukhangwa and Losang Tashi, exercised control in the capital. Assuming a legalistic approach which best suited its purposes, Peking ignored the Dalai Lama's investiture, which had taken place in Lhasa on November 17, on the grounds that he had not yet attained the legal age of eighteen. Thus, according to this view, the legal Tibet government remained in Lhasa under the Regent, Ta Dra. In an historical account of Tibet's relations with China, Peking's *Nationalities Research* does not admit that he assumed power from the Regent until the spring of 1951—that is, until after he had returned to Lhasa from Yatung and after a Chinese representative had been reinstalled in Lhasa. In this way the Chinese technically sustained the precedent in which the Chinese *Ambans*—or High Commissioners in the Court of the Dalai Lama—must be in attendance at the investiture ceremony.

Nationalities Research wrote about the Dalai's 1950 flight to Yatung: "A handful of reactionaries in collusion with the imperialists and foreign expansionists abducted the Fourteenth Dalai Lama to Yatung whence they planned to take him to a foreign country and await the outbreak of World War III before returning."[5] This was Peking's way of lessening the value of Tibet's trump card as well as keeping intact a significant symbol of suzerainty. It was important to prevent the Dalai from leaving his country and thus placing himself beyond Chinese control. Toward this end Peking's threatening propaganda exerted considerable pressure on India, leaving it in no doubt that Peking would consider admittance of the Dalai Lama a hostile act. But should these threats have failed, Peking would have found some solace in its legal position that the Dalai Lama had not yet come of age and could therefore not have legally assumed power.

China's warnings achieved their purpose. While the government of India was never put in the position of having to refuse the Dalai Lama political asylum in 1951, the government made clear that it would not welcome him nor support him in exile against the Chinese. For the Dalai this was an important sign that New Delhi's policy toward Tibet and China had departed from the traditional policies of British India; circumstances had changed since his Thirteenth reincarnation.

Peking dates the Dalai Lama's assumption of power and the resignation of the Regent from February 1951.[6] Ignoring the real investiture, this date was selected to coincide with the departure of a Tibetan negotiating team to Peking. The Chinese had to recognize the Dalai Lama's new position by February if they were to accept the credentials of the negotiating group which departed Lhasa in February.

Ngapo Ngawang Jigme, Tibet's Quisling, was named leader of the new Tibetan delegation. He was already in Peking when other members of the delegation, traveling overland via Kham and Chungking, arrived in Peking. The Panchen Lama—also slated to play an important role for the Chinese in Tibet—arrived to be on hand for the peace negotiations. Talks began on April 29 between Ngapo Ngawang Jigme and Li Wei-han, Chairman of the Commission of Nationalities Affairs for the Chinese People's Republic.

Members of the Tibet delegation were subjected to intense pressure to meet Communist terms. The Chinese presented the delegation upon arrival with a ten-point draft agreement and insisted that they agree to it. Only after strong resistance by certain members of the Tibet delegation did the Chinese substitute for this a relatively more moderate 17-article draft. This too was based on the same objectionable thesis that Tibet is an integral part of China. Although still unacceptable to the Tibetans, the draft was this time presented as an ultimatum and accompanied by unmistakable threats. Moreover the delegation was forbidden to request instructions from its government and was told that failure to accept the draft would bring further military action against their people. Yielding to this, the delegates not only signed but were forced to affix an official seal which had been forged in Peking.[7] The original, authentic seal had been kept in Lhasa as a precaution against just this type of coercion.

Negotiations—if they can be called this—ended on May 21. Without the courtesy of prior notification of the Dalai Lama, Peking announced that a resolution called Agreement on Measures for the Peaceful Liberation of Tibet between the Central People's Government and the Tibet Local Government had been signed on May 23, 1951. Peking's propaganda described the "Agreement" as a "brilliant achievement of the Chinese Communist Party and Chairman Mao Tse-tung in settling a very intricate domestic nationality question."[8] In a speech given at a dinner in honor of the signing, Mao Tse-tung set the keynote for Tibet when he crowed: "Unity has been achieved between the Dalai's forces and the Panchen's forces and the Central Government."[9] This was a two-to-one alignment with the Dalai Lama in the minority.

The outrage which had been perpetrated by the forced imposition of the 17-Point Agreement was not revealed publicly until the Dalai Lama reached Indian sanctuary eight years later. Shortly after His Holiness arrived in India in 1959 he announced that "consent of the [Tibetan government] was secured under duress and at the point of a bayonet." He claimed that his representatives were compelled to sign the agreement under the threat of further military operations against Tibet. The Dalai said, "We . . . decided to abide by its terms and conditions in order to save my people and country from the damages of total destruction."[10]

The 17-Point Agreement is a significant document since it not only provides a false front for the Chinese absorption of Tibet but an indication of China's true nationalities doctrine. As stated in a preamble, the agreement is in accordance with the "Common Program," but the next eight years in Tibet would see the discrepancy between theoretical doctrine and actual practice, as well as the role of doctrine in masking the discrepancy through the ingenious application of Communist semantics. Violations of the agreement, which became fully apparent after the Dalai Lama's flight in 1959, exposed the Chinese doctrine of nationalities as a screen behind which the Han Chinese could make good their consolidation of the greater China mainland.

The opening statements of the 17-Point Agreement humiliated the Tibetans. The very first sentence describes them as "one of the nationalities with a long history within the boundaries of China."[11] This incredible document explains how, over the last one hundred years, "imperialist forces" penetrated into China and "in consequence also penetrated into the Tibet region and carried out all kinds of deceptions and provocations." The preamble accuses Tibet of having adopted an "unpatriotic" attitude toward the "great Motherland." The language of the document is proof enough that it could only have been accepted under duress, yet the preamble concludes with the sentence: "The Chinese People's Government appointed representatives with full powers to conduct talks on a friendly basis with the delegates with full powers of the local government of Tibet."

The agreement calls upon the Tibetan people to drive out the imperialists and return to the "big family of the Motherland." It requires the Tibetan government to "assist the People's Liberation Army to enter Tibet and consolidate the National defenses." This latter point clearly violated instructions given Ngapo by Lhasa that agreement should not be given for Chinese forces to advance further into Tibet. In fact, it had been the Dalai Lama's main hope that his country could be spared Chinese militatry occupation, and this had led him in the first place to agree to negotiations.

Although the agreement calls for the "leadership of the Chinese People's Government," Point 4 states that it "will not alter the existing political system in Tibet" nor the "status, functions and powers of the Dalai Lama." This is a critical clause which shows Peking's intention to work ostensibly through the existing institutions and the monastic system of Tibet—the policy which China was to abandon after 1956 when it felt itself strong enough to rule directly.

It establishes the position of the Panchen Lama and his relationship to the Dalai Lama as that in force when the Thirteenth Dalai and the Ninth Panchen "were in friendly . . . relations with each other." Thus "Mao's Panchen," heretofore never recognized by the Tibetan government as the true reincarnation of the Ninth, was readmitted to Tibet and accorded full status. This was a major concession by Lhasa and one of the most damaging ones. Although Peking had accepted the existing religious and political framework, it had insinuated its creature, the Panchen, into a key position of this framework. He was intended as a control on the Dalai—a reminder of the alternative figurehead available to the Chinese if the Dalai Lama should refuse to cooperate. Peking in this way sought to revive the classic rivalry between the two lamas and split the Tibetans into hostile camps in order to facilitate Chinese control of a hostile population.

Although veiled by innocuous and misleading language, Points 8, 9 and 10 provide China with justification for cultural penetration and forced "reforms." Point 8 calls for the integration of the Tibetan armed forces into those of the People's Liberation Army. Point 9 provides that "the language and school education of the Tibetan nationality shall be developed step by step in accordance with the actual condition in Tibet." Point 10 calls for the improvement of Tibetan agriculture, livestock raising, industry and commerce "in accordance with the actual condition in Tibet." These clauses gave Peking an opening wedge with which to indoctrinate Tibet, militarize it and convert it ultimately to a Chinese province—culturally as well as politically. It was the abuse of these points which more than anything else finally incited the Tibetans to revolt.

Point 14 was of interest to the Government of India, concerned with its traditional trading rights and privileges. This point stipulates that the "Chinese People's Government shall have centralized handling of all external affairs of the area of Tibet; and there will be peaceful co-existence with neighboring countries and establishment and development of fair commercial and trading relations with them on the basis of equality, mutual benefit and mutual respect for territory and sovereignty."

Three clauses of the agreement deal with the role of the People's Liberation Army. Indicative of how these clauses would make regional autonomy a farce is the fact that they were not announced for several months. Point 15, for example, calls for the establishment of a "Military and Administrative Committee and a Military Area Headquarters in Tibet" to ensure the implementation of the 17-Point Agreement. This clause was a tip-off that Peking intended a military occupation upon which China's control would be based. Point 16 provides for maintenance of the People's Liberation Army and requires the "local" government of Tibet to help in the "purchase and transport of food, fodder and other daily necessities." This served later to justify the Chinese expropriation and depletion of Tibet's stockpiled grain supply. Point 13 promises that the People's Liberation Army "shall also be fair in all buying and selling and shall not arbitrarily take a needle or thread from the people."[12]

The Dalai Lama came very close to leaving Tibet for sanctuary in India rather than return to govern in the context of this agreement. On one hand he did not want to be a party to Communist administration in Lhasa. On the other hand he had an obligation to return to his people and do what he could to lessen the impact of Chinese occupation. Peking exerted maximum pressure on the Government of India to refuse him asylum. A Chinese Communist "Advisory Delegation" under Chang Ching-wu—newly appointed Chinese "Commissioner and Administrator of Civil and Military Affairs in Tibet"—was flown quickly to Calcutta and sought feverishly to find Norbu whom they suspected of arranging asylum details for his brother. The Chinese Ambassador in New Delhi also came to Calcutta, where he managed to track down Norbu and appeal to him with a combination of threats and promises.

What finally convinced the Dalai Lama to return was a delegation of three abbots from Sera, Drepung and Ganden monasteries in Lhasa who pled with him to seek guidance from the State Oracle. Twice the Dalai asked the Oracle for advice, and both times the reply specified that he should return.[13] It is likely that the Dalai found a mirror for his own conscience in the pleadings of the abbots and the verdict of the State Oracle, and that this more than the mystical response of the Oracle caused him to return.

The God-King returned to Lhasa on August 17, 1951, but not before he had met General Chang Ching-wu in Yatung to discuss their future relationship in Lhasa. Chang was Peking's first instrument to convert Tibet into a wholly subservient province of China. The Dalai recalls in his memoirs that his meeting with the general was cordial, but it is unlikely that this surface cordiality hid the real nature of the Chinese general's mission.[14] That Chang went to Tibet by way of India and Yatung rather than by way of the overland route from China can probably be attributed to his wish to project a general impression that his new mission had the cooperation and collaboration of the Dalai Lama.

On October 26, units of the so-called People's Liberation Army totalling three thousand troops entered Lhasa under the command of General Chang Kuo-hua. A second contingent of about equal size reached Lhasa on December 1, having entered from the northwest. Chinese propaganda alleged that they "were warmly welcomed by the Tibetan people, both lamas and laymen." The Dalai Lama to the contrary described how the people of Lhasa watched them come "with the apparent indifference which . . . is usually shown at first by ordinary people in the face of such national humiliation."[15] On November 4, 1952 Red troops occupied Chungchen in the north. Tibet's second largest city, Shigatse, was garrisoned by the Chinese on November 24, while the army reached Gyantse on November 29. Thus by the end of 1952 the Communist Chinese army was in effective occupation of Tibet.

The 17-Point Agreement had promised that the army would not take a "needle or thread," yet its demands increased daily. Two successive forced loans of barley demanded of the Tibetans threatened Lhasa with famine. Typical of the testimony given by Tibetan refugees to representatives of the International Commission of Jurists in 1959 were statements such as the following: "Supplies had to be carried from Phundo to Lhasa and the Chinese requisitioned transport animals for this purpose; some of the animals died and human beings had to replace them." Another refugee testified that "people were sent to carry the loads . . . of over one and a half *maunds* [110 lbs.] and they covered eight mule caravan stages [about 120 miles] in about twenty-four days. . . . about ten people died." A Tibetan from Diggong recalled that road construction began in 1953, so "one thousand people had to be sent and their provisions had to be supplied by the Tibetan people."[16]

The Chinese plan called for systematic diminution of the Dalai Lama's power and stature. Yet it had to be carried out subtly so it would not appear that the traditional monastic system was being tampered with or that the 17-Point Agreement was being ignored. Early in 1952 the Chinese forced the Dalai Lama to remove his two co-ruling Prime Ministers, Lukhangwa and Losang Tashi,* on the grounds that they were uncooperative and were inciting the people to disobey the occupation agreement. He did not replace them because, as he later observed, "it was no use having Prime Ministers

* Upon returning to Lhasa the Dalai Lama had named Lukhangwa Special Secular State Councillor in charge of the Cabinet while Losang Tashi, the Grand Steward, was elevated to the same rank for ecclesiastical matters.

if they were merely to be scapegoats for the Chinese."[17] Their departure, however, faced him with two troublesome alternatives—either to contact and guide the Cabinet directly or allow the Cabinet to rule without his close supervision. In the first instance, by entering more directly into administration and becoming more accessible, he would lose some of his divine aura. In the second instance he would relinquish lay authority to the Chinese. Either alternative suited Peking, which was intent upon lessening his authority.

The Chinese also made an effort to deprive the Dalai Lama of his control over the ecclesiastical court (Tse-kor) and forced him to serve co-equally with the Panchen Lama and the Tibetan Quisling, Ngapo, on the Chinese "People's Political Consultative Conference."[18] In matters of religious as well as lay protocol Peking tried to show the Panchen equal deference to that accorded the Dalai Lama. For the first time the Panchen was equipped with a private armed force with which to police his seat of rule so that for all practical purposes the Dalai's lay power and authority was confined to Lhasa Province, where he was closely observed and controlled by a large Chinese garrison.

In October 1951 the Chinese proclaimed monetary and economic reforms enabling them to confiscate properties belonging to Tibetan nobles. A branch of the People's Bank of China was opened, and all Tibet's trade was controlled by a Chinese-managed "General Tibetan Commercial Corporation." A cultural department was established which acted as the medium through which propaganda was disseminated and Marxist doctrine taught. This was augmented by several front organizations similarly designed to indoctrinate Tibetans in Marxo-Buddhism—a hybrid version of Marxism developed for Tibetan consumption. For example, a Tibetan branch of the New Democratic Youth Federation of China was opened in Lhasa on May 4, 1952, and a Cultural Association of Patriotic Youth founded a few months later.

Long realizing the inequity of Tibet's land tenure system, the Dalai Lama, upon assuming office, began to work on a land reform plan. He decreed the cancellation of agricultural debts and made provisions for seed loans to the peasants. Unfortunately the Chinese, who were anxious to gain mass support and thus isolate Tibet's ruling aristocracy, sought to divert credit to themselves by providing tax and debt relief and by taking over the Dalai Lama's seed loan program. Anti-landlord propaganda was disseminated in a complementary effort to sharpen the class cleavage.

Tibetans, regardless of class, clung to their traditional ways and resented Chinese innovations—even those few which benefited them. Near-famine conditions caused by the seizure of Lhasa's grain reserves was fanning public opposition to the Chinese. Peking's propaganda, obviously at variance with visible facts, angered rather than impressed Tibet's highly religious population, which resented an alien ruler. Rumors from the north that Chinese farmers were being given Tibetan land alarmed peasants and landlords alike.

Although the 17-Point Agreement solemnly promised that the People's Liberation Army would not take a "needle or thread," it gradually dawned on the Tibetans that a whole way of life might be taken from them. The Dalai Lama hoped that Tibet "might win back a degree of freedom in the end,"[19] but the true perimeters of Chinese policy as they were contained in the 17-Point Agreement provided little substance for this hope. As early as 1952 the embryo of organized resistance began to form in defiance to the alien master.

The events of 1950 and 1951 are entirely consistent with China's historical approach to its border lands—an approach which combined an obsession with the security of the Middle Kingdom and an urge for territorial aggrandizement. The vast Tibetan-Sinkiang area could not be allowed to slip from China's control and be divided between the Indians—still considered by Peking to be Western dominated—and the Russians, with whom China still competed for power and territory in Central Asia. With free access to Tibet India could dominate trade and sow dissension between the Tibetans and the Chinese. For that matter the ghost of Dorjiev had not entirely vanished. Sinkiang, which still seethed with anti-Chinese sentiment, was flanked by Tibet. Moreover, Lhasa, the Holy See of Lamaism, had influence over Mongolians as well as Tibetans. With Peking's historical perspective it was possible to conclude that the Soviet Union had at least residual interest in Tibet.

The Tibetan highlands not only represented a base for political action throughout the Central Asian borderlands but in the nuclear age it had a dangerous potential as a strategic base for bomber squadrons and missile launching pads aimed at China. Militarily, Peking could tolerate nothing short of total control. To achieve this,

Peking would have to proceed in three stages, all of which—scarcely veiled—were provided for in the 17-Point Agreement. First, road and air communication facilities between China and Tibet would have to be built. These facilities, according to Peking's plan, would orient Tibetan trade toward China rather than India. But, more important, they would facilitate mass Chinese immigration into Tibet, thus diluting the hostile Tibetan population. Such facilities would also permit China to support strong military forces in Tibet whose defensive function would be to protect Chinese immigrants, Chinese rule and the newly built supply routes.

The second stage of control would be the imposition of direct military rule in place of indirect rule through the Dalai Lama and the traditional theocratic machinery of government. This stage not only required a powerful military presence but it required a softening of the Tibet population through propaganda, education and weakening of the powerful Lamaist religion. A study of the 17-Point Agreement reveals the framework within which such a program could be legitimized and carried out under a variety of guises.

The third stage of control would be the Sinoization of Tibet. The Han saw as the ultimate solution to the ethnic problem of Tibet the eradication of the Tibetans. The evidence amassed by the International Commission of Jurists in 1959 and 1960 to support the charge that acts of genocide have been committed in Tibet by the Chinese is impressive. The Commission concluded that the Chinese "have systematically set out to eradicate . . . religious belief in Tibet, have killed religious figures because their religious belief and practice was an encouragement . . . to others, and have forcibly transferred large numbers of Tibetan children to a Chinese materialist environment in order to prevent them from having a religious upbringing."[20]

Like Curzon, Peking saw the role of a buffer state in the context of geopolitical realism. In the first instance a buffer had a defensive role. It could provide a belt of land—or a frontier in depth as Curzon described it—which could not be crossed without sounding the alarm of invasion. But while Curzon saw the Himalayan regions of Kashmir, Nepal, Sikkim, Bhutan and Assam Himalaya as an inner line of defense for India protected by a Tibetan buffer region, Communist China today views Himalaya as its outer line of defense, necessary for the protection of Tibet. Peking, which sees the Himalayan states as irredentist regions to be regained as soon as possible, also assigns to them an offensive role. They can be future bases for the subversion of India. But before China's real Tibetan and Himalayan policies could be realized there was much to be done. China needed time. India and the rest of Asia would have to be lulled into accepting Peking's peaceful pretensions while the wounds of Tibet healed.

CHAPTER 7

ENTER PANCH SHEELA

China has demolished . . . a buffer state. In international politics when a buffer state is abolished by a powerful nation that nation is considered to have aggressive designs on its neighbors.

Acharya Kripalani, Indian Parliamentary Deputy, 1954

China's occupation of Lhasa upset India's traditional relationship with Tibet. New Delhi recognized that it must be satisfied with some new kind of relationship with its northern neighbor. Moreover, it was obvious that China would dictate the terms of this relationship. Peking was quick to inform the Government of India that "problems relating to Sino-Indian diplomatic, commercial and cultural relationships with respect to Tibet may be solved properly . . . through normal diplomatic channels"[1]—that is, through Peking, not Lhasa.

Adjusting to the new situation, the Indian Foreign Office announced in September, 1952, that its representative in Lhasa would henceforward hold only consular rank and its trade missions would be considered extensions of the Lhasa Consulate General. The status of India's traditional trade and communication rights was nevertheless ambiguous. Certainly Peking had made it clear that it would no longer be bound by "unequal treaties" imposed on Tibet by "imperialists," yet it had not made clear to India what its new relationship with Tibet must be.

New Delhi was faced with an even more fundamental problem. It had to determine what its attitude and policy toward China itself would be. From England, India had not only inherited specific treaties governing its relationship with Tibet but it had inherited a fundamental geopolitical situation which neither the independence of India nor the Communist revolution in China had changed. In the traditional British view the Himalayan range was of strategic value as a defense barrier only if the Tibetan plateau behind it was kept from hostile hands. The security of the subcontinent thus required Tibet as a neutral buffer zone. Britain had gone to great lengths to prevent Tibet from falling under the control of Russia at the beginning of the century in the fear that the high plateau would be used as an invasion route to India. Lord Curzon may have exaggerated this threat, but few then denied that there was a line beyond which Russia could not advance in Central Asia without India being in jeopardy. That line ran along the northern borders of Iran, Afghanistan and Tibet, and as shown by Younghusband's expedition, Britain had been prepared to defend it with force of arms.

The failing Manchu dynasty and the disintegration of the Chinese Empire had raised the specter of a central Asian power vacuum which Russia seemed eager to fill. Sinkiang on Tibet's northern border was a particularly tempting target for the Czar. But if both Sinkiang and Tibet remained under the suzerainty of a weak China the subcontinent would be safe. This had been the reasoning of Imperial Britain.

The expansion eastward of the Russian Empire and the rise of the British *Raj* in India did nothing to change Peking's historical assumption that Tibet is part of China. The Anglo-Chinese Treaty of 1906 and the Anglo-Russian Convention of 1907 had paid proper lip service to Chinese supremacy in Tibet, but Peking still sought to define more satisfactorily the ambiguous term "suzerainty" through Chao Erh-feng's military occupation of the Tibetan plateau. Chao's ruthless campaigns had temporarily brought eastern Tibet under control while at the same time Chang Yin-tang, an aggressive Chinese *Amban*, had tried to re-establish Chinese authority in Lhasa. Chang blocked British trade into Tibet by forbidding English traders or their Indian agents to have contact with Tibetans and by denying them the right to acquire property. But, even worse, he provoked the British by intriguing in Nepal and Bhutan.

Communist China's attitude toward Tibet and India is basically the same as that of the Imperial Manchus—a fact which should have provided independent India with a body of experience with which to judge Chinese actions after 1950. To describe the acts of Chang

Yin-tang more than fifty years ago is to describe Chinese Communist actions during the last several years. Moreover, the reaction of British India to Chinese political action in Lhasa from 1906 to 1911 is strikingly similar to the reaction of Nehru's India to Chinese actions between 1950 and 1954.

In 1909 Peking had favored the return of the Dalai Lama after five years of exile in Mongolia, but it had been intended that he must henceforward remain under firm Chinese control and exercise his authority only with Chinese sufferance. As was to be the case in 1950, Peking saw the importance of not interfering with the monastic structure of society and realized that the God-King was the indispensable keystone to this system. Control over the Dalai Lama, of course, must be guaranteed by military force. When General Chao Erh-feng's army moved toward Lhasa, the Dalai Lama asked Great Britain to intervene militarily and stop the Chinese advance. But these pleas went unheeded and, just as in 1950, India would not go beyond protesting China's actions.

A parallel can also be seen in the efforts of the Chinese to bring back the Thirteenth Dalai Lama from Indian exile following Chao Erh-feng's entry into Lhasa in 1910 and their efforts to bring back the Fourteenth Dalai Lama from Yatung on the Indian border following the "People's Liberation Army's" invasion in 1950–1951. In 1910 the Chinese had first turned to the Panchen Lama to rule in the Dalai's stead but this proved to be no solution. The Panchen had had the wisdom to decline the offer, realizing that he could not hope to work with an antagonistic Tibetan National Assembly. Similarly in 1956 Peking realized that the Panchen Lama—popularly disdained as "Mao's Panchen"—was no substitute for the Dalai Lama. Thus strong efforts were made to bring the latter back to Lhasa.

Despite repeated Chinese violations of the 1904 Anglo-Tibetan Convention and the 1908 Trade Regulations—even despite the exiled Dalai Lama's pleas for help—the British government had refused to intervene in 1910. London's reaction to the military occupation of Tibet was expressed by Lord Morley, Secretary of State for India, who rationalized that China was only trying to make effective its recognized suzerainty. Forty-four years later Nehru was to adopt a similar point of view and state that India's posture reflected "recognition of the existing situation there [in Tibet]."[2]

Still another parallel exists between Great Britain's need to clarify the status of Tibet in 1913 and independent India's need to reach agreement with China over Tibet in 1953. Yet the circumstances and objectives were totally different and here the parallel diverges. In 1913 China had been weakened by the Republican revolution and was harassed by Russian pressure in Mongolia. Tibet had regained its freedom from Peking's control and found itself in a relatively strong position. British power in India and the Far East was formidable. In 1953, regenerated by an aggressive Communist regime and implicitly protected by the Soviet Union, China enjoyed military supremacy on the Asian mainland. Tibet had been overrun by Chinese forces and—unable to attract either U.N. or Indian help—was forced to cede complete power in a bilateral agreement with China. Independent India, still beset with a multitude of internal problems and faced on two frontiers with hostile Pakistan forces, was powerless to defend its northern neighbor.

In 1913 British India had sought formal agreement to its *de facto* power position in the Himalayas. The initiative was Britain's because the power was Britain's. In 1953 India took the initiative to formalize the status of Tibet, yet India's relative power position had weakened radically from the days of the British *Raj*. It is difficult to see what India stood to gain by negotiating from weakness. It is thus at this point that India swerved abruptly from the traditional Himalayan policy empirically tested by Britain. It is true that circumstances were different. There was indeed nothing India could have done to save Tibet in 1950 and 1951. But other reasons must be found to explain India's decision to press for a new treaty on Tibet. These reasons are traceable to the ideology of the new Indian government—not to its geopolitical, power position.

The role Nehru's advisers played in molding India's policies and attitudes toward Red China are important though not definitive. India's Ambassador to China, Sardar Panikkar, was among the first to justify Peking's actions in Tibet. In his book *In Two Chinas; The Memoirs of a Diplomat* Panikkar admitted his commitment to a preconceived position when he wrote, "Even before I started for Peking I had come to the conclusion that the British policy (which we were supposed to have inherited) of looking on Tibet as an area in which we had special political interests could not be maintained." Panikkar's influence on Nehru in 1950 cannot be ignored, but the exaggerated adulation of New China which shone through the dispatches from Peking perhaps did more to sour Nehru on Panikkar than sweeten him on China.

Of more significance was Krishna Menon. If Panikkar was intent on improving China-India relations, Krishna Menon was playing for larger and more meaningful stakes. As co-architect with Nehru of neutralism as a positive force in international affairs, Krishna Menon saw in Tibet an irritant which could not be allowed to spoil India's function as bridge between West and East.

India's Governor General Rajagopalachari and Deputy Prime Minister Sardar Patel saw the Tibet crisis in a more realistic way. Both counseled caution in the recognition of Red China. Both saw Tibet in the light of Indian self-interest. As Panikkar recalled in pique, "There was . . . support in the External Affairs Ministry for the view that India should act vigorously to protect Tibet—even Sardar Patel . . . felt called upon to make an unfriendly speech [about China]." Panikkar confessed he was nervous lest his government "take some hasty step"[3] against China. The Indian Ambassador had little cause for fear on this score, however.

Many Indian intellectuals—probably Nehru himself—have held a somewhat idealized image of China. Much has been made of alleged Chinese-Indian cultural affinity and common colonial experience. The two peoples are supposed to be bound together by the common heritage of Buddhism. In 1944 Nehru wrote of the "commerce of scholars" between the two countries during the Buddhist period. Typical of the tendency of Asian intellectuals to seek an identity in a common colonial experience, Nehru also wrote:

> After being cut off from each other for many centuries, India and China were brought by some strange fate under the influence of the British East India Company. India had to endure this for long; in China the contact was brief, but even so, it brought opium and war.[4]

The Indian leader rhapsodized further, "Pilgrims of a new kind cross or fly over the mountains . . . bringing their messages of cheer and good will and creating fresh bonds of a friendship that will endure."[5] Nehru had visited China for the first time in August, 1939, on the eve of World War II. Obviously impressed, he observed a "new China . . . rising rooted in her culture, but shedding the lethargy and weakness of ages."[6]

After the Communist revolution Indian and Chinese spokesmen made much of their two countries' two thousand years of good neighborliness and more than two thousand miles of common border. Too often overlooked as the critical factors of peace were the most forbidding geography in the world and the buffer role performed by Tibet. In Nehru's eyes the Communist revolution in China was an historically correct development. It was yet another stage in a long effort to be free from Western influence and the corrupt practices of a feudal system. He was elated at the new climate for Asian solidarity. Unseen were the true meanings and objectives of the ideological doctrine which China now preached. Nehru always believed that the Communist overlay in China had not fundamentally changed the basic drives of Han nationalism or the influences of an ancient, deep-rooted culture. There is much truth in this analysis, but he perhaps could not then fully appreciate that the expansionist tendencies of international Communism were aggravated rather than muted by Han nationalism. Unheard were voices of dissent which said that "Asianism" had limitations and India's political and cultural heritage was equally rooted in Western ideals and principles.

India's leaders found too much comfort in the fact that China faced domestic problems as formidable as India's. Logically both countries needed to devote all of their energies to solving terrible economic problems, to adjusting to rapid social change and to defending themselves from external enemies. It was reasonable to assume that neither country in their common predicament could afford to be antagonistic toward the other. But neither logic nor reason was the guide.

India's posture as arbitrator between East and West and Nehru's role as champion of peace obscured the true dimensions of the Chinese threat. New Delhi followed a super policy which can be briefly described as the effort to preserve world peace and to enhance India's international prestige as a force for peace and for prestige's sake itself. The role of international arbitrator for peace appealed to Nehru's ego and by extension to India's national ego. Moreover, an emotional rejection of the Western world which had so long been associated with colonialism and an attraction for the Utopian world of Fabian socialism made it difficult for Nehru to view the Communist world objectively.

Nehru also aspired to the role of pathfinder for Asian solidarity.

He had an historic vision of India as holding the "pivotal position between Western Asia, Southeast Asia and the Far East."[7] To play this role India had to be on good terms with China. Nehru seemed to have sensed early the competitive complications of the two countries' relations. He realized that two entirely different economic systems were on trial. The uncommitted countries of Asia were watching to see which system would prosper and which would fail. But Nehru did not fully recognize that conflict is inherent in this kind of competition. He accepted at face value the Communist slogan "competitive co-existence" and did not fully appreciate the purely tactical significance given it by China.

There were unmistakable clues to Peking's real policy and plans from the outset, but they are of course clearer in hindsight. The keynote was struck in 1949–1950 when Communist China showed complete contempt for India's capitalist domestic system and neutralist foreign policy; Nehru was branded a "running dog of imperialism." A Chinese editorial in 1949 lumped Nehru with Bao Dai, Syngman Rhee and Chiang Kai-chek as among the "dregs of mankind."[8] China's occupation of Tibet was in itself an expression of supreme unconcern for Indian sensibilities. Then toward the end of 1952 Peking responded to India's efforts to mediate the prisoner-of-war issue in Korea with scorn when Krishna Menon's compromise plan was described by an uncompromising China as an "illegal resolution which has as its basic content the United States' principle of voluntary repatriation under an Indian cloak."[9] Chinese publications repeatedly printed maps showing large areas of India as part of China. And Mao Tse-tung encouraged an already insurrectionist Communist Party in India by telling them that "India will certainly not remain long under the yoke of imperialism." Mao promised Indian Communists that "like free China, a free India will one day emerge in the Socialist and People's Democratic family."[10]

Nehru's commitment to India's super policy caused the Indian government during this period to subordinate all other considerations to bringing peace in Korea. India sought tirelessly to mediate between China and the United Nations forces in Korea and took the leading role in trying to seat Communist China in the U.N., where it believed peace could be found through negotiation. The imbalance in India's neutrality became apparent during this period when India bought China's goodwill at the cost of opposing nearly all Western positions in the Far East. India opposed the United

Nations resolution branding China an aggressor in the Korean War, criticized United States actions to neutralize Taiwan in 1950 and attacked the peace treaty with Japan because it had been negotiated by the United States without reference to China. Moreover India was to be highly critical of United States policy and actions in Southeast Asia during the Indo-China War and to show sympathy for the Chinese-backed Vietminh forces.

Only after the Korean truce talks began did Peking's policies begin to shift toward a more conciliatory line. But this shift was not a response to India's policy of conciliation toward China. Instead it reflected a general shift in international Communist tactics. A treatise by Stalin entitled "Economic Problems of Socialism in the USSR" published in October 1952—just before the 19th Communist Party Congress was convened—launched the new line, which stressed economic growth in the Communist camp and economic competition with Western capitalism. This line, which called for "competitive co-existence," gained its real momentum after Stalin's death. Although "co-existence" would ultimately provoke a serious doctrinal split between the Soviet Union and China, the latter declared in October 1952 that "countries with differing social systems and ways of life can coexist peacefully."[11]

India welcomed the thaw in China's policy and may for this reason have believed the time was propitious to define formally a new relationship between the two countries. Goodwill gestures such as the exchange of cultural delegations were useful as mood-setters, but only serious negotiations could resolve the differences between the two countries raised by the Tibet situation.

Another factor which may have specifically influenced New Delhi to seek a treaty agreement with China at this time was knowledge that the United States was planning to extend military assistance to Pakistan. From November 1953 India-U.S. relations deteriorated in anticipation of the Pakistan military program, although the latter was not formally announced until February 25, 1954.

India had legitimate concern for its trade rights in Tibet. Since the Chinese occupation in 1950 traditional border trade had drastically fallen off. It was clear that Peking was determined to divert Tibet trade from India to China. New roads being built into Tibet would not only permit military equipment to be brought into Tibet but would make overland trading between Tibet and China economically feasible. With the completion of the Lhasa-Chamdo road goods could reach China within a matter of days rather than the customary five weeks which it usually took the caravans to reach Chamdo. And by virtue of its control of Lhasa's administration, Peking could and did impose currency restrictions and state trading methods which favored trade with China.

Before the Communists had extended their revolution to Sinkiang and forbidden Indian trade into that area, New Delhi had traditionally maintained a Consulate General in Kashgar. India had hoped to reopen trade routes between Kashmir and Sinkiang through Ladakh. But on December 8, 1953 Nehru stated in Parliament that the Kashgar Consulate would not be on the agenda of the forthcoming negotiations with China because the latter considered Sinkiang a closed area. As the negotiations were to reveal, China not only refused India permission to reopen its Kashgar office but demanded the right to open three new Chinese trade missions in India. Only later would it become clear that traditional Sino-Soviet competition for control of Sinkiang was again entering a dangerous phase and that this was an important reason to keep India out of the area.

It is significant that no representative from the Ministry of Commerce and Industry was included in the negotiating group which India sent to Peking. Not only was there little likelihood that India could have regained its previous trade through negotiations, but it was certain that India would have had to relinquish many of the old treaty privileges enjoyed by the British. In sum, negotiations could result in only one thing—formal compliance with the new status of Tibet imposed by China. There was nothing of a material nature or nothing in India's traditional self-interest to be gained.

Negotiations were begun in Peking on December 31, 1953. Although quick agreement was expected, the negotiations dragged on for four months. One point of contention concerned the number and location of Chinese trade agencies to be permitted in India. China demanded the same number of agencies which India had in Tibet. Dr. Krishnalal Shridharani, *Amrita Bazar Patrika's* well-informed political analyst, speculated that India—unable to consider Tibet "an absolutely foreign country"—wanted to maintain its trade agencies even though this right exceeded normal diplomatic privileges, while China wanted "to show that India cannot inherit the traditions left behind in Tibet by British imperialism."[12] Specifically China insisted on matching India's trade agencies in Gartok, Gyantse and Yatung with Chinese agencies in Simla and Almora as well as the existing one in Kalimpong. But unwilling to see Chinese installations in these strategic western hill stations, India confined China to trade offices in New Delhi and Calcutta, where Chinese personnel could be better watched.

Foreshadowing the boundary dispute with India was an argument over the ownership of several border passes. Vice-Foreign Minister Chang Han-fu, Chinese representative at the 1954 negotiations, is alleged to have told Indian Ambassador Raghavan that the Chinese did not wish to touch on the boundary question. Nevertheless, it is likely that not only the specific issue of the border passes but the larger and more crucial problem of the boundary delimitation at least came up for discussion. In fact, it was probably a point of contention that China refused to incorporate into the agreement an acceptance of the Indian-claimed alignment.

The negotiations lasted longer than expected. It took four months for agreement to be reached, and apparently the chances of total failure were great enough for Nehru publicly to minimize the importance of the negotiations until they were successfully concluded on April 29, 1954. The *Eastern Economist* of Bombay speculated that the signing of the accord was timed by the Chinese to coincide with the Colombo Conference in Ceylon, while the *Hindusthan Times* linked the sudden successful conclusion of negotiations with the opening of the Geneva Conference on Indo-China. Certainly the Geneva Conference began at a moment when China could benefit from Indian goodwill and the euphoric atmosphere created by the accord. If this was China's motive, it was realized.

The formal title of the Sino-Indian pact on Tibet is Agreement between the Republic of India and the People's Republic of China on Trade and Intercourse between the Tibet Region of China and India. By acceding to this agreement India formally abandoned its traditional position that Tibet should be an autonomous buffer zone.

But the most important feature of the agreement is its preamble, which enunciates the now well-known "five principles of coexistence," or *Panch Sheela*, as they are called in the Hindi language. These principles, which provided a façade for Communist China's political and economic offensive in East Asia, are:

1. Mutual respect for each other's territorial integrity and sovereignty
2. Mutual non-aggression

3. Mutual non-interference in each other's internal affairs
4. Equality and mutual benefit
5. Co-existence

Describing the agreement in Parliament, Nehru pointed to the preamble as being of utmost significance. His words, so sincere and hopeful, sound strange in retrospect. The Indian Prime Minister asked the members of Parliament to accept the vows of peaceful co-existence contained in the preamble "not only with respect to India and China but also the other countries of Asia," promising that "this atmosphere of fear which is haunting us will gradually go away." Nehru added, "We have done no better thing than this since we became independent."[13]

Nehru's critics in Parliament were outspoken in condemnation of the agreement. During a foreign policy debate on May 15, opposition deputy Acharya Kripalani declared prophetically, "China has demolished a buffer state; in international politics when a buffer state is abolished by a powerful nation that nation is considered to have aggressive designs on its neighbors." Kripalani cited China's maps, which incorporated large areas of India, as further evidence of aggressive intentions. He criticized Nehru, saying, "I do not say we should have gone to war [with China] but this does not mean that we should recognize the claims of China on Tibet."[14] Kripalani later described the 1954 treaty as being "born in sin because it was enunciated to put the seal of our approval upon the destruction of an ancient nation which was associated with us spiritually and culturally."[15]

Parliamentary and public reaction in India to the new pact was nevertheless generally favorable. The press gloried in India's new approach to international affairs. The *Times of India*—prematurely as it turned out—lauded the "recognition by Peking of the economic ties that indissolubly link Tibet with India."[16] In view of China's cartographic provocations there was audible relief expressed for the boundary guarantees falsely believed to be implicit in the agreement. Nehru was given credit by *Amrita Bazar Patrika* for "getting a tacit Chinese approval of the McMahon Line,"[17] while reference in the agreement to "territorial integrity" was hopefully interpreted by the *Times of India* to mean that China respected the boundary. The *Indian Express* went even further in its optimism: "It is now seen that the alleged maps establishing Chinese claims to certain tracts this side of the McMahon Line were the products of the malicious imagination of mischievous outsiders."[18] Few newspapers reflected the healthy skepticism and foresight of the *Lucknow Pioneer*, which thought that "territorial integrity" was not adequately defined and that agreement should have been demanded from China for an acceptable map of the boundary to be officially prepared.[19]

The wishful thinking of the Indian press bespoke the government's official view—later to be revealed more directly during the 1960 Sino-Indian boundary discussions. During these discussions, for example, the Indian Foreign Office reasoned that normal relations between India and Tibet could not have been established by the 1954 agreement if the Chinese government had in mind "claims to large areas of Indian territory contiguous to the Tibet region."[20]

In answering his critics Nehru revealed much of his own thinking. Mindful of comparisons being made with the 1914 Simla Convention which had last fixed Sino-Indian relations as they pertained to Tibet, Nehru replied in Parliament to one critic saying, "As to the treaties and maps which Dr. Satya Narayan Sinha* has presented, let me tell him: after all, these treaties and maps were all prepared by British imperialists."[21] This was an unfortunate denigration of the very maps upon which India must a few years later defend its boundary against Chinese claims and intrusions. Nehru also failed to see then the importance of the 1914 Simla Convention in delimiting the eastern sector of the India-Tibet boundary, known since that treaty as the McMahon Line.

What seemed to have intrigued the Indian Prime Minister was the awesome spectacle of China on the move. His admiration for this phenomenon made it difficult for him to see the immediate threat to India. Nehru said before Parliament: "Now we must realize that this revolution that came in China is the biggest thing that has taken place in the world at present. . . . In a period of only a few years a country the size of China has moved and arisen from slumber and for the first time in several hundred years of history China now has a strong central government."[22] China's occupation of Tibet could thus be excused as part of the awakening process.

Parliament ratified the Sino-Indian Agreement on June 3, 1954, but the public debate continued. The opposition Praja Socialist Party was particularly critical of Nehru, and its press organ *Janata*

* Sinha was at that time a member of Parliament. He is author of *The Chinese Aggression* (New Delhi: 1961).

accused Nehru's speech of being "apologetic." Pointing out that India was committed to a plebiscite in Kashmir—"more rightfully Indian than Tibet was Chinese"—*Janata* asked why the same could not be done in Tibet to determine whether China should continue to hold it.[23]

Nehru described the 1954 agreement as a recognition of the existing situation in Tibet. Within limits this was true. Chinese control over Tibet was a fact beyond India's ability to change. The pact—together with an accompanying exchange of notes—formally eliminated the extra-territoriality which India had enjoyed as inheritor of British treaty rights. For example, the military escorts stationed at Yatung and Gyantse were no longer to be permitted, and the Indian telephone and telegraph link into Tibet was to be sold to China. This was inevitable, and Nehru had a point when he said, "What right does India have to keep a part of her army in Tibet, when, by the terms of the 1908 treaty with Tibet and China, Great Britain had agreed to withdraw the escorts when they ceased to be required for the protection of traders."[24]

Treaty guarantees which protected Indian traders against Chinese trade monopolies could not of course be retained in the 1954 agreement. Under the terms of the Anglo-Tibetan Trade Regulations of 1914, most of these rights would have terminated unilaterally anyway by January 3, 1955. India was able to retain its trade agencies at Yatung, Gyantse and Gartok in exchange for Chinese agencies at Kalimpong, Calcutta and New Delhi, but this did not provide Indian traders with trade protection or favorable treatment.

While the 1954 agreement did recognize an existing situation, Nehru did not make clear why treaty formalization was required, particularly since nothing significant seemed to have been gained for India by it. China achieved formal recognition of its right to absorb Tibet; India gained no discernible *quid pro quo*.

The 1954 agreement was not a non-aggression pact, and the platitudes contained in the *Panch Sheela* preamble are meaningless without clear agreement on the delimitation of the boundary. Many Indians may have been heartened by an absence of Chinese comment on the boundaries and may have interpreted this as acquiescence to the Indian-claimed boundary, but subsequent events proved all too well that this interpretation was wrong. In 1914 Sir Henry McMahon had believed that "the political status of Tibet could not be discussed . . . until the limits of the country were defined."[25] How much better it would have been if Nehru had insisted on the same prerequisite.

What cannot be calculated accurately is the effect which the 1954 agreement had on other countries bordering China. Nepal, for example, must have been influenced by India's posture toward China, and subsequent Nepal-China relations doubtless reflect this influence. Burma too was affected, and its willingness to enter into boundary negotiations on Peking's terms can probably be traced in part to the 1954 Sino-Indian Agreement.

New Delhi's rationale for this pact certainly included the belief that *Panch Sheela* was a major step forward in international morality and gained for India greater stature in the international community. Unfortunately it did not work out this way. The Praja Socialist weekly newspaper *Vigil* expressed it well at the time when it editorialized, "It is rather an irony that a treaty which guarantees between India and China peaceful coexistence and mutual respect for each other's territorial integrity and sovereignty should be the first international document to set a seal on the abolition of Tibet's autonomy."[26] It added in its next edition: "We think the Prime Minister need not have gone out of his way to give China a kind of moral certificate in regard to her action in Tibet . . . we think there should be some way for big nations to acquire friendship and create a 'peace area' without extinguishing the independence of a small nation that might have the misfortune of lying between them."[27]

It could have been argued that Tibet was a fair price to pay for the moral containment of China, particularly since the legal extent of Tibet's independence had always been a debatable subject. But Peking's words and actions consistently indicated that China had no intention of being contained, morally or otherwise. It was not publicly known until 1959 when India published its first "White Paper" on relations with China that Chinese forces violated Indian soil but a few weeks after the *Panch Sheela* agreement was signed!

On July 17, 1954 the Counsellor of the Chinese Embassy in New Delhi delivered a note to the Indian Ministry of External Affairs accusing "over thirty Indian troops armed with rifles" of crossing "the Niti Pass on 29 June 1954 and intruding into the Wu-je area of the Tibet Region of China." On August 13 the Chinese charged that a unit of thirty-three Indian troops were erecting tents in the Wu-je area.[28] This was China's way of throwing down the gauntlet and was a very practical way of claiming Indian territory. India denied the Chinese allegations and countercharged that Tibetan officials had tried to cross into [Indian] territory in the Hoti Plain [Wu-je] . . . without proper documents.[29] Then on June 28, 1955 India protested a Chinese encampment at Hoti. Chinese claims and intrusions continued without interruption from this time until such incidents escalated into a full-scale boundary war in 1962.

CHAPTER 8

THE BANDUNG SPIRIT

The Afro-Asian Conference should make us a little more circumspect and cautious in our moves. There is no particular reason why we should be coaxed into pulling Peking's chestnuts out of the fire for the doubtful benefit of getting our fingers burnt.

The Lucknow Pioneer, April 26, 1955

Although the aggressive tactics of the Chinese in Korea and Tibet were followed by a series of provocative violations of Indian soil, this facet of Chinese policy was not then visible to the rest of the world. Clearly evident, instead, were the meaningless rituals of *Panch Sheela*, particularly Chou En-lai's visit to New Delhi and Nehru's return visit to Peking.

With the problem of Tibet apparently eliminated as an irritant in Chinese-India relations, there seemed no reason why Peking's "peace offensive," launched under the slogans of "peaceful co-existence" and "Asian solidarity," should not succeed in India. Indeed, Peking's adoption of peaceful co-existence was particularly welcome in New Delhi since it seemed to vindicate Nehru's stance of non-alignment and to rationalize India's sponsoring of China for membership in the United Nations. Above all a peaceful China would provide the tranquillity necessary for India's economic development.

"Asian solidarity," on the other hand, raised danger flags in New Delhi. This theme as inspired by India was a noble dream, but used as an instrument of Chinese policy it was suspect. Nehru had always recognized that India's and China's political-economic systems were competitive in the sense that whichever proved most successful would be emulated by other Asian nations. But during this period he must have begun to realize that China was a more direct rival for ideological and even political leadership of Asia.

While addressing the Geneva Conference on April 28, 1954, Chou En-lai had made a highly significant plea for solidarity. He had urged the countries of Asia to "consult among themselves with a view to seeking common measures to safeguard peace and security in Asia."[1] Two months later when Chou visited New Delhi from Geneva, he discussed with Nehru this same theme, suggesting the concept of an "Asian Consultative Committee" and the extension of a "peace area." While Nehru himself had earlier proposed a series of bilateral non-aggression pacts among non-aligned nations, he was definitely opposed to China's concepts of solidarity. The All India Congress Committee—policy-making body of the Congress Party—faithfully reflected Nehru's views in this regard when in July 1954 it rejected China's proposal for a collective peace treaty among all Asian countries. The *Lucknow Pioneer* commented on the difference between India's belief in co-existence and China's broader ambition. Probably reflecting the views of the government, the paper wrote: "India subscribes wholeheartedly to the demand of 'Asia for the Asians' but she will not tolerate the domination of the continent by a single great power in the name of unity."[2]

A joint communiqué issued on June 28 at the conclusion of discussions in New Delhi between Nehru and Chou En-lai stressed the theme of peaceful co-existence. Their mutual reason for meeting was ostensibly to bring about a "greater understanding of the problems of Asia and to further a peaceful and cooperative effort." Asian solidarity, in the sense of specific Asian collective action and cooperation, was pointedly omitted.

The five principles of co-existence endorsed by both countries in the 1954 agreement on Tibet were reaffirmed in the communiqué. Curiously (but prophetically) the adjective "mutual" was omitted from the second and third principles, which had originally read "mutual non-aggression" and "mutual non-interference in each other's internal affairs."[3]

A measure of the extent to which Peking was willing to give the illusion of compromising doctrinal orthodoxy for the sake of the new tactic can be seen in a highly significant statement made by Chou En-lai during a press conference in New Delhi on June 27:

> The rights of the people of each nation to national independence and self-determination must be respected. The people of each nation should have the right to choose their own state system and way of life, without interference from other nations. *Revolution cannot be exported* [italics mine].[4]

Contrast this statement with Peking's definitive and historic doctrinal announcement of December 31, 1962*—made in the context of the Moscow-Peking breach. On the question of co-existence Peking then specified:

> It is inconceivable that peaceful co-existence can be achieved without a struggle. It is still less conceivable that the establishment of peaceful co-existence can eliminate class struggles in the world arena and can abolish the antagonisms between the two systems, socialism and capitalism. . . . But Comrade Togliatti and those [principally the USSR] who attack China, hold that through "peaceful co-existence" it is possible to "renew the structure of the whole world" and to establish "a new international order." . . . In reality they are substituting class collaboration for class struggle . . . advocating a fusion of the socialist and capitalist systems.[5]

Clearly Peking's position on co-existence enunciated for Nehru's and Asia's benefit in 1954 obscured the true doctrine. This was unmistakable by 1959 when serious border incidents betrayed China's fundamental hostility toward India; but not until 1963—while indicting the Soviet Union's "soft line" of peaceful co-existence—did Peking formally uncover its real doctrine. Thus what seemed to Nehru in 1954 to be a genuine pledge of peace and non-aggression was in reality an act of deception.

A *Times of India* editorial on June 29, 1954 struck a note of wisdom in commenting, "It is too seldom recognized that the present threat to international peace arises not from the existence of various and even contradictory political and economic systems, but springs from the assumption that the irreconcilability of theories must inevitably be paralleled by the mutual hostility of states loyal to different ideologies." Neither the *Times of India* nor Nehru then realized that despite pronouncements to the contrary Peking believed profoundly in the thesis that mutual hostilities between states

* The statement was formally entitled "The Difference Between Comrade Togliatti and Us" and first appeared in the Peking *People's Daily* on December 31, 1962.

of different ideologies are inevitable. Moreover Nehru may not yet have realized that Chou En-lai's definitions of "sovereignty" and "territorial integrity" were very different from his own. There were few Indian observers who then had the skepticism and foresight of A. D. Gorwala of the *Statesman* newspaper. Gorwala quoted Lenin's statement that it was "unthinkable" for the Soviet Republic and the imperialist states "to exist side by side for a long time." Gorwala warned prophetically that the freedom of countries lies not in talk of peaceful co-existence but in having sufficient strength confronting the Communists to deter them from launching aggression.[6]

Nehru had a very specific reason to give China the benefit of the doubt and accept at face value its declarations favoring peaceful co-existence. The Geneva Conference was at the moment close to achieving agreement on peace terms for Indo-China. While negotiating behind the scenes in Geneva, Krishna Menon had thoroughly committed New Delhi's prestige to underwriting China's faithful observance of the peace terms in the Southeast Asian crisis. Indeed, on July 18 the delegates at Geneva had agreed to name India chairman of an International Supervisory Commission made up of Indian, Canadian and Polish representatives to police the settlement in Indo-China.

The Madras *Hindu* editorialized that India's role in the settlement was a "logical sequence to . . . the principles enunciated by the Nehru-Chou En-lai talks at New Delhi midway through the Geneva Conference." The choice of India to chair the armistice commission was viewed by the *Hindu* as the "fruition of the policy of impartial and independent judgment in international relations." This was perhaps the highwater mark of New Delhi's prestige and success, but Nehru looked forward to a greater triumph—the acceptance of *Panch Sheela* by all nations in Asia and Africa and the resultant creation of a vast area of peace whose ideological center would be New Delhi. This would hopefully be accomplished at the forthcoming conference of Asian and African nations to be held in Bandung, Indonesia.

Nehru in an address to Parliament predicted that the conference would be a "striking example of co-existence" and described *Panch Sheela* as a guide for the conduct of nations. But even before Bandung Nehru made a state visit to Peking, and he must have been increasingly concerned by areas of friction with China which were already becoming apparent. But the buildup for Bandung could not lose its momentum—Nehru's Peking visit must be made to appear as another step toward Asian peace. In reality peace was still a long way off for in September the Chinese Communists began heavy bombardment of the Nationalist-held offshore islands of Quemoy and Matsu and thus precipitated still a new crisis in the Far East.

No complete record of Nehru's visit to China in October 1954 has yet been made public. Ostensibly he was simply returning Chou's visit to India, but the Indian Prime Minister admitted that "one always discusses problems." One such problem was certainly China's cartographic claims against Indian territory. Since 1950 Nehru had been troubled that the new Communist regime persisted in publishing official maps showing large areas of his country as belonging to China. He chose the occasion of his visit to Peking to complain.

According to Nehru's version of the conversation, Chou dismissed the offending maps as reproductions of "pre-liberation" maps which China had not had time to revise.[7] According to another official Indian record of the conversation which appeared in the 1960 report on Sino-Indian boundary discussions Chou stated that similar alignment errors appeared in the depiction on Chinese maps of the frontiers with the Soviet Union and Outer Mongolia.[8] Presumably this remark was meant to reassure Nehru, but it would have been less reassuring had the Prime Minister been able to glimpse the future and know that China's cartographic claims against Moscow would be pursued seriously in 1963. The official Chinese version of the 1954 conversations on the boundary problem alleges that Chou "made it clear that the boundary had yet to be delineated," and China would not make changes without a survey or without consulting the countries concerned.[9] This argument did not appear until 1960 and it is thus likely that Nehru was not left with the impression that China intended to press its cartographic claims.

There is also evidence to suggest that during their discussions in Peking Chou and Nehru again disagreed on the concept of collective action in Asia, the latter privately fearing that China would dominate any organized Asian grouping. Reports originating in Peking during the meetings of the two leaders indicated that a competitor to SEATO had been suggested by Chou, who was reportedly even willing to extend *Panch Sheela* to Pakistan or other SEATO members.[10] Nehru believed to the contrary that "fear could be overcome only by expounding and enlarging the five principles of co-existence."[11] The *Lucknow Pioneer* confidently predicted that Nehru would impress upon the Chinese India's opposition to "any development of 'pan-Asianism' based on active hostility to the West." The Indian leader soon thereafter did in fact deny publicly any intention of creating a new Asian military alliance.

Nepal was still another point of contention which the two leaders discussed. In public the Prime Minister would only admit that India's "special position" in Nepal received attention during the talks, but it is likely that Peking's desire to establish a diplomatic mission in Nepal introduced a substantial element of friction. A Kathmandu announcement that Nepal intended to renegotiate its relationship with China was in itself enough to make Nehru publicly re-assert for Chou's benefit India's paramount claim in Nepal.

On balance Nehru's visit to Peking must have been a disquieting experience—one which caused him to recognize that there were potentially serious points of difference between the two countries which could not indefinitely be masked by Peking's "peace offensive." Despite well-staged mass rallies of welcome the Indian Prime Minister must have left with a feeling of apprehension. Not only were there probably nagging fears that China had designs on Indian territory and intended to usurp India's special position in Nepal, but there was Chou's proprietary approach to Asian solidarity, which labeled him a serious rival for Asian leadership. The Bandung Conference would be a critical indication of Chou's role in Asia. Nehru must have suspected at least that he was walking into a dilemma. In an effort to sell non-alignment and co-existence to Asia and Africa he was in effect sponsoring Chou En-lai at Bandung and presenting Communist China as a peaceful member of the Asian community. Yet by so doing he was promoting his own rival.

The Asian-African Conference convened by the five "Colombo Powers"* brought twenty-nine nations together at Bandung. The announced purposes of the conference were to promote goodwill and cooperation; to consider social, economic and cultural problems of special interest to Asian and African peoples; and to view the position of Asia and Africa in the world today and the contribution they could make to the promotion of world peace and cooperation. Nehru saw the conference as an expression of co-existence. He announced before the Indian Parliament, "*Panch Sheela* is the challenge of Asia to the rest of the world," and he hoped "this question

* India, Burma, Indonesia, Pakistan and Ceylon.

will be posed by the Asian-African Conference in all its straightness and boldness."[12]

Nehru's dream of Afro-Asian cooperation perhaps begun in 1927 when he attended a meeting in Brussels of the Congress of Oppressed Nationalities. As the delegate representing the Indian National Congress he exchanged ideas with a variety of leftist and Communist political exiles from the colonial world. The 1927 congress was funded mainly from two sources—the Mexican government, which sought sympathy in its struggle against United States domination of Central America, and the Chinese Kuomintang Party, which was similarly struggling against British influence in the Far East. The Brussels congress was thus an early example of Latin America's identification with the Afro-Asian anti-colonial cause. It is interesting to recall that Nehru's report to the All-India Congress Committee on the Brussels meeting took note of the "rising imperialism of the United States" and predicted that American expansion would pose a more serious danger than British imperialism.[13]

Nehru was elected to the presidium of the Congress for Oppressed Nationalities and acquired with his new job a taste for international leadership. He thereafter was a devout believer in the role of Indian leadership in Asia and frequently took the initiative in organizing other conclaves devoted to the cause of Asian independence. Addressing an American audience in 1949, Nehru described India's "pivotal position between Western Asia,* Southeast Asia and the Far East" which made India "the central point of the Asian picture." His early sense of destiny—national and personal—has been justified by history. Yet the Bandung Conference—a culmination of his efforts to create an Afro-Asian influence for peace in a troubled world—would reveal that not only were the areas of agreement small but the competition for leadership great.

The delegates to Bandung from India, Egypt, Burma and Communist China had met in Rangoon en route to Indonesia. If, as the *Hindusthan Times* editorialized, "Nehru, U Nu and Nasser were at Bandung to sell China to the rest of the Asian-African fraternity and the Western World" it was natural that they felt the need to caucus before the conference began. But the propriety of this secret session is in question. It tended to dramatize the rivalry between the non-aligned group which sponsored China and the other delega-

* Middle East.

tions even before the conference began. If the flood of general statements made by several leaders at the beginning of the conference raised the ideological disputes with China and thus irritated the Indian delegation, Nehru must accept some of the blame himself.

Many delegates came to Bandung determined to prevent domination of the conference by either China or India. The representatives from Turkey, Lebanon, Iraq, Iran, Thailand, Pakistan, Ceylon and the Philippine Islands were particularly outspoken and forceful in defending their positions. This group fought hard, for example, to have the Soviet satellite system specified as one type of colonialism opposed by the conference. The compromise phraseology in the final communiqué which called for opposition to "colonialism in all its manifestations" represented only a partial victory, but at least the issue had been aired.

Nehru and Chou—both caught off balance by the intensity of anti-Communist and anti-neutralist attacks—must have been particularly startled by the refusal of the conference to endorse *Panch Sheela* and "peaceful co-existence." The five principles as specifically phrased and itemized in *Panch Sheela* had come to symbolize Indian—and by extension neutralist—collaboration with Communist China and were unacceptable to those who opposed Peking. The conference finally adopted a ten-point declaration which incorporated the points of *Panch Sheela* but avoided the endorsement of an objectionable doctrine born of China and India on the occasion of Tibet's loss of independence.

Also unacceptable because of its original Communist sponsorship was the word "co-existence." Ironically, Chou En-lai, whose posture throughout the conference was characterized by reasonableness and moderation, suggested the alternate slogan, "living together in peace," which he had borrowed from the United Nations Charter. After the conference Nehru reported to Parliament simply that "in the Bandung Declaration we find the full embodiment of these five principles."[14] This statement, of course, purposely avoided the real significance of the ten-point declaration and the omission of the phrase "peaceful co-existence."

The concept of collective defense became still another troublesome issue at the conference, although a formula was finally found to meet the obviously divergent views of the delegates. Specifically,

Article 5 respects the right of each nation to "defend itself singly or collectively in conformity with the charter of the United Nations," while Article 6A calls for abstention from the use of collective defense to serve the particular interests of any big powers. At least a clear loophole was thus left to accommodate defense arrangements such as SEATO. In reporting to Parliament Nehru emphasized that the collective defense clauses were consistent with the provisions of the United Nations Charter, but it is likely he realized that the compromise was an expression of opposition to Indian and neutralist policy on this score.

Bandung provided Asian and African countries with a forum for self-expression and made them more aware of their own emergence. It proved that the underdeveloped countries could exert an important influence on world affairs, not only in this kind of regional conclave but in the United Nations itself. It is significant that the Bandung Declaration was careful to recognize the position of the U.N. and the need to subordinate Afro-Asian consciousness to a consciousness of belonging to the world community of nations. The countries represented at Bandung did find common cause on a variety of issues, but it was apparent that the areas of actual and potential disagreement were greater than the areas of agreement.

Of lasting concern to Nehru was his personal failure at Bandung. He had made certain mistakes. The pre-conference meeting in Rangoon with Chou En-lai, Nasser and U Nu was one. Another was his attempt to impose a conference agenda at a time when the heads of several important delegations were absent. His unsuccessful effort to prevent opening speeches by heads of delegations also antagonized many of them and provoked them to more aggressive opposition to India. Frustrated by opposition, Nehru was frequently irritable and occasionally lost his temper, which only reduced his effectiveness even more.

Chou En-lai by contrast was able to project a new and entirely favorable image of himself. Constantly emphasizing the theme of peace, Chou conveyed to the delegates China's desire to cooperate with its Asian neighbors. In a speech on April 19 he promised that China had no intention of subverting its neighbors.[15] He declared on another occasion that "the Chinese delegation has come to seek unity and not to quarrel." The *Times of India* columnist "Onlooker" summed up Chou's position at Bandung: "Brought in as a rakish wolf amid a flock of embarrassed and suspicious sheep, he succeeded by his lamb-like demeanor in making the rest look far more wolf-like than he."[16]

Chou skillfully used Bandung to communicate with countries which China normally found difficult to reach. He was, for example, able to lay the groundwork for a new relationship with Nepal. The Chinese leader also took advantage of Bandung to reach agreement with Indonesia on the question of overseas Chinese. But the most dramatic gesture of Chou's peace offensive at Bandung was his offer to negotiate with the United States on relaxing tensions in the Taiwan area. This announcement stole the spotlight from the concluding declaration of the conference and earned for Chou the laurels of the hour as peacemaker.

Nehru confided to Parliament that before Bandung he had held several conversations with Chou En-lai relating to the Formosan problem. Moreover, Krishna Menon had, on Nehru's instructions, held exploratory conversations in Peking, Washington, London and Ottawa in an effort to find a formula for easing the Formosan crisis. Bandung provided another opportunity for backstage talks with Chou on this subject. Nehru had come to Bandung prepared with certain suggestions on Formosa which had been discussed earlier in London between Krishna Menon and Britain's Foreign Minister, Anthony Eden. But if Nehru found satisfaction in his and Krishna Menon's behind-the-scenes role at Bandung, there were others in India who were not so sure it was useful. The *Lucknow Pioneer*, for example, cautioned: "The Afro-Asian Conference should make us a little more circumspect and cautious in our moves. There is no particular reason why we should be coaxed into pulling Peking's chestnuts out of the fire for the doubtful benefit of getting our fingers burnt."[17]

Recognizing the success with which Chou increased China's influence at Bandung and resenting the personal competition he offered, Nehru was always understandably cool to suggestions that subsequent Asian-African conferences be convened. It is perhaps significant that in his report to Parliament on Bandung Nehru placed stress on his avoidance of "any provisions for setting up additional machinery of international cooperation."[18] Bandung had shown the Prime Minister that such machinery can be exploited by China to the detriment of Indian aspirations in Asia.

The educated public of Asia and Africa found satisfaction in

Bandung and felt that despite disagreements a new spirit of peace and cooperation had been born. Perhaps epitomizing Indian views was K. R. Ghosh's exhuberant article in *Eastern World* which credited China and India with "acting as midwives of the new trend in history." Even the Indian Praja Socialist Party organ *Janata*, normally critical of Communist China and Nehruian India, commented:

> Asian and African nations did not quite agree with the United States and her allies when they branded People's China as an aggressor . . . Now their [Asian and African] stand has been vindicated at Bandung. People's China has once again, as she had done at Geneva, demonstrated her willingness to steer clear of the Moscow axis, at least, insofar as Asian affairs are concerned.[19]

How strange that sounds today when it is Moscow which poses as the defender of peaceful co-existence while China insists on the inevitability of war. Still another editorial which was accurate in its prediction of Peking's independence of Moscow but which was wrong in estimating China's devotion to peace appeared in the *Times of India*. "Onlooker" in his column gave Nehru credit for creating "an Afro-Asian area of peace which would include China." Nehru saw a world in which "China would be a member not of the Russian but of the Asian orbit, with a Communist government owing neither allegiance nor subservience to Moscow but building up its own Marxist structure of society conditioned entirely by Chinese needs."[20]

The real spirit of Bandung can be seen from China's actions—not from Chou En-lai's charade at Bandung. Aside from the obvious exhibition of Chinese militancy in the offshore island crisis (which Asians were prone to blame on the United States), there were even then increasing signs of Chinese hostility toward India. That these signs were kept from the Indian people and Parliament until 1959 makes them no less significant.

In 1955—the very year of Bandung—Chinese troops violated Indian territory in two places, Bara Hoti and Damzan, in the state of Uttar Pradesh. In the following year Red laborers began construction of a permanent road from Sinkiang to Gartok in western Tibet which crossed deep into Indian Ladakh.[21] Also in 1956, Chinese patrols willfully crossed three times into India over the Shipki Pass in the border province of Himachal Pradesh and an armed party camped on Indian territory near Milang in Uttar Pradesh.[22] During the following year Chinese troops reached Walong in the Lohit frontier sector of India's Northeast Frontier Agency.[23]

In September 1958—shortly after Nehru announced India's support of Peking's claims to the offshore islands—Chinese soldiers arrested an Indian police patrol in the Aksai Chin corner of Northeastern Ladakh. The prisoners were maltreated while held in custody for five weeks.[24] During the same month Red troops began construction of permanent barracks on Indian soil at Bara Hoti. A detachment of Chinese also entered the Lohit frontier area for the second time.[25] In October construction was begun on new Chinese military outposts at Lapthal and Sangchamalla in the Uttar Pradesh border area.[26]

These incidents were the subject of an acrimonious exchange of notes between Peking and New Delhi. The tone of this correspondence, which was certainly out of phase with the spirit of Bandung, grew steadily more hostile. Peking's diplomacy in Nepal from 1954 onward must also have been disturbing to India's leaders. The 1956 agreement with Kathmandu permitting China to open a consulate and three trade missions, as well as a subsequent Chinese aid agreement, seriously challenged India's traditional supremacy in Nepal. Yet it was Tibet which provided the issue on which India and China broke.

The anti-Chinese Tibetan underground and Khamba tribal insurgency in eastern Tibet had by 1958 reached dangerous proportions. In July of that year China officially protested to India, alleging "subversive and disruptive activities against China's Tibet region, carried out by the United States and the Chiang Kai-shek clique in collusion with fugitive reactionaries from Tibet using India's Kalimpong as a base."[27] But even before this, the circumstances surrounding the Dalai Lama's trip to India on the occasion of the Buddha Jyanti celebrations—or 2,500th anniversary of Buddha's birth—had placed a dangerous strain on Sino-Indian relations. After going to considerable lengths to dissuade the Dalai Lama from accepting the Indian government's invitation to visit New Delhi for the ceremonies (including at first failing to tell him that the invitation had arrived), Peking reluctantly permitted him to go. But he was sternly warned not to discuss the India-Tibet border or the anti-Chinese resistance movement operating in his country.[28] Inevitably, the God-King's presence in India served to excite exiled Tibetan leaders, who stepped up their anti-Chinese propaganda efforts. His arrival also focused Indian attention and sympathy once again on the Tibetan situation.

Sorely troubled by the growing opposition to China in Tibet, the Dalai Lama earnestly sought Nehru's advice. Tibet's leader was torn between a sense of duty which beckoned him back to Lhasa where his presence might avoid bloodshed and the exhortations of Tibetan exile leaders in India who feared for his safety if he returned to Tibet. Moreover, the resistance leaders realized that if he returned the Chinese would exert intolerable pressure on him to use his influence against the resistance movement. But Nehru advised him to return and to work peacefully toward carrying out the 17-Point agreement.[29] Implicit in his advice was a promise that India would use its influence to see that Peking honestly fulfilled the terms of the agreement.

Chou En-lai, who found it prudent to visit India at the same time, met with the Dalai Lama and reassured him that their agreement would be honored. Chou also made it clear that the Dalai Lama must return soon to Lhasa. The Dalai later recounted in his memoirs how Chou had described the deteriorating situation in Tibet and had threatened forceful suppression of any popular uprising should it occur.[30]

The Dalai Lama did return to Tibet and two years later found himself the rallying symbol of the very kind of mass uprising which the Chinese had feared. His visit to India to honor the 2,500th anniversary of one of the world's greatest disciples of peace had in fact ignited sparks of conflict. His visit had made Peking realize that he could not be relied upon to front for the Chinese subjection of Tibet and that when the inevitable test of strength came, Indian sympathies would be on the side of the Tibetans. The "Bandung Spirit," as hopefully expressed by Asians and Africans after their memorable conference, was wholly illusory; it was a product of Chinese deception. Following the fateful visit of the Dalai Lama to India, China's collision course with India was charted.

CHAPTER 9

COLD WAR COMES TO INDIA

If the heart be stout, a mouse can lift an elephant.
Old Tibetan Proverb

Although guerrilla resistance had been fought in southeast Tibet for more than five years with casualties estimated as high as 80,000, neither Peking nor New Delhi was prepared for the events which were to take place in Lhasa in March 1959. Nehru hinted on March 17 that there were disturbances in Lhasa, but he had then minimized their importance. During a routine parliamentary debate the Prime Minister told the Lower House that he was not "happy" about Tibet and mentioned that a "clash of wills" had taken place, but he assured Parliament that "no major violence had occurred!"

There had been a large influx of Khamba tribesmen from eastern Tibet into Lhasa during the summer of 1958. Estimates ran into the thousands. Many had simply been displaced by the chronic fighting in their home area, but some were semi-organized guerrillas who had secretly infiltrated Lhasa as part of the resistance strategy. The Chinese were well aware of this activity and, in prudence, could not tolerate for long the tribesmen's presence in Lhasa. The Chinese garrison had in fact put considerable pressure on the Dalai Lama to denounce the resistance and order Tibetan army units to move against the Khambas. By thus pitting Tibetan against Tibetan and reviving the traditional antagonism between U (Lhasa) and Kham provinces, Peking hoped to break the militant aspects of the revolt without using military force. This was both militarily and politically desirable.

The Dalai Lama steadfastly refused to move against his own people and this, of course, strengthened a growing Chinese realization that he would not serve as puppet. It is likely that Peking reached its decision to rule directly in Tibet rather than continue to appease the powerful monasteries and rule through the God-King sometime shortly after the latter had visited New Delhi in 1956. But before this decision could be implemented, Chinese garrisons had to be greatly increased. Peking by then knew that direct rule would precipitate a showdown with the Tibetan people as well as with the Dalai Lama. Through painful experience the Chinese had become aware that their existing garrisons were inadequate to suppress the Khamba irregulars, much less cope with an all-out popular uprising, which would surely be set off if the Dalai Lama were removed.

Peking needed time to prepare. This time was bought by promises to live up to the 17-Point Agreement and leave the Tibetan way of life unchanged. Chinese promises were to prove empty, but on February 27, 1957 Chou En-lai gave the appearance of backing down when he announced, "It has now been decided not to proceed with democratic reforms in Tibet during the period of the second Five-year Plan."[1] This conciliatory message was accompanied by an official assertion that troops were being withdrawn from Tibet—but in fact reinforcements were steadily coming in. Three divisions were believed to have reached Lhasa by March 1959.

Despite the military force which Peking could maintain on this inhospitable plateau, the person of the Dalai Lama was still the main obstacle to direct rule. The obvious and classic solution would have been to keep him under secure control in China where his sanction for Chinese rule in Tibet could be extracted under pressure or if necessary forged. Since his return from India in early 1957 the occupation authorities in Lhasa had put pressure on him to pay another "visit" to Peking. They specifically wanted him to attend the Chinese National Assembly to dramatize the solidarity of minority groups. Fearing detention in China he evaded Chinese "invitations" by pleading special religious duties which demanded his presence in Lhasa. But by January 1959 it was becoming more difficult to stall and he found himself in the position of having to make an outright refusal to leave Tibet. The pressure was such that the Dalai and his closest advisers finally concluded that the Chinese, on one pretense or another, would force him to travel to Peking. It had, in fact, been publicly announced that His Holiness would attend the National Assembly even though he had not given his consent.

The atmosphere in Lhasa on the Tibetan New Year's Day (February 18, according to the Western calendar) has been described by refugees as tense and, in view of the upheaval soon to take place, it could hardly have been otherwise. The city was jammed with monks, who customarily flock to the capital from all over Tibet for the celebrations, and there was still a large concentration of Khamba refugees. Khamba partisans were reported to be active in the Yamdrok Lake area and by March they controlled the entire region from the Brahmaputra River southward to the Bhutan-Indian frontier east of Shigatse and Gyantse.

This was the setting when the Chinese authorities in Lhasa suddenly and curiously made plans for a "theatrical program" which it was seemingly important for the Dalai Lama to attend. The Dalai later described how two junior Chinese officers on March 1 insisted on interrupting him in the midst of a most important religious examination to ask him to set a date for attending the "theatrical performance." He refused to do so at that time, but when pressed again a week later he finally agreed to the date of March 10.[2] The formal invitation, issued the day before the performance was scheduled, specifically excluded the ministers and the contingent of ceremonial bodyguards which customarily accompany the God-King on such occasions. Shakabpa, one of the Tibetan emigré leaders in India, later testified before the International Commission of Jurists' investigative commission that in late 1959 "a number of incidents had happened when high personages believed not to be sympathetic to the Chinese were invited to parties by the military commanders."[3] The Dalai Lama similarly stated in his memoirs that four high lamas had been invited to parties by Chinese military commanders and had never been seen again. Furthermore, these mysterious disappearances were widely known throughout Tibet. It is thus understandable how rumors of a Chinese plot to seize the Dalai Lama at the "theatrical performance" could sweep through the city so quickly.

On March 10 thousands of Lhasans surged toward the Norbulingka summer palace. The mob's intention was simple and spontaneous: protect their Dalai Lama and prevent the Chinese from taking him from Tibet. The quisling, Ngapo Ngawang Jigme, whose version of that eventful day was given before the plenary meeting of the National People's Congress in Peking, reported that "the rebels deceived the people in Lhasa by alleging that the invitation to the Dalai Lama to go to the military area command to attend a performance was aimed at carrying him off by force to the interior." He added that "on the same day, at the gate of Norbulingka where the Dalai Lama lived, the reactionaries killed Kenchung Sonam Chatso, member of the religious affairs committee of the Preparatory Committee for the Tibet Autonomous Region, wounded Sampo Tsewong-rentzen, Vice Commander of the Tibet Military Area Command, and occupied by force the inner and outer walls of the living quarters of the Dalai Lama."[4]

Tibet's leader himself described the day as the most momentous Lhasa had ever seen. The crowds were in a state of turbulent excitement and in a fury against the Chinese. Although the Dalai Lama announced that he no longer intended to go to the "theatrical performance," the crowds would not be dispersed. Mass rallies were held that day throughout the city denouncing the 17-Point Agreement and calling for a complete withdrawal of the Chinese. The Dalai recalled in his memoirs that about seventy members of his government met within Norbulingka later the same afternoon and endorsed the public declarations repudiating the 17-Point Agreement.

On March 12 a mass meeting of thousands of Lhasans was held below the Potala to celebrate Tibet's newly-declared total independence—a brave but futile performance. Independence Day was documented and a letter was sent by courier to the exile leaders in India requesting that the decision of the Tibetan people to declare themselves fully sovereign be announced to the world. (This letter never reached India—probably because of the confusion of the times and because the Chinese had closed most of the passes to India through which the courier could have traveled.) On the same day an estimated five thousand Tibetan women marched to the Indian Consulate General to enlist India's backing for Tibetan sovereignty. From here they marched on the Chinese Foreign Bureau where they screamed their demands.

The first intimation that the Chinese meant to meet public opposition with all-out force came to the Dalai Lama in a letter from the Quisling Ngapo who had remained under Chinese protection throughout the disturbances. Ngapo wrote on March 16 that he had learned of the people's "evil plan" to abduct the Dalai Lama and warned against allowing this to happen. He asked him to inform General Tan Kuan-san* exactly which building he planned to occupy so that it would not be damaged by the Chinese.[5] Also on March 16 reports were received by the Tibetans that the People's Liberation Army had moved up heavy guns and brought in additional troops. These preparations provoked the people to a state of near panic.

The Chinese troops shelled Norbulingka Palace on March 17. Three mortar shells were initially fired, two of which were duds, but the third exploded very close to the palace walls. All possibility of conciliation between the Dalai Lama and the Chinese had passed. Open warfare between Tibetan citizens—now joined by Khamba guerrillas—and the alien occupiers was taking place in the streets of Lhasa. The Chinese version of the main outbreak which erupted on the 20th was given by Ngapo Ngawang Jigme in a speech at the National People's Congress in Peking on the 22nd. Ngapo said:

> At 3:45 before dawn on March 20 the rebels launched armed attacks against the People's Liberation Army units stationed in Lhasa and the offices of the central government agencies in Tibet. In order to safeguard the unification of the motherland and the security of the Tibetan people, the People's Liberation Army could not but begin to counterattack at 10:00.[6]

This contrasts sharply with eyewitness reports by surviving refugees which accuse the Chinese of provoking the outbreak when they began bombarding Norbulingka in earnest on March 20. The Potala was also shelled and severely damaged. Neighboring monasteries were attacked by the Chinese, particularly the famous monastery of Sera, which was badly damaged, and the Sera Medical College, which was razed. According to the Dalai Lama's information "thousands of Tibetan bodies could be seen inside and outside Norbulingka." He later observed ruefully that the Chinese had "ruined Norbulingka, believing that I was still inside it . . . they no longer cared whether they killed me or not." He concluded that "because Tibet's ordinary people had finally—eight years after the invasion began—convinced the Chinese that they would never willingly accept their alien rule, the Chinese were trying to terrify them by merciless slaughter into accepting this rule against their will."[7]

* Political Commissar of the Tibet Military Region.

By the end of the day on March 20, Chinese troops had fought their way into Norbulingka and with great bloodshed subdued the Lhasan defenders. Peking estimated that two thousand Tibetans were killed, but is likely that, in an effort to minimize the extent of their brutality, they underestimated the casualties just as they had underestimated the number of participants in the revolt.

It was Nehru's March 23 statement in Parliament which provided India and the world with the first apparently accurate and relatively full statement of events in Lhasa. Thirteen days had elapsed between the time disturbances first began in Lhasa on March 10 and Nehru's official announcement on the subject. Tight Chinese control conspired to keep all news of Tibet from the world press and the government of India had been cautious about making statements before it had all the necessary facts. At stake was India's national security.

Indian Consul General Chibber in Lhasa had been able to maintain uninterrupted wireless contact with his government, so New Delhi had information from Lhasa within hours after the first signs of trouble on March 10. Nehru announced in Parliament on March 30, "The . . . only news that has come to us or to the wide world . . . was from our Consul's telegrams to us."[8] But Chibber's perspective was limited because of his and his staff's confinement by the Chinese. As India's Prime Minister added, "The Consul General reports by and large what he sees from the window of his consulate." Neither Chibber nor New Delhi could thus be expected to evaluate immediately the extent and significance of the uprising or, for that matter, decide when it had become an uprising rather than a minor disturbance. The Government of India needed facts. It also wanted to have the benefit of Peking's official attitude toward the uprising before announcing its own.

The Chinese government fired off an irate note to New Delhi on March 22, which complained: "The local government in Tibet under instigation and support of the imperialists and foreign reactionary elements have torn up the agreement on the peaceful liberation of Tibet and begun armed revolt by attacking many of the offices of the central government and the central government's troops." The note warned: "This is entirely an internal affair of China and we shall never permit interference from outside. Tibet is an integral part of China's territory and any intrigue aimed at splitting Tibet away from China is doomed to total failure."[9]

Nehru had learned much from the Hungarian uprising in 1956. He could not again allow public opinion to race too far ahead of him. It is likely that he felt an emotional response to the plight of the Tibetans which he had not felt with the same intensity in the case of Hungary. And Tibet, as India's northern neighbor along a 2,500-mile frontier, brought reality closer than ever before. China, which officially claimed considerable areas of India's northern territory and had total control of a militarized Tibet, presented India with a very serious threat.

Nehru's first major statement on the Lhasa crisis—on March 23—was made one day after receiving Peking's note. It is to his credit that he made a public announcement before Chou En-lai took the initiative to do so. Consistent with India's policy of keeping news of its chronic dispute with China from its own people as well as from the world in general and probably in an effort to keep public tempers cool at this critical moment, Nehru made no direct mention of Peking's belligerent note nor of the extent of his own very grave concern.

It was during the same session of Parliament that a Praja Socialist Party opposition deputy moved to condemn China for its action in Lhasa. The Speaker of the House ruled the motion out on the grounds that it was improper to discuss the internal affairs of a "friendly" state. This was a stand soon to be ignored by an angry parliament which did not consider China's actions friendly and which felt the pressure of public sympathy for Tibet and public outrage toward Peking. In fact, the right of the Indian Parliament to discuss anything it pleased was to become a principle which Nehru, himself, was soon to support publicly.

Peking remained silent on events in Lhasa until March 28, when the New China News Agency finally issued a long communiqué. This was broadcast over the NCNA domestic and international services as well as the Peking home service. Broadcast at the same time over the same services was the text of a document called "State Council Order," which officially abolished the Tibet government. Also released and transmitted was a proclamation issued by the Chinese "People's Liberation Army,"[10] calling on Tibetans to assist in the suppression of "reactionary" Tibetan resistance and warning those who didn't. These first statements by Peking to the world provided the basis for Peking's subsequent propaganda barrage.

Between March 19 and March 29 Peking's home service broadcasts in the Tibetan language were particularly conspicuous for their failure to mention anything about Tibet, much less discuss the uprising in Lhasa. On March 29 the Tibetan language transmissions beamed at Lhasa broke silence and carried in full the communiqué, the People's Liberation Army proclamation and the State Council Order. No signals of any type had been sent from the Chinese-controlled Lhasa broadcasting station between March 19 and March 27. On the latter date—preceding Peking's first official announcements on the Lhasa uprising by one day—a Lhasa broadcast threatened dire punishment to Tibetan officials, while the Dalai Lama himself was given assurances that no harm would come to him.[11] The phrasing of this message was such as to indicate that the Dalai Lama was not in Chinese hands. Thus the world was provided with its first clue that the God-King was in flight and still safe from capture.

The shelling of the Dalai Lama's residence on March 17 had convinced the Tibetan Cabinet that the only alternative to flight was imprisonment by the Chinese. The Cabinet was also convinced that it was necessary for the God-King to leave quickly if his escape were to be successful. As the Dalai later recounted, there was no certainty that escape was physically possible. He recalled that "everything was uncertain, except the compelling anxiety of all my people to get me away before the orgy of Chinese destruction and massacre began."[12] The Dalai Lama certainly recognized the gravity of his decision to leave. His refusal to accept exile on two previous occasions—1951 and 1956—despite the danger implicit in his remaining in Tibet is proof enough that he considered flight a last resort.

Disguised as a humble Lhasan, the Dalai Lama with his mother, sister and younger brother had slipped out of Norbulingka Palace on March 17. Accompanied by certain key officials who were a party to the escape plan, the members of the family cautiously picked their way through Chinese lines and forded the Kyi Chi River, where they were met by an armed escort of loyal Tibetan troops.

Only after interrogating and in some cases hideously torturing remaining attendants of the Dalai Lama were the Chinese finally convinced that the God-King had slipped through their hands. They still did not know how he had penetrated the human wall of Tibetans faithfully protecting him nor how he could have made his way through the Chinese lines two hundred yards beyond the

Palace. Although the Chinese did not know which route the escape party had taken they could assume that his destination was India. Immediately before his escape from Norbulingka on the 17th the Dalai had, in fact, left instructions with a trusted official to inform Indian Consul General Chibber of his escape and through him to request asylum from the Government of India.

The Dalai Lama and his party reached Lhuntse Dzong, a village near the Indian border, after a week of hard traveling. This stop had significance since it was here that a free Tibetan government was formally established. By this act the Dalai hoped that the Tibetans would take heart.[13] The Lhuntse regime was soon to be swept before Chinese forces; most of its members found refuge in India and later joined their leader in Musoorie. This government's existence in Tibet—brief as it was—had symbolic value to the Tibetan resistance and assured the people that their God-King had not abandoned his countrymen.

The Dalai Lama's party left behind its armed bodyguards and crossed into Indian territory on March 31 at an obscure location just south of the Tibetan village of Mangmang where he had received Indian permission to enter as a political exile. China was the first to announce the Dalai's entry into India—a phenomenon which did not go unnoticed by the Indian press, which credited this scoop to the efficiency of Peking's espionage. The Indian government's tardiness was generally attributed to a conscientious effort to protect the security of the escape party.

On April 6 the Dalai Lama was welcomed by the monks of Towang Monastery—the largest monastery outside of Tibet—where the relics of the mother of the Sixth Dalai Lama are enshrined. No official Indian spokesman directly took note of the fact that the party traveled for nineteen days through Indian territory south of the McMahon Line which is claimed by China (and which in 1962 was occupied by China) before he safely reached Tezpur in Assam. The drama and excitement of the God-King's entry into India obscured the political risks implicit in his pursuit by Red troops through territory claimed by Peking. The Indian government had not lost sight of these risks, and units of the Assam Rifles were sent immediately to the point of entry on the McMahon Line as a "precaution against pursuers." The *Times of India* news service reported on April 5 that Indian authorities in Shillong, Assam "still appeared concerned about the safety of the Dalai Lama, members of his family and entourage although they were now well inside the McMahon Line."

Tezpur—normally an obscure and sleepy tea planters' town in Assam—suddenly found itself host to a platoon of high Indian officials and nearly two hundred newsmen. Aside from two small official rest houses given over to the visiting bureaucrats, hotels were non-existent. The Tezpur Station Club, once the private reserve of British tea planters, opened its doors to as many visitors as could be packed into its club rooms. Newsmen were obliged to curl up on chairs, sofas and billiard tables to catch fitful rest and to rely on the badly stretched food stocks of hospitable local planters and missionaries. An engraving of Napoleon's surrender to Britain hung over the bar, by all odds the most popular spot in town. During the several-day wait for the Dalai Lama's arrival newsmen passed the time filing stories of local color and jockeying for position at Tezpur's hopelessly overtaxed telegraph facilities. Abortive efforts were made to charter aircraft with which to overfly the Dalai Lama's party as it traveled down from the last pass before Tezpur. Tezpur's only two taxis were hired on standby at exorbitant rates by the first two newsmen to discover their existence.

The Dalai Lama entered Tezpur on April 25, climaxing the drama begun weeks before when he stole out of Lhasa. The exodus of Tibet's God-King had the stuff of a religious epic as well as being politically momentous. No more dramatic way of bringing Sino-Indian tensions to a head or announcing the bankruptcy of *Panch Sheela* can be imagined. Tezpur in its one moment of glory had a carnival air about it, yet throughout India there was a sense of impending disaster. Rumors had been heard that thousands of Tibetan guerrillas, whose ranks had been swollen by monks from Lhasa's beleaguered monasteries, were being pushed toward India's borders by a Chinese punitive drive bent on finally eliminating Tibet's resistance.

A staff reporter of the *Hindusthan Standard* commented in that paper, "The apprehension that India and China may be involved in a dispute of a serious nature in the near future over the northern portion of the territory now commanded by the Northeast Frontier Area administration seems to prevail in official circles." How correct this observation was! But it was to be several months before the full impact of India's longstanding border dispute with China was to be felt by the Indian people, and even longer before China would actually attack India to press its claim. But with the escape to India of the Dalai Lama the cold war of words began in earnest.

China's first communiqué of March 28 revealed careful drafting intended to establish the basis for its case on Tibet and provide the line for its subsequent propaganda. It absolved the Dalai Lama of guilt, portraying him instead a prisoner of the "upper strata reactionary clique," henceforward the official Chinese euphemism for Tibetan resistance leaders in Communist semantics. Here was mentioned for the first time the three letters allegedly written by the Dalai Lama to General Tan Kuan-san, Acting Representative of the Central People's Government in Tibet.[14] These letters, which play an important part in subsequent Chinese propaganda, were calculated to provide proof that the Dalai Lama tried his best to govern loyally in accord with the terms of the 17-Point Agreement but was prevented from doing so by resistance elements which abducted him.

The "Order of the State Council," issued by China on the same day as the communiqué, dissolved the Tibet local government and placed the Panchen Lama in charge of the Preparatory Committee. This officially ended whatever semblance of autonomy Tibet had enjoyed under Chinese rule. It also confirmed the Communist line portraying the Dalai Lama as an aggrieved party, abducted by "reactionary elements in Tibet."

The third official document was a proclamation of the Chinese People's Liberation Army, dated March 20. It announced that the army was charged with putting down the rebellion. It also appealed to the "rebels" to give themselves up, claiming that "no account will be taken of the past misdeeds of those who desert the rebellious bandits and return to us; . . . those who persist in error and carry out stubborn resistance will be punished strictly."[15] This statement, suggesting the size and universality of the resistance, belies the other two documents which blame the resistance on only a small band of "upper strata reactionary" Tibetans and "feudal lords." In this connection, Nehru recalled that Chinese Communist sources themselves spoke of the magnitude of the revolt, "whose basis must have been a strong feeling of nationalism which affected not merely the upper class but other classes too."[16] Again, on May 8, Nehru referred to the subject during a parliamentary debate in which Deputy Suchila Nayyar asked if there were any "feudal lords" among the ten thousand refugees. Nehru replied pointedly: "It is hardly likely that Tibet will produce ten thousand landlords."[17]

The People's Liberation Army release was clearly intended for Tibetan and domestic consumption. It is understandable that the People's Liberation Army proclamation, unlike the other two documents, was omitted from radio transmissions in the Asian languages. Peking certainly realized that public opinion in the Buddhist countries of Southeast Asia would react adversely to news revealing widespread military action against unarmed Tibetan people. But for the peoples of the Chinese People's Republic—particularly the minority groups—a stern object lesson was necessary.

The pivotal figure throughout the Tibetan crisis had been the Dalai Lama. It was his presence in Tibet which required the Chinese to work cautiously through the monastic system, and it was his exalted image which prevented them from ignoring his wishes or bypassing his authority. His escape created for the Chinese an internal security crisis not only in Tibet but among all minority and nationality groups in China. The propaganda theme that the Dalai Lama had been abducted appeared ridiculous to the outside world once the Dalai Lama had safely reached India. But as unbelievable as it may have seemed outside of China, the line had to be defended by Peking if a total upheaval in Tibet was to be prevented and if serious unrest in adjacent areas of China, particularly Sinkiang, was to be avoided. What better launching platform for the "abduction" line than the Dalai Lama letters to Commissar Tan Kuan-san?

Peking's March 29 release of the alleged exchange of correspondence between the Dalai Lama and General Tan Kuan-san was meant to provide proof and substance to Peking's charge that His Holiness had been abducted by resistance leaders. In the letters the Dalai sounded a conciliatory note and implied that he had not been able to carry out Chinese instructions because of obstruction by his Tibetan advisers. He wrote in one letter that "reactionary, evil elements are carrying out activities endangering me under the pretext of protecting my safety." In another he promised that in "a few days when there are enough forces that I can trust, I shall make my way to the Military Area Command secretly."[18]

Not until Nehru's press conference in Musoorie, following his first meeting with the Dalai Lama on April 24, was specific reference made to the letters. Giving the refugee Dalai as his source, the Indian leader acknowledged that the letters were authentic. He felt that "on the one hand, the Dalai Lama was trying to avoid a break with the Chinese . . . on the other hand, he was in a highly distracted state and was being pulled in different directions."[19] Clarifying what he meant by "different directions," Nehru said that the Dalai was being pulled by his Tibetan feelings while at the same time trying to avoid an open break with the Chinese.

The Dalai Lama's own straightforward explanation of the letters, given in his memoirs *My Land and My People*, is more enlightening. He admitted that he had replied to General Tan Kuan-san's letters "to gain time—time for anger to cool on both sides and time . . . to urge moderation of the Lhasan people." He added that it had been his duty to prevent a totally disastrous clash between "unarmed people and the Chinese people."[20] To have revealed anything but total compliance with Chinese wishes at this critical time would have courted arrest. As it happened, the Dalai Lama was able to escape only because he had the benefit of complete secrecy. The letters, therefore, were useful to cover his last-minute escape.

The best proof that the Dalai Lama had not been abducted or spirited away to India against his will was his unfettered presence in India—fully visible to all who would behold him. This was evidence which the Chinese could not rationally dispute. Yet for reasons of policy Peking's party line had to be maintained. Not only was China concerned about internal reaction to the Dalai Lama's flight but, for the sake of plans not yet revealed, India had to be shown guilty of conspiring with reactionary Tibetans to cause the Tibetan revolt and abduct the Dalai Lama. India had to be proved guilty of violating *Panch Sheela*, the five pillars of co-existence.

CHAPTER 10

EXIT PANCH SHEELA

If we believe in Panch Sheela, we follow it, even if no country in the wide world follows it. Of course, it cannot be easily followed in a one-sided way.

Jawaharlal Nehru

"Though they love peace and cherish friendship over 600 million Chinese people . . . will never allow foolish hogs to poke their snouts into our beautiful garden."[1] This homely parable, quoted by a Chinese spokesman in April 1959, refers to alleged interference by a "reactionary" India in the internal affairs of China. It summarizes in a phrase the propaganda line fed to Asia by Peking to meet the problem created by the flight of the Dalai Lama to India. It was a line clearly meant to brand India the aggressor and portray China as victim.

Peking's torrent of words placed the main burden of guilt on India. The United States and Nationalist China, normally Communist China's prime enemies in the Far Eastern cold war, were lesser accessories to the crime. The Dalai Lama was absolved of guilt entirely. Peking claimed that he was abducted, held under duress and victimized by "reactionary, rebellious" Tibetan upper-class elements working in collusion with Indian "expansionists." This left the door open for his return and provided a means for him to save face if he did.

"Indian expansionists" was a new phrase added to Communist semantics. The epithet "expansionist" was invented by Chinese propagandists perhaps because no other term quite applied to the Indian case. To use "imperialist" would be stretching credulity because of Nehru's image as champion of colonized countries. "Reactionary" applied in this case to internal enemies—upper-class

Tibetans—and this term did not convey the idea that India was interfering in the internal affairs of China.

The new term also had to support the subsequent charge that China's frontier had been violated, a charge which was later to prove so important. No epithet in Communist semantics adequately described the special crime for which India had to be condemned and found guilty. "Expansionist"—a milder term than "aggressor"—seems to convey the idea of a self-perpetuating centrifugal thrust riding on some initial momentum. In this case the initial momentum was generated by pre-independence British imperialism. According to Peking's reasoning, an expansionist India, however innocent as prime mover, was guilty of not arresting the imperialist momentum set in motion by the British *Raj*. India must deny its heritage or become China's enemy. In Communist semantics "expansionism" describes a fault which can be cured by policy change, while "imperialism" connotes a fundamental ideology which cannot be changed without proletariat revolution. Peking perhaps did not yet consider Nehru to be among the incurables, but it sternly put him on notice that he must take the cure.

By April 1959 the specifics of China's approach to the Tibetan crisis were clear. As the Sino-Indian Agreement of 1954 on Tibet had inspired the five principles of peaceful co-existence, the Lhasa uprising and the Dalai Lama's flight to India inspired five major charges by China against India of violating these principles. The first four provided the basis of Peking's propaganda campaign to neutralize the damaging effects of the Dalai Lama's escape and his condemnation of China. Briefly summarized they are:

1. India aided the Tibetan resistance movement by allowing its command center to operate from Indian soil (Kalimpong).
2. The Dalai Lama was abducted and held under duress by reactionary Tibetan elements acting in collaboration with India.
3. The Indian government was interfering in the internal affairs of China by allowing widespread press comment and public demonstrations against China and by allowing anti-Chinese criticism in its parliament.
4. By aiding and sympathizing with the reactionary, feudal resistance elements in Tibet, the Indian government revealed its own reactionary nature.

The fifth charge, which did not emerge until August 1959, brought into the open China's longstanding boundary dispute with India. It went beyond the first four to accuse New Delhi of actual physical aggression against China on the grounds that Chinese territory was occupied and defended through force of Indian arms.

To accuse India publicly in 1959 of aggressive acts against China when no hint of such accusations had been contained in the 1958 exchange of notes or in the 1956 informal Nehru-Chou En-lai talks, was to engage in propaganda with all the nuances of falsehood which this word implies. Even though the Indian press and Parliament were, in April 1959, as yet unaware of the note exchange and the discrepancy between truth and hypocrisy which this exchange revealed, they reacted fiercely to Peking's charge that India was responsible for harboring the Tibetan resistance command center.

It was during the spring of 1959 that Indian public disapproval of the alien-directed Communist government of Kerala was beginning to erupt in angry public demonstrations throughout that South Indian state. The President of India was to dismiss Kerala's government within a few weeks and to call for new elections because of the Communists' inability to maintain order in the face of widespread popular opposition. Indians could understandably wonder about the location of the command center for Kerala's Communists. Nehru himself criticized Indian Communists for their implicit disloyalty to India. While referring to the Party's Peking line, the Indian Prime Minister commented distainfully: "What they [Communists] are, I don't know—they cease to be Indians if they talk in this way."[2]

The Dalai Lama's dramatic arrival in India occurred the week before he had been scheduled to participate in the Second National People's Congress in Peking. Having attacked the Indian Parliament for using its floor to make statements hostile to China and thus "interfering in Chinese affairs," China now apparently felt that it had license to use the People's Congress to reciprocate. In the keynote speech Chou En-lai expressed his "deep concern" over the Dalai Lama. Chou commiserated, "Now while we are having this happy get-together here, the Dalai Lama is being held in duress by the rebels and is outside our country."[3] On cue the Panchen Lama echoed this line, deploring "the abduction of the Dalai Lama by rebels in collusion with Imperialists."[4] Ironically, it was while the Dalai Lama was making his first statement to the world from India that Chou En-lai and the Panchen Lama referred to him as a prisoner.

Arriving in Tezpur after his epic escape from Lhasa and miraculous journey over the Himalayas, the Dalai Lama delivered a full and frank statement to the battery of newsmen from all over the world waiting to hear him. Deploring the Chinese failure to live up to the terms of the 17-Point Agreement and describing the growing resistance to the Chinese by the Tibetan people, the God-King explained why he had fled. He unequivocally denied Chinese charges of abduction and stated categorically that he had left Lhasa and Tibet and come to India of his own free will.

The definitive Chinese criticism of Nehru and India was reserved for an editorial appearing in the May 12, 1949 edition of the *Peking Review*. The article, entitled "The Revolution in Tibet and Nehru's Philosophy," authored by the editorial department of the *People's Daily*, summed up Peking's propaganda case against India in general and against Nehru in particular. After a lengthy justification of its own action and policy in Tibet, the editorial answered Nehru's detailed statement on Tibet given before Parliament on April 27 and explained how India had, by its reaction to events in Tibet, interfered in internal Chinese affairs. Apparently forgetting that the Chinese line had heretofore exempted the Dalai Lama from any blame and still officially recognized him as Tibet's spiritual and temporal leader, the editorial asked: "Did not the impressive welcome extended to the Dalai Lama by the Indian Government and the visit to Mussoorie by Prime Minister Nehru himself mean giving a welcome to and holding a meeting with the leader of a rebellion in a friendly country?"

The editorial specifically attacked Nehru, blaming him personally for India's attitude. By inference the Prime Minister was held responsible for irresponsible press attacks accusing the Chinese government of practicing banditry and insulting China's head of state as an "abominable snowman." It also made clear that China believed India had not yet rid itself of a British colonial attitude toward Tibet.

The conviction that New Delhi was still dominated by Western "imperialism" was at the heart of China's fear and makes more understandable the importance China placed on defining its minority doctrine for Tibet. The following passage in the *Peking Review* editorial is most revealing:

> Certain political figures in India have followed the tradition of the British Government of the past—they only recognize China's

> "suzerainty" over Tibet, like India's "suzerainty" over Bhutan and Sikkim. What they call "autonomy" for Tibet is different from national regional autonomy as laid down in clear terms in the Constitution of China—different from the national regional autonomy practiced in Inner Mongolia, Sinkiang, Kwangsi and Ninghsia. Rather it is a kind of semi-independent status. True, Tibet is not a province but an autonomous region of the People's Republic of China, with greater powers and functions than a province as laid down in the constitution . . . but it is definitely no protectorate . . . the big bourgeoisie of India maintains innumerable links with imperialism and is, to a certain extent, dependent on foreign capital. Moreover, by its class nature, the big bourgeoisie has a certain urge for outward expansion. This is why, while it opposes the imperialists' policy of intervention, it more or less reflects consciously or unconsciously certain influences of imperialist policy of intervention.[5]

Public demonstrations condemning Chinese action in Tibet were held in various places throughout India. But it was parliamentary reaction to the Tibetan crisis—particularly statements by Nehru and other government spokesmen—which provoked Peking to accuse India of adopting a hostile attitude contrary to the spirit of *Panch Sheela.*

Nehru had been cautious. A March 30 speech before Parliament describing his government's attitude toward granting political asylum to the Dalai Lama had been full of vague circumlocutions. He tried on one hand to appease an angry parliament and on the other to avoid provoking an angry China.

Then suddenly—as though he had perceived the questioning thoughts of House Members—Nehru took an excursion into history to justify his stand:

> The previous [British] Government of India took an expedition to Lhasa under Colonel Younghusband fifty-five years ago. It very much interfered. . . . All kinds of extra-territorial privileges were imposed on Tibet because Tibet was weak. . . . With variations we inherited these special . . . privileges when India became independent.
>
> Regardless of what happened in Tibet or China or anywhere, we could not, according to our own policy, maintain our forces in a foreign country even if there had been no change in Tibet. . . . What I am venturing to say is that the policy we adopted toward Tibet would have been adopted regardless of what China did . . . we could not do anything in Tibet either in law, constitutionally or practically.

Nehru's concluding words were tougher. He exhorted Parliament not to "submit to any kind of dictation." To shouts of "Hear, hear!" the Indian leader denied that there had been unlawful activities directed toward China from India and he unequivocally rejected Peking's complaint that hostile parliamentary comments were tantamount to interference in China's affairs. He wanted to make it clear that "Parliament is not going to be limited in the exercise of its right of discussion . . . by an external or internal authority—whoever it may be."[6]

The Communist members of Parliament, like the rest of the Party, had been caught unprepared by the Tibet crisis. But on March 31 a full statement clarifying the Party line was published. As the *Hindusthan Standard* commented, it was "not even a colorful paraphrase but . . . a mere stringing together of the very phrases used by the Chinese authorities."

The Communist Party's statement, with its treasonous overtones, ignited an outburst in Parliament on April 1. Had Nehru been there his presence would have exerted a pacifying influence, but he was out of New Delhi that day and Parliament indulged itself in a rare orgy of emotion. An adjournment motion—a procedure frequently used to attack the government, criticized the Chinese Embassy for having distributed copies of an offensive editorial from the *People's Daily* accusing India of harboring the Tibetan resistance headquarters.

Members of Parliament—usually cautious and restrained in discussing foreign affairs—fiercely denounced Peking and the Communist Party of India. As Communist MP's jumped up to defend the position of their party, they were hooted down by cries of "Shame, shame!" Kripalani, a leader of the Praja Socialist Party, deplored remarks released by the Communist Party to the effect that its members would "welcome the Chinese" into India if the latter invaded India to stamp out alleged Tibetan resistance centers; and Home Minister G. B. Pant rose to express agreement with him.

Mrs. Lakshmi Menon, Deputy Minister of External Affairs, spoke for the Indian government in the absence of Nehru. Referring to the indiscreet circulation of Peking's editorial, Mrs. Menon considered it "highly improper for any mission posted in any country to make any critical statement about the government of that country or its activities." She asserted that the government took "very strong exception" to Communist China's charge that Kalimpong was being used as the center of subversive activities in Tibet, and she accused the Communists of lacking "integrity and honesty" by repeating Peking's allegations after Prime Minister Nehru had denied them. She added that a memorandum denying the charge had been sent to Peking on August 2.[7] This, incidentally, was Parliament's first intimation that the Indian government and the Chinese People's Republic had officially corresponded on this subject eight months before. Five more months would elapse before the verbatim exchange was surfaced for public consumption in a White Paper reviewing India-China correspondence since 1954.

The April 1 debate had been concerned with two main themes: (1) denial that India harbored in Kalimpong the headquarters of the Tibetan resistance movement—or, in effect, denial that India was guilty of interference in China's internal affairs, and (2) criticism of China for distributing in India a reprinted Peking editorial attacking the Indian government—i.e. criticism of Chinese interference in India's internal affairs. The deeper significance of the debate was that Parliament made clear that India would tolerate neither Peking's charges nor Chinese aggression against India. Parliament's expression also gave Nehru a clear mandate to take a strong stand against the Chinese.

Peking's cold war language had succeeded in arousing India's people and legislators. The positions of the antagonists were clear; the battle lines were drawn. The months ahead would see a different kind of cold war—one which only incidentally involved the East-West issue. It would be a cold war between the founding partners of *Panch Sheela*, who had so long hidden their serious and inevitable incompatibility.

The war of words was but an angry accompaniment to more sinister harassment of India which began soon after the Dalai Lama's flight from Lhasa. China's first objective was to eliminate Indian rights in Tibet which had been guaranteed by the 1954 Agreement on Trade and Intercourse. That agreement, incorporating the famous five principles of peaceful co-existence, had ostensibly been reached because India and China wanted to promote trade and cultural intercourse between Tibet and India and to facilitate pilgrimage travel between the two countries. But by its actions during the early summer of 1959 Peking soon made clear its intention to remove every vestige of Indian presence in Tibet—to deprive India of even the normal rights enjoyed by one country in another.

In May 1959 India began rebuilding its trade agency building at Gyantse which had been washed away during the terrible floods of 1954. But Chinese interference provoked the government of India to complain officially that the laborers working on the site were being harassed and intimidated by firing practice which took place over their heads! New Delhi also complained that transport facilities were denied and unfair restrictions were placed on the movement of Indian Trade Agency personnel.[8]

More important were Chinese actions which directly interfered with Indian trade and which ultimately brought to a halt all commercial relations between India and Tibet. In July 1959, for example, the Chinese imposed new currency regulations in Tibet which made illegal the traditional acceptance of Indian currency and pegged the value of Tibetan currency 25 percent lower than it had been. This was a mortal blow to Indo-Tibetan trade, and overnight many Indian traders were ruined.

There also arose a problem of citizenship for many Indians, long resident in Tibet. After the 1959 Lhasa uprising such expatriates were anxious to register as Indians and gain some measure of protection from the hostile Chinese administration. They were, however, not even allowed to see the Indian Consul in Lhasa, and in many cases extreme pressure was exerted on them to renounce their Indian citizenship. In response to Indian official protests the Director of the Chinese Foreign Bureau* in Lhasa accused Indian Consul Chibber of an "unfriendly act of instigating the Chinese people to break with China by means of external forces." He expressed surprise that "Mr. Chibber should have raised . . . the problem that they are Indian nationals at a time when our troops had put down the rebellion unleashed by the former local government and the reactionaries of the upper strata in Tibet."[9]

Harassment of Indian trade and traders caused Indo-Tibet commerce to wither and die. It thereby destroyed that which the 1954 treaty sought to achieve. But more serious were subsequent acts of aggression which destroyed the whole concept of co-existence enunciated in the 1954 agreement and thus destroyed the basis of

* The formal name of this office is Alien Affairs Bureau of the Tibet Autonomous Region Preparatory Committee.

Sino-Indian relations. *Panch Sheela* called for "mutual respect for each other's territorial integrity and sovereignty," but a series of Chinese-instigated border incidents created a crescendo of tension which in the end made a sorry shambles of this doctrine. These incidents brought down the whole flimsy façade which had hidden for so long two incompatible ideologies—two irreconcilable points of view—and a fierce rivalry for Asian leadership.

The Indian government had been puzzled and annoyed by Communist China's publication of maps showing large areas of Indian territory within China. Even though Nehru had been assured personally by Chou En-lai in 1954 that these were simply reproductions of old maps which had not yet been revised, Peking's motives were clearly suspect. More disquieting had been the Bara Hoti incidents which culminated in Chinese forces establishing a camp on Indian territory in the boundary regions of Uttar Pradesh (State) and the Khurnak Fort incident in July 1958 which heralded a succession of Chinese intrusions in the Ladakh region of Kashmir.

On July 28, 1959 an Indian police detachment carrying out border reconnaissance near Spanggur in the western Pangong Lake area of Ladakh, encountered a force of 25 Chinese soldiers within Indian territory. Replying to a note of protest sent by India when the scouting party did not return, the Chinese Foreign Office accused the Indians of intruding into Chinese territory and alleged that the patrol refused to heed warnings to withdraw. "Out of friendly considerations" China agreed to return the hapless policemen and warned India to take effective measures to prevent a recurrence of similar incidents."[10]

Most ominous of all was the Chinese construction of a permanent road deep into Indian territory crossing the Aksai Chin bulge of Ladakh. India officially claimed knowledge of this road in October 1958[11] but probably knew of it earlier. Clearly implicit in all incidents were major Chinese claims to Indian territory. But not until later, when Chou En-lai first would make explicit China's territorial pretensions in a letter to Nehru, could India comprehend the full meaning and long-range implications of Peking's actions.[12]

The Lhasa revolt and the flight of the Dalai Lama to India had introduced a new and dynamic element into Sino-Indian relations. Boundary incidents and cartographic claims must henceforward be viewed by New Delhi in a more serious context. Were border violations meant to be punitive in nature, the consequences of China's fury because India had granted asylum to the Dalai Lama? Or were Chinese-provoked border incidents the first manifestations of a new turn in Peking's policy? These were the questions which confronted Indian leaders in August 1959, when trouble struck at the opposite end of the border.

A strong detachment of Chinese troops crossed into India on August 25, at a spot south of Migyitun in the border region of India's Northeast Frontier Agency. According to India, the Chinese force fired without notice on an Indian picket. In the melee which followed one Indian was killed and three captured. The Chinese detachment then probed deeper and attacked an outpost at Longju, two miles south of the boundary line. By the following day the Indian defenders were forced to abandon their outpost in the face of a stronger Chinese force.

An incredulous Indian government protested to China on August 28, requesting that Chinese troops be withdrawn immediately.[13] This incident is significant, not only because the first blood was shed in defense of Indian soil, but because it provoked Nehru to admit to his people for the first time that China had violated Indian territory. The Indian Prime Minister acknowledged before Parliament that there had been cases of "petty intrusion" of the border areas by Chinese troops during the last two or three years.[14]

New Delhi still did not know for certain what lay behind China's new belligerence, but Nehru promised that the government would "naturally be prepared for any eventuality and, without fuss or shouting, keep vigilant." Not only was "fuss and shouting" ruled out for the moment, but so was parliamentary debate. Deputy Braj Raj Singh from Firozabad felt the subject was worth "a two-hour discussion" but Nehru "did not see how a discussion of this case will serve anyone's purpose" and, taking his cue, the Speaker refused to allow debate on the subject.[15]

India's official policy toward China was nevertheless hardening behind the scenes. In view of the Migyitun-Longju incident and lesser incidents at Khinzemane, located at the western end of the Northeast boundary, the entire Northeast Frontier Agency (NEFA) was placed under military rule. Previously it had been administered by the Ministry of External Affairs and policed by the Assam Rifles which that ministry—not the army—controlled. Nehru reported to Parliament on August 31 that, henceforward, India would follow "a double policy—one, of course, defense and the other was to settle these matters by conferences." He added significantly, "It is not possible . . . to prevent an incursion over a two thousand mile frontier but it is possible to take steps to repulse that incursion and to strengthen our defenses. . . ."[16]

If China's threatening border actions did not speak eloquently enough for themselves, Chou En-lai dispelled any remaining ambiguity by a letter to Nehru dated September 8, 1959. The tone was set by Chou's allegation that India had demanded that "the Chinese Government give formal recognition to . . . the British policy of aggression against China's Tibet region as the foundation for the settlement of the Sino-Indian boundary question." The Chinese leader accused the Indian government of "not even scrupling against the use of force to support this demand." He made clear his country's view that the Sino-Indian boundary had never been formally delimited, and he described China's position on the different sectors of the boundary in dispute. Chou accused India of trying to change unilaterally the long-existing state of the border between the two countries by "pressing forward steadily across the eastern section of the Sino-Indian boundary."[17]

Now India, at least, knew where it stood. The full significance of nearly ten years of cartographic aggression and five years of sporadic border violations became clear. China was claiming thousands of square miles of territory long considered part of India and would clearly not hesitate to occupy key parts of its claim by force. Nehru felt that Chou's letter was serious enough to take "Parliament and indeed the public into our confidence" and a White Paper was published describing the long history of India's many disagreements with China including the boundary quarrel.

Chou's letter not only made claim to Indian soil but by strong implication questioned India's treaty rights and position in Sikkim and Bhutan. The Communist leader, while making reference to a passage in Nehru's letter of March 22 concerning the boundary between China and Sikkim, wrote that "China is willing to live together in friendship with Sikkim and Bhutan without committing aggression against each other and has always respected their *proper* relations between them and India [italics mine]."[18] Peking's concept of "proper" relations and the reasons why it refused to discuss Sikkim and Bhutan in the context of the boundary dispute were later to emerge more clearly. But this hint that China questioned the legitimacy of India's treaty relationships with these two strategically-located border states served as adequate warning. Nehru felt it necessary to establish that the subject of Sikkim and Bhutan did very much fall within the scope of future discussions.* He reminded Chou that India had undertaken certain responsibilities for the defense of Sikkim and Bhutan if they were attacked, saying, "If something happens on their borders, it is the same thing as an interference with the borders of India."[19]

It must be assumed that Nehru's disillusionment with China had been in gradual process for a long time. Seeds of doubt must have been planted as early as 1950 when Communist China first set in motion its plan to seize control of Tibet and vilified India as a "running dog of imperialism." The Bari Hoti border incident of 1954 re-awakened fears which may have been momentarily stilled by the *Panch Sheela* agreement on Tibet. Unmistakably, the events following the Lhasa uprising and flight of the Dalai Lama placed Sino-Indian relations on trial. But Chou En-lai's words, contained in his September 8 letter, unequivocably marked the end of *Panch Sheela* or "peaceful co-existence" as a basis for Sino-Indian relations. It was probably at this point—if not before—that a more realistic estimate of China must have crystallized in Nehru's mind. He admitted before Parliament on September 10: "I have been surprised at recent developments. . . . They [the Chinese] have valued India's friendship only to a very low extent. . . ."[20]

Chou En-lai telegraphed Nehru on October 6 that recent difficulties between the two countries were but an "episode in our age-old friendship." This struck an apparent note of conciliation, but words are cheap and Chou's message had no such significance. Still another tragedy was to occur on India's border.

Karam Singh, an Indian officer of the Tibet Border Force, and a party of constables on border patrol near Kongka Pass in Ladakh became witnesses and victims of a new level of ferocity in Chinese aggression against India. A reconstruction of a serious incident in which they took part shows the very low extent to which China "valued India's friendship" and explains why the already aroused Indian public reacted as violently as it did. Moreover, China's handling of the Kongka Pass incident provides a further glimpse of Communist China's cold war techniques, particularly its effort to

* Nehru's remarks were made on September 12, 1959 in reply to a debate on India-China relations in the *Lok Sabha.*

brainwash Indian captives and force them to testify in support of Chinese propaganda.[21]

Kongka Pass lies forty to fifty miles within Indian territory at the southern end of the disputed Aksai Chin bulge of Ladakh which China claims and through which China had earlier constructed a motorable road. A force of about sixty constables, commanded by Karam Singh and belonging to the India-Tibet Border Force, set out on October 21, 1959 to investigate the disappearance of a patrol which had been reported missing in this sensitive area.

Five miles east of a place known as Hot Springs hoofmarks were noted. On the assumption that they belonged to the horses of Chinese intruders, Karam Singh and a detachment of twenty men followed them while the main party remained behind. Suddenly a Chinese soldier was spotted on a hill above the party signaling the group to surrender. Shouts of protest from Karam Singh were met by a volley of fire, forcing the patrol to scramble for cover and fire in self-defense. Ali Raza, one of the Indian constables, made good his escape and notified the main force left behind.

Toward evening heavier Chinese fire killed some of the beleaguered Indians and Karam Singh surrendered to the Chinese rather than risk further casualties. The patrol leader's own words give dispassionately the flavor of the tragedy which occurred immediately after his surrender:

> Five of us were made to carry the dead body of a Chinese soldier who had been killed. Constable Rudra Man and I were asked to help Makhan Lal, who had been injured seriously in the abdomen. . . . We carried him for two miles where the Chinese soldiers ordered us to leave him on the bank of the Chang Chenmo River. . . . From this place I and Constable Rudra Man were made to carry heavy loads. We were completely exhausted and were finding it difficult to walk with this heavy load but we were repeatedly prodded by rifle butts to move on. We reached the Chinese Kongka La post (above 16,000 feet) at about 2:00 A.M., on the 22nd of October 1959. We were all put together in a pit six feet deep, seven feet wide and fifteen feet long, normally used for storing vegetables. It was covered with a tarpaulin which left several openings through which ice-cold breezes penetrated. We had to spend the night on the frozen ground without any covering. No water for drinking was provided nor were we permitted to ease ourselves during the night and the following day. . . . For the first three or four days we were given

> only dry bread to eat. The intensity of the cold and our conditions of living were more than sufficient torture to demoralize us. By then I and three constables were suffering from frostbite and our repeated requests for medical attention and hot water were disregarded.

On October 24 Karam Singh was shown the corpses of the nine Indian constables killed by Chinese fire and was asked to identify them. On the following day the Chinese began a twelve-day course of intensive interrogation in an effort to make him admit that the Indians had fired first and provoked the incident.

Singh recalled:

> At first they asked me to narrate the entire incident. As soon as I came to the point that firing was opened by the Chinese, their senior officer present became wild and shouted back that it was incorrect and that I must confess that the Indians fired first. I refused to accept this despite repeated and constant threats that I would be shot dead. Ultimately, they made me say that I could not judge at that time as to who fired first.

The Chinese also tried to make Singh and others among the Indian prisoners admit that they had known before the incident took place that they had intruded into Chinese territory. Unable to extract such a confession, the Chinese anyway attributed to Singh the statement: "I have now come to know that the area where the encounter had taken place is under Chinese occupation."

The Patrol Leader was then pressured to acknowledge that the Indian Border Force had never before patrolled this particular area. This later became more understandable when, during the 1960 Sino-Indian boundary discussions, China attempted to prove its ownership of the disputed area by showing that India had never patrolled nor otherwise exercised authority in it.

Karam Singh reported that during the interrogation "the Chinese officer lost his temper and threatened to take out his pistol and shoot [him]" for refusing to admit that the gesticulating Chinese soldier had tried to warn the Indian party to leave during the first encounter. The Chinese were of course anxious to frame the testimony in such a way as to make it appear that the Indians—not the Chinese—had provoked the incident.

Singh's testimony provides a good picture of Chinese interrogating technique:

> This interrogation lasted from 4:00 A.M. to about 4:00 P.M. . . . By this time I was almost frozen and mentally and physically exhausted because of cold, persistent interrogation, intimidation, threats, angry shoutings and lack of sleep. In this condition I was compelled to sign the statement recorded by the Chinese. At the end of this interrogation the Chinese then brought all the other captured personnel before me and read out the statement and several photographs were taken.

The interrogation continued on October 27 and 28 when the Chinese extracted order of battle information concerning the Indian border forces. On October 28 all of the Indian prisoners were taken to the Chang Chenmo River where photos were taken by their captors as they washed the bodies of dead colleagues in accordance with Indian custom. Photos were taken also of the prisoners being issued with warm clothing, padded in the Chinese style. Karam Singh stated that on the 29th he and others among the prisoners were taken to the original scene of the incident and there forced to re-enact the events which had taken place. The incident was staged according to the Chinese version of events while photographs were taken which could be used as evidence in support of the Chinese allegations that the Indian patrol had provoked the incident.

A capsule summation of India's ideological errors was included in an indoctrination lecture delivered to the Indian prisoners on November 7. The Chinese lecturer stressed that "even now when India was a free country, the British and Americans owned a number of industrial concerns and that there were still a number of Indian capitalists and landlords." This little talk, delivered in the biting cold of the high Karakorums to a huddle of miserable Indian policemen, speaks volumes for Peking's attitude toward India. While the Western world has fretted over Indian neutralism with its occasional bias in favor of Communist positions, Peking—blinded by a rigid and doctrinaire ideology—has totally rejected India's bona fides as a neutral. When China branded India a "running dog of Anglo-American imperialism" it was expressing a real conviction, not simply mouthing propaganda calculated to shame India into drawing closer to its orbit.

On November 14, Nehru's birthday, the Chinese returned to India the three Indian police who disappeared on October 20, the seven surviving policemen who had been in Karam Singh's captured search party and the bodies of nine constables killed in the October 21 action near Kongka Pass. Constable Makhan Lal—last seen by Karam Singh in Chinese custody lying wounded on the banks of the Chang Chenmo River—was never returned nor accounted for. Presumably he died because his wounds were neglected.

China rejected India's strong and carefully documented protests on the Kongka Pass episode. Peking insisted that the Indian personnel had been given "friendly and generous treatment by the Chinese frontier guards" and alleged that "interrogations of them were always made in a free and unrestrained atmosphere." Producing the forced and fabricated confessions of the captured Indians and boasting that "the Chinese People's Liberation Army has a tradition of treating prisoners magnanimously," Red China had the evidence it needed to prove that India, not China, was guilty of scrapping *Panch Sheela.*

CHAPTER 11

COLD WAR AT THE CONFERENCE TABLE

As China was prepared to accommodate the Indian point of view in the eastern sector, India should accommodate China in the western sector.

Chou En-lai

The Kongka Pass incident brought Indian fury and frustration to a new pitch of intensity. China's callous disregard for Indian life at Kongka Pass aroused the people to a greater extent than the more ominous political significance of the act ever could have. The frustration of being helpless to oppose China's aggression was vented in increased press attacks against Nehru and Defense Minister Krishna Menon. The *Hindusthan Times* thundered, "Inaction now can make war inevitable," and the *Indian Express* complained that Nehru had "sadly underestimated the real menace of Han expansionism and Communist imperialism." Typifying a growing body of opinion which believed that India must resolve its differences with Pakistan in the face of the greater common threat, the *Express* urged Nehru to drop non-alignment and "look around for allies with common defense policies and problems." Certain Indian leaders suggested breaking relations with China while Rajagopalachari, India's respected elder statesman, was among those who urged outright alignment with the West.

Confronted with strong public, press and parliamentary criticism, Nehru was forced to defend his government's policy. On November 2, 1959 he declared publicly that the "talk of leaving non-alignment is utterly wrong and useless."[1] He found vindication of peaceful co-existence in a momentary lessening of international tensions. The prospect of a summit conference scheduled for Paris encouraged Nehru, who alleged that "everyone" in America and Europe wanted to put an end to the cold war. The Indian Prime Minister was convinced that affirmation of Indian policy had been "tremendous." Unfortunately the U-2 incident, which was soon to occur and be used by Khrushchev to wreck the Paris conference, would make Nehru's optimism premature.

India-Pakistan relations had also been thawing. On October 23, the two countries had reached final agreement on a long-pending boundary dispute in East Pakistan, and Nehru mentioned that Pakistan's new President, Ayub Khan, had expressed a desire to find peaceful solutions to as many disagreements as possible. The latter did, in fact, propose a common defense pact which he felt was possible to conclude without "changing the foreign policies of either country." In Ayub Khan's opinion it would simply mean defending their respective frontiers and the frontiers of each other in the case of aggression. He predicted that "the Indo-Pakistan subcontinent would become militarily vulnerable in five year's time" and if any Chinese invasion of India took place, "Pakistan—being in the way—would have to save India to save itself."[2]

Nehru rejected any consideration of a joint defense accord. While expressing appreciation for Ayub's "friendly approach," he was convinced that "common defense is always intimately connected with foreign policy" and he reminded newsmen at a press conference that India is "rather allergic to military alliances with anybody."[3]

Even with the new stimulus of Chinese belligerency the two countries could not find common cause. Realistically, no common defense agreement could be reached until India and Pakistan solved the badly-festering Kashmir dispute. Ayub Khan admitted in October that joint defense would have application against Afghanistan and the USSR as well as China. Because of New Delhi's need for Soviet friendship as a protection from China, this would obviously be unacceptable, but the problem was even more basic. Nehru could not join in a military alliance with Pakistan or any other country without repudiating his ideological opposition to collective security. The Prime Minister was not yet ready to accept a doctrine to which he was so totally opposed.

Nehru still hoped that China would withdraw and negotiate an honorable settlement on terms acceptable to India. Encouraging him were early indications that Moscow did not approve of Peking's hostility toward India. He believed that Khrushchev would ultimately bring pressure on China to abandon its aggressive policy toward the subcontinent. Nehru found solace in continuing Soviet cordiality and could rationalize from it that *Panch Sheela* was still a valid policy toward the Communist world despite Peking's maverick performance.

During the Kongka Pass crisis the Indian Prime Minister was faced with a journalist's question: "Do you consider the series of Chinese incursions as part of world communist strategy—something inseparable from Communist theory and practice—or as pure aggression by the Chinese Communists?" His reply is revealing:

> Chinese activities on our border have nothing to do with world strategy of communism or communism itself or Chinese Communism. It has to do with Chinese expansionism . . . it is essentially an element which China has exhibited many times in its past history of 2,000 years. . . .[4]

Nehru thus believed China to be simply a periodically delinquent nation and not currently the product of a compelling ideology.

Perhaps a measure of Moscow's embarrassment over increased Sino-Indian tension was a delay of nine days before the Kongka Pass incident was mentioned in the Russian press. On October 29, *Tass* finally broke the story, printing side by side the Indian and Chinese versions without comment. Two days later Soviet Premier Khrushchev, speaking before the Soviet Parliament, called for a peaceful solution. In a significantly neutral vein he regretted "the incidents on the Indian-Chinese frontier" and hoped "the difficulties will be solved by negotiating." Within a week the Soviet leader again commented neutrally on the crisis, saying that to him the situation was incomprehensible "since there are no people living in that area" and there is no strategic value to it.[5] While it may have had little strategic value for India, it was enormously valuable for China as it helped secure the vital route from western Tibet to Sinkiang. For this reason, if no other, it should also have been of considerable interest to the Soviet Union, whose relationship with China in Sinkiang was still unsteady.

There had been previous occasions when the Soviet Union showed displeasure with Chinese actions by a lack of comment and support, but this was the first time that Moscow volunteered neutral commentary on a situation involving another Communist country.

Implicit in this was criticism of China's action, an early manifestation of what would later be revealed as serious tension between Moscow and Peking. A Soviet diplomat in Switzerland was more explicit in a news interview on December 18. He referred to Chinese activity along the Indian boundary as "more than just untimely" and added that the Soviet government was not very happy about the situation.[6]

In highlighting "marked differences" between the Soviet Union and Communist China in their approach to world problems, Nehru observed: "I do not think there is any country in the world today . . . which is more anxious for peace than the Soviet Union . . . but I doubt if there is any country which cares less for peace than China."[7] But if Nehru counted on the Soviet Union to exercise influence on China in India's favor, he ignored the possibility of just the opposite occurring.

Peking was resentful that Khrushchev planned to meet President Eisenhower at Camp David in October and was probably determined to deprive Khrushchev of any mandate to discuss Far Eastern affairs. According to members of a Polish delegation who had just returned from Communist China's Tenth Anniversary celebration in October, this may even have been one of the motivations behind the Chinese government's decision to provoke India and thus remind the Soviet Union that Asian issues could only be settled through Peking.[8]

The Soviet leader's objective in seeing Eisenhower had been to lessen East-West tensions aggravated by the highly charged Berlin crisis. But more alarming to Peking than the doctrinal heresy implicit in Khrushchev's retreat on Berlin at Camp David was the fear that the Soviet leader and the American President had made important decisions pertaining to Far Eastern problems without prior reference to Peking. China was later to complain that Khrushchev, upon his arrival in Peking following the Camp David meetings, had unashamedly sought Chinese acceptance of the "two China" thesis and the removal of Taiwan as a point of East-West tension. Even more provocative was the Soviet Union's unilateral abrogation of its nuclear assistance treaty with China soon after the Camp David talks. Peking could reason that the price of Khrushchev's policy of reducing tensions was a reduction of Chinese power.

President Eisenhower's state visit to India in December 1959 and the unprecedented public acclaim accorded him also had considerable significance in connection with India's border crisis. President Eisenhower's genuine concern for India and his sympathetic reaction to India's need for massive economic assistance must have given Nehru comfort in this time of crisis.

China suddenly came forward with a plan for easing the tension which it had created. In November Chou En-lai proposed that the armed forces of China and India each withdraw twenty kilometers from the McMahon Line in the east and from the line "up to which each side exercises actual control" in the west; and that both sides refrain from again sending armed personnel into the zones from which they had been evacuated. The Chinese leader also suggested that he meet with Nehru to discuss the boundary question and "other questions in the relations between the two countries."[9]

This signaled a shift of tactics by Peking; a pretense of conciliation and negotiation would replace border intimidation. But it was to be negotiation from strength and negotiation with the benefit of possession. Nehru recognized and commented informally that the proposal by Peking for demilitarizing the Indian-Chinese frontier would not be advantageous to India. In fact, Chou's formula would have made India's defense of Ladakh more difficult and would have ceded the strategic area of Aksai Chin to China.

Nehru rejected Chou's offer but substituted one of his own. In the Northeast the Indian Prime Minister proposed a suspension of border patrols by both sides. But he felt that "Longju was a different case altogether" and he pointed out to Chou in a letter that since Chinese armed forces had attacked and ousted Indian personnel from Longju, India could not agree to any arrangement which would permit China to hold this region—even temporarily.[10] In the western—or Ladakh—sector Nehru proposed that, as an interim measure, India withdraw its personnel to the west of the Chinese claim as shown in the 1956 Chinese map while Chinese personnel be withdrawn to the east of the line claimed by India.

The Indian Prime Minister also rejected Chou's suggestion that they meet together to discuss their differences. Chou En-lai, in turn, could not accept Nehru's counterproposal which he described as unfair. He reiterated his conviction that talks between them would be a desirable prerequisite to further efforts at settlement and specifically suggested that they meet either in Peking or Rangoon on

mutual w'd from disputed area!

December 26. But Nehru still could not see merit in a meeting to reach an "agreement on principles when there is such complete disagreement about the facts."[11]

As part of its new tactic, China began talks with Nepal, Burma and later with Pakistan aimed at settling by negotiation long-standing boundary disputes with these countries. An important reason for Peking's actions and the particular timing of them was to isolate India from its neighbors and portray it as the only neighboring country unwilling to negotiate its differences.

Agreement was reached with Nepal to negotiate its boundary of more than five hundred miles on October 28 and Nepal's Minister of Development, Dr. Tulsi Giri, obtained as sweetener promises of further economic assistance for Nepal. Three months later Burma—reversing an earlier refusal—signed a treaty of non-aggression as well as a boundary agreement. In the case both of Nepal and of Burma the Chinese had exerted strong pressure for agreements which neither country could indefinitely resist. Like India, both countries had long been victims of border incidents and Burma, two years earlier, had suffered major incursions by China not unlike those which took place on Indian soil in 1959. Peking saw in its new pact with Burma "a stunning blow to the United States" and may also have believed that the agreement helped to counteract the effects in Asia of the American-Japanese Mutual Security Pact. But more importantly, China saw in its treaty with Burma a means of encouraging India to negotiate.

The arrival in New Delhi on January 20, 1960 of Marshal Voroshilov, heading a high-ranking Soviet delegation to participate in India's Tenth Anniversary celebration, introduced an impressive and significant Soviet presence at this critical time. Nehru, who pointedly hailed the Soviet Union's "striving for peace," certainly found the visit helpful and timely. But of much greater significance was an informal visit to India by Premier Khrushchev three weeks later. This was interpreted by most Indians as a direct reaction to Chinese pressure on India, and it was widely hoped and expected that the Soviet Premier would exercise a moderating influence on Chou. It thus came as a great disappointment when Nehru, after his first talks with Khrushchev, announced in Parliament on February 12, "I see no bridge between the Chinese position and ours. The present positions are such that there is no room for negotiating on that basis."[12]

Suddenly, on February 16, Nehru announced that he had extended to Premier Chou En-lai an invitation to visit New Delhi for the purpose of discussing the boundary dispute. In the face of widespread public criticism of this step the Indian Prime Minister denied that there had been a reversal of his stand against negotiating India's boundary. He told Parliament that his invitation could be interpreted to mean only that he was willing to "meet anybody and everybody to find a way to peaceful settlement."[13] The coincidence of Nehru's announcement of a "summit" meeting and Khrushchev's visit nevertheless was more than the opposition parties could accept. There were cries of "Sellout" and the non-Communist opposition moved to consider the "sudden and unwarranted reversal of the Government's policy which had been approved and endorsed by Parliament." They found it difficult to accept Nehru's differentiation between a "meeting" with Chou and "negotiations" with him.

The government denied emphatically that Khrushchev had anything to do with Nehru's change of mind. It was officially pointed out that the letter inviting Chou was drafted and signed six days before the Soviet Premier had arrived, while the delivery and thus the announcement was delayed (until a date after Khrushchev's departure) only because Nehru wanted the letter handed personally to Chou by the Indian Ambassador to China.

Despite this nimble explanation there was still a temptation to conclude that—far from being used by Nehru to exert pressure on Peking—Khrushchev was used by Chou to influence Nehru. Nehru could ill afford to resist Khrushchev's entreaties to negotiate—assuming they were made—since he still believed the Soviet leader to be his main lever against Peking. Regardless of fine distinctions between "meetings" and "negotiations," Chou had won his objective—a summit conference which would serve as a propaganda forum for China to posture in a falsely conciliatory light.

Before Chou En-lai's visit the stage had been set by recently concluded Chinese boundary agreements with Burma and Nepal. An agreement with Pakistan was to follow. The implications to India were clear; by reaching pacts with India's neighbors China could more easily place on India the onus of intransigence. Peking's prerequisites for negotiations were unacceptable and prejudiced India's case from the start, but this could be obscured by Red propaganda and Chou could proceed with the summit gesture in an aura of right and reasonableness. If the meeting proved unsuccessful—as it surely would—Peking would place the blame on India since it could be made to appear that Chou had sought and achieved a summit meeting despite Nehru's reluctance. China had everything to gain and nothing to lose by the forthcoming New Delhi talks.

At the time of the Nehru-Chou meeting Peking set forth definitively and with clarity its true doctrinal position on peaceful co-existence. This made a mockery of any Chinese effort to talk out its differences with India. In a series of newspaper articles—two of which appeared in the theoretical journal, *Hung Chi* (Red Flag) and one in *Jen Min Jih Pao* (People's Daily)—Communist China served notice that it would support and foster Communist revolutions throughout the world by armed uprisings where necessary. Peking declared that war was inevitable and made the astonishing statement that nuclear war need not be feared by the Communist camp because "on the debris of dead imperialism a superior civilization could be built."[14]

The public atmosphere in New Delhi was as chilling as Peking's doctrinal pronouncement. On April 17 an estimated five thousand Indians, chanting in parody "Chou En-lai—*hai, hai,*"* marched to Nehru's residence to protest the imminent meeting of the two leaders. At a mass rally organized by the political opposition Nehru was warned to be firm in his discussions with Chou and the press still railed at the Government for going ahead with talks before China relinquished the Indian territory which it had seized. The Chinese leader arrived in this hostile atmosphere on April 19. In his opening speech he observed, "Both . . . China and India are now engaged in a large-scale and long-term construction. . . . Both of us need peace." He added that he saw "no reason why any question between us cannot be settled reasonably through friendly consultations" as called for by the five principles of co-existence.[15]

Predictably, the talks ended in complete deadlock. Neither side would modify its stand to a point acceptable to the other. In a relatively short joint communiqué concluding the visit it was stated simply that "the talks did not result in resolving differences that had arisen." Some inkling of China's unrealized objective can be gained

* Loosely translated from Hindi this means "Chou En-lai—death, death." It is also a parody of the earlier slogan "Hindi-Chini, *bai, bai,*" which means "Chinese and Indians are brothers," a slogan used during the period of good relations between India and China, particularly at the time of Chou En-lai's first visit to New Delhi.

from Chou's suggestion that his country might have been prepared to relinquish its claims to 36,000 square miles in the eastern sector if India would have recognized China's claim to 15,000 square miles in the Ladakh sector.[16] China's attitude was without doubt a reflection of the importance with which the Aksai Chin road was viewed and was connected with fundamental strategic considerations, the same ones which caused China to build the road in the first place.

In an effort to keep the spirit of peaceful settlement alive and to lessen the impact of total failure, the two Prime Ministers agreed that "officials of India and China should meet, examine all available evidence and draw up a report for submission to the two governments."[17] The resulting boundary discussions of 1960 represented an effort to find firm enough ground on which to begin serious negotiations toward a settlement. It was an act of good faith even though India never had much hope that it would succeed. As it turned out, India's pessimism was justified; firm ground was not found. But, more discouragingly, the boundary discussions and the sum of diplomatic correspondence which preceded them revealed that bilateral discussion in the hands of China is but another propaganda technique, a cynical tactic in its cold war with India. The discussions provided China with still another medium by which to publicize its spurious case. In the judicious and objective atmosphere of the 1960 boundary discussions China gained all too much legitimacy for irrelevant, pseudo-legal or completely fallacious arguments in support of its claims.

Peking had its reasons for claiming more than 50,000 square miles of Indian territory. But the reasons, based partly on Communist doctrine and partly on more traditional Han expansionist tendencies, bear little relationship to the pseudo-legal case argued with India. Part of China's case had an air of plausibility when viewed in the context of erroneous assumptions and accommodating definitions; much of the case is spurious, regardless of context. Only a small part could serve as a legitimate basis for meaningful boundary negotiations with India. Certainly Peking's case, as reflected in diplomatic correspondence and discussion, obscured a fundamental and very serious question: What are China's real and ultimate objectives in India?

Chinese negotiators tried to influence the very structure of debate so as to favor its side. By determining the terms of reference of the discussions they were able to channel them along lines of their choosing which did not always bear on the problem but usually served to show India's case in a bad light. Recognizing that its own claimed alignment could not be supported, the discussions were framed in such a way that the burden of proof fell on India. Whereas China sought principally to prove that no valid boundary delimitation exists, India was made to prove its boundary alignment, inch by inch. Peking's logic—distorted and wholly inequitable—seemed to insist that until India was willing to negotiate a settlement formally delimiting a common boundary, it would have to respect China's unilaterally determined boundary.

A serious and very significant disagreement took place between the Chinese and Indian representatives in determining which sectors of the boundary should be discussed. India described the sectors as: (1) western—the boundary between Jammu and Kashmir of India and Sinkiang and Tibet; (2) middle—the boundary between the states of Punjab, Himachal Pradesh and Uttar Pradesh of India and the Ari district of Tibet; (3) eastern—the boundary between the Northeast Frontier Agency of India and Tibet; and (4) northern—the boundaries of Bhutan and Sikkim on one hand and Tibet on the other. China insisted that its boundaries with Bhutan and Sikkim "do not fall within the scope of the Sino-Indian boundary question."[18]

The implications of this stand were ominous, and China's attitude toward Sikkim and Bhutan since 1960 has done nothing to allay New Delhi's fear that China has territorial designs on these border protectorates. India, which has responsibility for the foreign relations of both countries and which had specifically been asked by Bhutan to represent it on matters pertaining to its interests in Tibet, submitted data on this sector anyway even though China refused to acknowledge the competence of the officials to discuss it.

Perhaps just as ominous for India was China's refusal to discuss the boundary west of the Karakorum Pass in the approaches to the Pamir mountains.[19] This area is currently beyond India's *de facto* jurisdiction since it falls within Pakistan-held territory north of the Pakistan-Indian cease-fire line in Kashmir. For China to have discussed it with India would have been to acknowledge the latter's claim as the more valid one in the chronic India-Pakistan dispute over Kashmir. Clearly China did not want to do this lest it lose its option to use the Kashmir dispute for its own purposes in its quarrel with India. As it turned out, New Delhi's fear that Peking's attitude presaged its intention to use Pakistan as a pressure lever against India was entirely justified. On March 3, 1962, to the accompaniment of renewed Chinese firing in Ladakh, China and Pakistan announced their intention to negotiate the boundary west of the Karakorum Pass.[20]

CHAPTER 12

NEPAL: INDIA'S LOST BUFFER

Tibet is China's palm. Nepal, Bhutan, Sikkhim, Ladakh and the Northeast Frontier Agency of Assam are the five fingers. Now that the palm has been restored to China, the fingers should go with it.

Chinese Communist propaganda

Using alternately pressure and largess, Communist China has sought to exploit Nepal as a weapon against India. Traditionally a shield of protection against intrusion from the north, Nepal has instead become a vulnerable flank. It is an irredentist territory, one of the "five fingers" which should be attached to the Tibet "palm" according to Chinese propaganda. Should Nepal fall under Chinese control the entire Gangetic plain of India would be exposed and what little meaning the Himalayan barrier has left in the jet age would be lost.

Nepal's precarious existence between two giants is once again threatened, but this time by a modern colossus whose compelling ideology is aggression; and, unhappily, there is no counterbalancing power strong enough to protect it. A century of safety in the protective shadow of Great Britain came to an end with Indian independence. While India inherited from Britain the same need for a buffer area along the southern slopes of the Himalayas it did not inherit the circumstances permitting continued control of Nepal's external affairs. As a result there exists a weak but independent country, chronically resentful of Indian half-measures to influence it and unable to resist indefinitely full measures which China will certainly take to do so.

Nepal's history is that of a secluded, inaccessible kingdom which until recently has enjoyed the luxury of isolation. Its sudden immersion in the mid-twentieth century cauldron of power politics and

Soviet Premier Nikita Khrushchev confers with India's Prime Minister Jawaharlal Nehru at Nehru's official residence in New Delhi, February 1960. (Wide World Photos.)

High point of the coronation ceremony of King Mahendra, ruler of Nepal. (Wide World Photos.)

Nehru addresses Indian troops during the 1962 Chinese invasion of India.

(*Below, left*) Young Indian women train to defend their homeland against the Chinese invasion.

(*Below, right*) Evacuation of wounded from Northeast Frontier area, October, 1962.

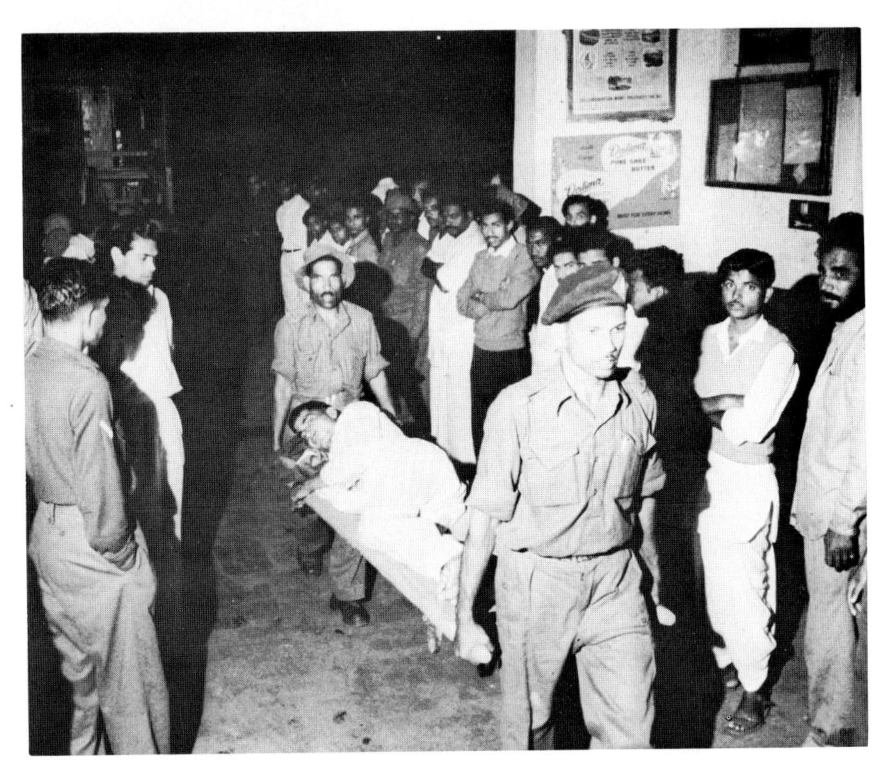

Ladakh: Sikh sentries guard a Himalayan pass at the time of the 1962 Chinese invasion. (Photographed by W. E. Garrett, ©National Geographic Society.)

Kunwar Inderjit Singh, Nepalese revolutionary during the 1950's. (Wide World Photos.)

Photographed by W. E. Garrett, ©National Geographic Society

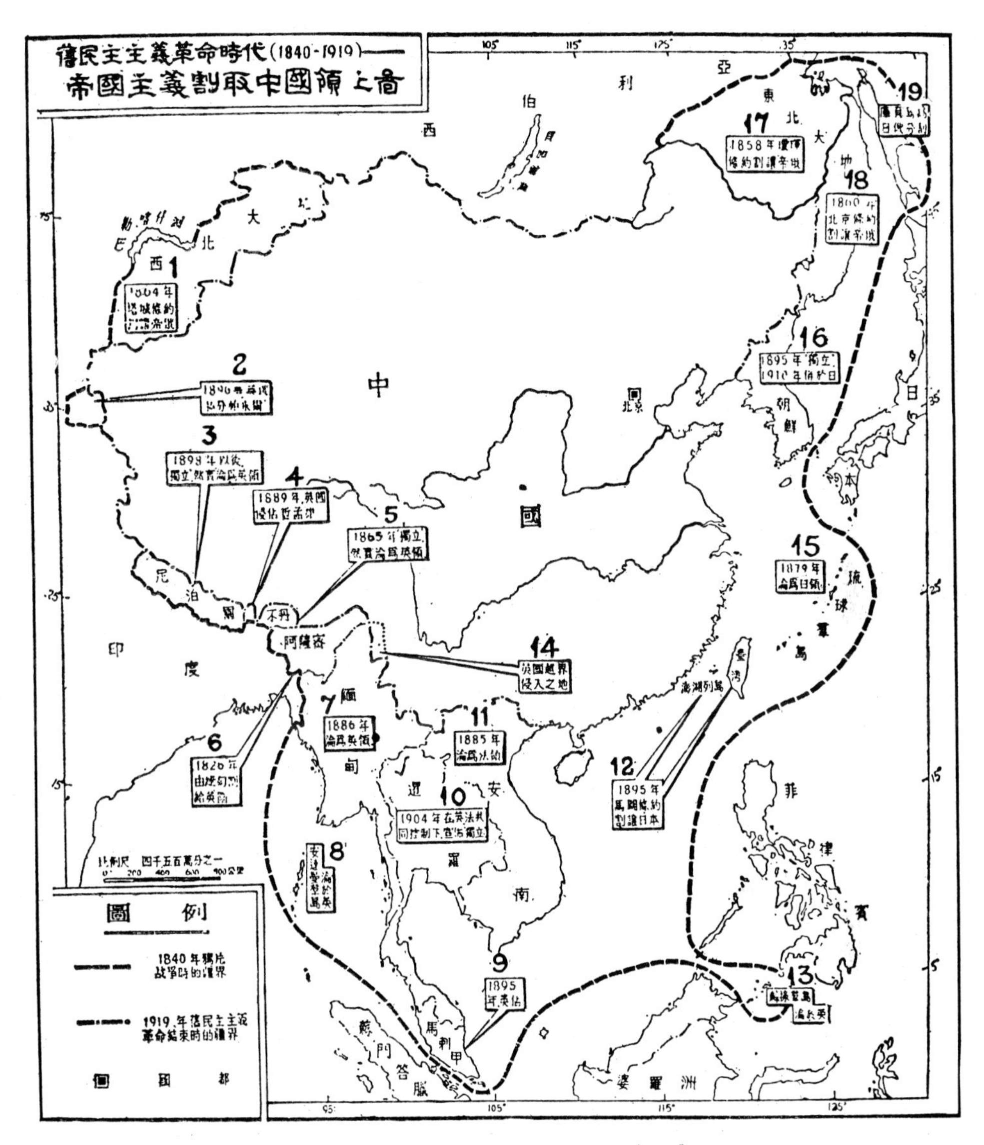

Chinese territorial claims as shown in a 1954 Chinese textbook. The Chinese text claims that the numbered territories were dominated by Peking before the 1820's. An accompanying caption lists numbers 3, 4, 5, and 6, all pertinent to India, as having been acquired by Britain through unfair treaties. (After Liu P'ei-hua (*A Short History of Modern China,* Peking, 1954.)

Indian Prime Minister Lal Bahadur Shastri, left, Pakistan President Mohammed Ayub Khan, and Soviet Premier Alexei Kosygin at the 1966 summit conference in Tashkent, USSR. (Wide World Photos.)

competing ideologies creates problems from which it may not emerge intact. Certainly nothing in its little-known history would have prepared it for this experience.

In 1837 there emerged a legendary figure in Nepal named Jang Bahadur. Ruthless in his drive for power, he is said to have massacred fifty-five nobles on a single occasion to eliminate opposition. His durability was phenomenal. Several attempts were made on his life, but an uncanny sense of survival saved him in each instance. According to one story he had the foresight to stuff mattresses in the village well so, when henchmen of the royal heir sought to murder him in the traditional way by throwing him down it, he landed softly and unbruised. By 1846 Jang Bahadur had consolidated his power in Nepal and had begun a new dynasty of hereditary "Rana" prime ministers who thereafter kept the royal line of kings in the background as powerless figureheads.

Realizing the necessity of being on friendly terms with his powerful southern neighbor, Jang Bahadur sought to improve Nepalese-British relations, which had been bad since the rise of the Gurkha dynasty under Prithvi Narayan Shah in the 1760's. As a peace gesture he offered the British six regiments of Gurkha troops for use against the Sikhs who had been harassing them both. Although the offer was declined, his gesture accomplished its purpose and a period of close Nepal-India relations began.

In 1854 Gurkha soldiers from Nepal—always warlike and aggressive—again attacked Tibet. Peace was finally restored with a treaty signed in 1856, which provided the basis of Tibet-Nepal relations for the next century. According to the terms of this agreement, Tibet was required to pay annual tribute to Kathmandu. But the most significant part of the treaty in light of the situation today is the preamble in which both Nepal and Tibet agreed to "respect" or "obey" the Emperor of China (depending on which translation of the treaty is accepted). As recently as 1908 the Chinese *Amban* in Lhasa reasserted China's claim of suzerainty over Nepal on the basis of the preamble. In a message to Kathmandu, for example, he commented that Nepal and Tibet—"being united like brothers under the auspices of China—should work in harmony for mutual good."

If a true state of suzerainty existed at all, it had no practical validity after 1912, by which time Chinese troops had been driven from Tibet. Like Tibet, Nepal viewed its special relationship as a phenomenon relating only to the Manchu emperors—not to China.

Tibet, which had recognized Manchu suzerainty since 1720, considered Manchu emperors to be incarnations of the Buddha of Wisdom. Nepal's leadership, which has been Hindu—not Buddhist—never felt the same religious link with the Manchus nor had a patron-priest relationship, but for a while recognized a Manchu suzerain on the basis of political expediency. It found the Chinese Emperor to be a useful control on British domination. Nevertheless, the parallel between Nepal's status and that of Tibet was close enough to make the government in Kathmandu apprehensive when it found a strong and modern Chinese army permanently encamped along its northern border. In 1939 Mao Tse-tung wrote that the "imperialists" had stolen many of China's territories.[1] Specifically included in the list were Nepal and Bhutan. Peking had also described parts of Nepal as irredentist Chinese territories on several maps which it had published.[2]

Nehru reassured the Indian Parliament in March 1950 that "it is not possible for any Indian government to tolerate any invasion of Nepal from anywhere." In order to discourage Chinese aggression and to forestall Peking's claims, India and Nepal hurriedly concluded two new pacts. The first, signed on July 31, 1950, was a treaty of friendship guaranteeing Nepal's sovereignty and calling for consultations in the event either country was threatened. The second was a trade agreement concluded in October which guaranteed free transit through India of goods whose destination was Nepal.[3]

The Communist Chinese occupation of Tibet inevitably excited political tensions within Nepal. With the introduction of freedom and democracy in India the autocratic rule of the hereditary Rana prime ministers in Kathmandu had become an anachronism in the subcontinent. The anti-feudal propaganda which seeped through the passes from Tibet further nourished the discontent of the Nepalese. But, perhaps most important of all, New Delhi had become convinced that the continuance of reactionary Rana rule made Nepal dangerously vulnerable to Chinese Communist influence. Even while the Nepalese Prime Minister was in New Delhi negotiating new treaties with India, Nehru pointedly told Parliament: "Freedom interests us in the abstract. . . . If it does not come, forces that will ultimately disrupt freedom itself will be created and encouraged. We have accordingly advised the Government of

Nepal . . . to bring themselves into line with democratic forces that are stirring the world today."[4]

Suddenly Nepal's King Tribhuvan fled his palace in dramatic protest against Rana misrule and autocracy. He found sanctuary in the Indian Embassy in Kathmandu until he could be safely evacuated to New Delhi by air. This event, which took place in November, signaled a mass uprising in Birgunj Province led by Nepali Congress Party liberals and a coordinated revolt in western Nepal led by an obscure Nepalese revolutionary named K. I. Singh. India's official reaction to the revolution was reflected by Nehru in Parliament, where he said, "there can be no peace and stability in Nepal by going back to the old order."[5]

Pressed hard by the insurgents, the Rana government was forced to relinquish power and negotiate a peace. The Government of India, which clearly favored the insurgents and whose backing of the King had been obvious, acted as mediator. The negotiations resulted in complete capitulation of the Ranas. With the full blessing of the Indian government, King Tribhuvan returned victoriously to Kathmandu on February 15, 1950 to preside over a Council of Ministers of his choosing. For the moment Indian primacy was protected. New Delhi could rationalize its only slightly disguised intervention in Nepalese affairs by its compelling need to deny Nepal to the Chinese.

The enigmatic figure of Dr. K. I. Singh momentarily dominated the scene. Claiming that Nepal's revolution had been betrayed, Singh refused to abandon his insurrection and with a group of armed followers continued to defy the new government in Kathmandu until he was finally subdued with the help of Indian troops. During this very brief interlude Singh became something of a legendary figure in Nepal. He captured the imagination of a newly liberated people hungry for heroes. His personality was dynamic and his nationalist fervor—real or feigned—found response in a people who disliked Indian paternalism as much as Rana autocracy. Singh was thus not forgotten when he escaped into Tibet with his band of followers and, to the discomfort of India, found political asylum in Red China.

The Indian *Panch Sheela* agreement with China on Tibet concluded in 1954 made Nepal's need to renegotiate its own relationship with China more urgent. Only a few days after the conclusion of the Sino-Indian pact in April, Nepal's Foreign Minister Regmi announced that his government would soon raise with Peking the matter of a new agreement. He acknowledged that until 1912 Nepal had considered Tibet as being under Chinese suzerainty and that even after 1912 the treaty negotiated under Chinese auspices (1856) still regulated Nepal's relationships with Tibet. The Foreign Minister promised that if the Chinese "approach us formally we will do the right thing at the right moment."[6]

Nehru was widely believed to have discussed Nepal with his Chinese hosts when he visited Peking in October-November 1954. It was reported that Chou En-lai had agreed to continued Indian paramountcy in Nepal but had made clear China's intention to establish diplomatic relations with Kathmandu. Nehru's comment on these reports upon his return from Peking was to note specifically India's "special position in regard to foreign affairs in Nepal. . . ."[7]

Nepalese Prime Minister C. P. Koirala certainly had the full benefit of Nehru's private as well as public views on this question since he met with the Indian Prime Minister both before and after the latter's trip to Peking. Direct discussions were held in Kathmandu between Nepalese and Chinese government representatives during July 1955. This was but a few months after King Tribhuvan had died and been succeeded by his son, Mahendra Bir Bikram Shah Dev. On August 1, 1955, an agreement was signed providing for the establishment of diplomatic relations between China and Nepal and specifying that a treaty would be negotiated based on *Panch Sheela*—the five principles of co-existence.

Seemingly as a gesture of goodwill and conciliation, the Chinese also made arrangements for the return to Nepal of K. I. Singh. This stimulated the *Hindustan Times* to editorialize optimistically on August 3 that a "chapter of distrust is now closed and Nepal and China can look forward to increasing co-operation in the cultural sphere." Actually, it is likely that India—perhaps Nehru during his trip to China—played the mediator's role in arranging for the return of Nepal's "hero" rather than to see him exposed to continuing Chinese influence in Peking or exploited by the Chinese for further adventures in Nepal. Part of the deal clearly specified full amnesty for Singh, and this was granted by royal decree soon after he crossed into Nepalese territory from Tibet on September 4. His public welcome in Kathmandu on September 13 was very impressive, and a public meeting which he held on September 24 to describe his political plans rallied one of the largest crowds in Kathmandu's history.

Singh had captured the public's imagination, particularly in the West. But he was still an enigma to Indian observers, who could not be sure of the extent—if any—of China's secret backing. Nehru's opinion was that "K. I. Singh is no communist—just a free-booter who tried to seize power and failed."[8] Whatever the case, he made plans to canvas the country in a grass roots political campaign which was to prove unique in Nepal's history.

The appointment of Tanka Prasad Acharya as Prime Minister in 1956 ushered in a period characterized by a highly defensive attitude toward India. Acharya's party newspaper *Samaj*, for example, ran a series of editorials critical of India. One called for a revision of the Indo-Nepalese trade treaty. Another went so far as to impugn India's allegiance to peaceful co-existence, claiming that India at least did not practice this doctrine in its relationship with Nepal.

Apprehension was felt in New Delhi's official circles when in September 1956 China and Nepal negotiated an agreement entitling China to open a consulate in Kathmandu and establish trade agencies in three other locations within the country.* While the need for Nepal and China to determine anew their relationship in Tibet had been recognized as a logical corollary of the Sino-Indian agreement of 1954, the specter of Chinese representation throughout Nepal was a disturbing one. The agreement also specified that direct telegraphic communications would be established between Kathmandu and Lhasa. This meant that, henceforward, New Delhi need not serve as way station in the conduct of Nepal-China relations.

Prime Minister Tanka Prasad Acharya returned from a visit to China in October 1956 with a promise of substantial aid. To New Delhi's consternation Nepal was to receive 60,000,000 rupees (approximately $12,000,000) in budgetary assistance and machinery with "no strings" attached. With Nepal's first national elections scheduled to be held in less than a year, the cash grant (approximately one-third of the total) particularly disturbed the Indian officials, who feared that the funds might be used for strictly party purposes to perpetuate a regime antagonistic to India. New Delhi reacted by sending President Rajendra Prasad on a state visit to Kathmandu in October. While implying that India had no intention

* The trade agencies were, in fact, never established.

of relinquishing its special position in Nepal, Prasad indicated that his country was prepared to support an economic development program.

Another event in October which revealed India's hardening attitude toward Nepal was K. I. Singh's visit to New Delhi and the surprisingly cordial reception given him there. The timing was also significant since Singh arrived while Prime Minister Tanka Prasad Acharya was still negotiating in Peking. There was much speculation in New Delhi as to the meaning of highly partisan political speeches critical of Acharya given by Singh and how they related to his private talks with high Indian government officials.

Two months later Prime Minister Acharya visited New Delhi. In a public address he declared that Nepal's role was that of a neutral which should help tie the bonds of friendship between India and China. This was a euphemistic way of saying that Nepal would profit by China's new propinquity and use it to lessen Indian influence. The situation was ripe for Peking's exploitation. Doubtless conscious of the importance of timing, Chou En-lai visited Nepal during the last week in January 1957. He called the Nepalese "blood brothers" of the Chinese—a reference to the fact that many of the Nepalese are racially akin to the Tibetans. His speeches also stressed the theme of Afro-Asian solidarity, while the joint communiqué urged "Asian and African countries . . . to rise above minor differences between them." This could be interpreted as a pointed reminder to India that friendship and forbearance toward China was the wisest policy.

Chou's emphasis on Afro-Asian solidarity could also have been calculated to deprecate the United States aid efforts in Nepal. The U.S. aid mission—first sent to Nepal in 1951—had brought the American presence to China's border. It is likely that Peking took advantage of this program to justify its own program and rationalize for India's benefit China's economic penetration of Nepal. Chou found a ready listener to his "Afro-Asian solidarity" line in Prime Minister Acharya who expressed concern that most of the countries of Asia were underdeveloped or non-developed, so "are at times liable to forget unity and solidarity and be led astray by considerations of petty gains."[9] This remark certainly suggested criticism of the U.S. aid program and probably reflected Chou En-lai's personal agitational activities in Nepal.

Ironically it was K. I. Singh—long suspected of being a Chinese tool—who briefly restored to Nepal's government a pro-Indian bias. Upon replacing Tanka Prasad Acharya as Prime Minister in 1957, he made it clear that he disapproved of the recently concluded Sino-Nepalese agreement on Tibet and gave his blessing to the continued recruitment of Gurkha soldiers in Nepal by both the Indian and British armies. He also publicly supported India's stand on Kashmir. But Chinese influence continued to infiltrate across the long common border. Many of the Nepalese in the frontier areas found access to Tibetan market places easier than those in Nepal and in certain of the more remote areas the authority of the central government had traditionally been weak. Episodes such as the petty revolt by the Raja of Mustang in May 1957 were symptomatic of the control problems faced in Kathmandu.

The Tibetan uprising in 1959 created a situation dangerous to Nepal as well as to India. Particularly disturbing were Chinese claims to certain boundary areas. Widespread press reports that China was massing troops along the Nepal border may have been exaggerated in the confusion of the times, but they increased the tension in both Kathmandu and New Delhi. On November 27, 1959 Nehru climaxed a long foreign policy debate in Parliament by a dramatic pledge to defend Nepal against aggression. Having earlier guaranteed the security of Sikkim and Bhutan—also believed threatened—Nehru declared that aggression against Nepal would be considered aggression against India.[10] Kathmandu's official reaction to Nehru's pledge was indicative of the country's traditional suspicion of India's motives; B. P. Koirala, who had succeeded K. I. Singh as Prime Minister, asserted that Nepal would seek help from the United Nations rather than from India in the event of an attack by China.

Nepal tried hard to remain neutral between India and China. Ignoring reports of Chinese border violations, Koirala described India and China as both good friends of his country. In mid-December a Nepalese parliamentary delegation toured India as a goodwill gesture, and a month later Prime Minister Koirala himself visited New Delhi at Nehru's invitation. The joint communiqué issued at the conclusion of the visit was significantly devoid of any reference to joint defense but, despite his refusal to side with India in the latter's dispute with China, Koirala received from India at this time 180,000,000 rupees for development programs.

Prime Minister Koirala balanced his Indian visit by one to Peking in March 1960. Chinese officials on this occasion assured him that China had only the friendliest intentions toward Nepal. Of more substance than such platitudes were two agreements, the first of which called for a scientific demarcation of the China-Nepal boundary. Peking assured Nepal that the latter's traditional border would not be disturbed. In this agreement both parties also promised to keep armed personnel out of a frontier zone extending twelve and a half miles on each side of the traditional boundary. While en route home Koirala spoke publicly in Calcutta, expressing his hope that the newly concluded pact would "provide a very good background" for the settlement of the Chinese-Indian boundary dispute.[11] This must have been exactly what Peking wanted him to say. China's motive in reaching an agreement to delimit its boundary with Nepal on the eve of Chou En-lai's "summit" meeting with Nehru on the Sino-Indian boundary question was clearly to keep the pressure on India to negotiate.

The other agreement—a sweetener for the first—provided for Chinese economic assistance to Nepal worth 100,000,000 rupees (approximately $21,000,000). This sum is nearly as much as that which India granted Nepal two and a half months earlier. Koirala's spring tours had been very profitable and for the moment at least neutralism seemed to pay.

Koirala stopped short of signing a non-aggression pact despite Chinese efforts to promote one. Such an agreement would have been redundant in view of the Sino-Nepal treaty of 1956 which included "mutual non-aggression" as one of the five points of co-existence. It would also have been very provocative to India. But the principal reason behind Koirala's refusal to sign a new non-aggression pact was a disagreement over the ownership of Mount Everest. This difference had soon become evident during the Peking discussions. By claiming the world's highest peak, Chou generated a highly emotion-charged reaction in Kathmandu. Upon his arrival in Nepal's capital on a state visit in April to patch up relations, the Chinese leader was greeted by angry posters bearing slogans such as "Everest is ours." Soon thereafter he was flown to a remote palace in the Pokhara Valley where public hostility was not visible. Following his talks with Koirala, Chou issued a statement of compromise in which he agreed to accept Nepalese maps showing Everest's summit to be squarely on the border, but Koirala was not yet ready to concede that Nepal must share the world's highest peak with China.

Dramatizing Peking's claim to half the summit was an announcement on May 19 that a Chinese-Soviet mountaineering expedition—heretofore unpublicized—had reached the top of Everest by way of the difficult north slope.* It is interesting to note Soviet participation in this feat and to speculate on its significance. Did the USSR insist that Russians be included for prestige reasons? If so, was this another manifestation of growing Sino-Soviet rivalry in Central Asia and the subcontinent? Certainly Sino-Soviet tensions were clearly on the increase in 1960.

Contributing to the Sino-Nepalese tension created by the Everest issue were reports in June 1960 that one border patrol officer had been killed and fifteen soldiers captured by the Chinese in the troublesome Mustang border area. Kathmandu sent a strongly worded protest to Peking demanding release of the captured Nepalese and withdrawal of Chinese troops to the agreed-upon distance from the border. Peking candidly admitted that Chinese troops had been on the border rather than twelve and a half miles back as required by the terms of the March 21 temporary boundary agreement, but excused the violations on the specious grounds that a new Tibetan rebellion in the area had required the deployment of Chinese in the demilitarized boundary zone.[12]

China was simultaneously exhibiting an equally aggressive attitude toward Bhutan. This too may have been provoked by lingering Tibetan resistance fighting which the Chinese were finding difficult to mop up. But Peking soon disclosed that it had serious claims to Bhutan's territory just as it had to Indian territory. China was reported to have used the cultural, religious and economic ties between Tibet and Bhutan as an excuse to serve an ultimatum demanding that Bhutan break its special treaty ties with India. It is also significant that Peking's negotiators refused to discuss the Bhutan border during the 1960 Sino-Indian boundary talk even though the Maharaja of Bhutan had specifically requested Nehru to do so.[13]

* Perhaps one reason the Chinese were anxious to scale Everest by way of the north slope was a Nepalese official argument that ownership of the peak should be based on the way the mountain "inclines." A Nepalese spokesman assumed that it must incline southward toward Nepal since this was the direction from which it had always been climbed.

Nepal's King Mahendra and Burma's Prime Minister U Nu were both guests of Peking during National Day festivities in October, 1961 and both signed border agreements. This was played up by Chinese propaganda as being in contrast to India's attitude of intransigence, blamed for the impasse in the China-India boundary dispute. By this agreement Nepal gained Chinese acceptance of its traditional boundary. The troublesome issue of Mount Everest was resolved to the satisfaction of both parties by vague wording which simply included Everest as one of the Himalayan mountains through which the boundary runs. The only comfort which New Delhi could find in the new boundary treaty was that it tended to uphold the "watershed principle" which has provided an important basis for India's own boundary case. But this was small compensation for an otherwise direct assault by China on Indian primacy in Nepal.

An economic agreement was also reached. It called for Chinese help in constructing and financing a road from the Tibetan border to Kathmandu which would link Nepal's capital with Lhasa. The strategic value to China of such a road is obvious. Equally obvious is its significance in diverting Nepal's trade from India to China and reducing Nepal's economic dependence on India. In the joint communiqué signed by King Mahendra and Chou En-lai, China upheld the rights of small nations and, as an oblique slap at India, promised not to assume an attitude of "great nation chauvinism" toward Nepal.

India became increasingly critical of King Mahendra after December 1960, when he dismissed Nepal's first elected government headed by B. P. Koirala and returned to direct rule. Conversely, King Mahendra was vexed by India's willingness to provide haven for expatriate members of Koirala's Nepalese Congress Party. Particularly disturbing was hostile guerrilla action organized from Indian sanctuary by Nepali Congress exiles. Mahendra and some of his principle advisers believed with bitterness that the Indian government had done nothing to stop Nepalese rebel action and might even have encouraged it. He was also dissatisfied with the scale of military assistance provided by India. Because the Nepalese government lost patience with Indian foot-dragging on this score, it bought military equipment from the USSR in early 1962 and—more pointedly—accepted from China in May 1962 three single-engine transport planes. Later Nepal acquired more significant quantities of military aid from the United Kingdom and the United States.

King Mahendra visited New Delhi in April 1962, when an effort was made to resolve the differences between the two countries. Upon his return to Kathmandu the King did in fact reshuffle his ministers in what appeared to be an effort to jettison those who were particularly objectionable to India. But Nepal otherwise made no compromise with his policy of "neutrality" between India and China. Its leaders meant to oppose Indian paternalism and continue to encourage Chinese assistance as a counterbalance. This was a classic equation and Peking was prepared to exploit it.

CHAPTER 13

THE PAMIR KNOT: CROSSROAD OF CRISES

The future danger for Russia from this empire [*China*] *of 400,000,000 is beyond all doubt. The most vulnerable part of the Russian frontier, as 800 years ago, remains that great gateway through which the hordes of Genghiz Khan poured into Europe.*

General Kuropatkin, Russian Governor General of Russian Turkestan in 1916

The "Pamir Knot"—a jumble of high peaks which tower over the junction of Chinese Sinkiang, Soviet Kirghizistan, Afghanistan and Kashmir—has long been an area of critical importance in Asia. Here three empires clashed little more than a half-century ago. Today it is still an uneasy area where three major territorial disputes—those between India and Pakistan, India and China, and China and the USSR—overlap, one with another, to create and compound serious tensions.

Probably the most significant of these disputes from a global point of view is that between the Soviet Union and Communist China. Obscured until recently by the inaccessibility of the area and the secrecy which shrouds all events in Communist Central Asia, this bitter territorial quarrel provides a geopolitical rationale for the ideological crisis which has split the Communist world into two antagonistic camps. Less obvious has been the impact of Soviet-Chinese tensions—particularly in Sinkiang—on China-India relations. Interacting indirectly through the India-Pakistan dispute over Kashmir as well as more directly, Sino-Soviet tensions have done much to shape the form and determine the timing of Chinese aggression against the subcontinent.

The massive Pamir peaks and tributary ranges nearby now create a cockpit of conflict, but during most of the nineteenth century the Pamirs provided British India a certain illusion of security. Thomas Gordon, an Indian army officer who led a reconnaissance mission into the Pamirs in 1873 to assess the Russian military threat, concluded that these "lofty mountains between Eastern Turkestan and Ladakh barred the passage of a modern army in that direction."[1] It was not until the last decade of the nineteenth century that Britain fully awoke to the Russian threat in the Pamirs. Russian flirtation in 1890 with Safar Ali, the Mir (or ruler) of a sliver-like frontier principality known as Hunza, led to a bloody showdown between Imperial Britain and the Mir. Safar Ali was forced to flee, but the Hunza sector of India's frontier with Sinkiang remained unsettled. The Great Game of secret reconnaissance and tribal intrigue by both Britain and Russia kept the area in chronic ferment.

In 1896 Russia—always alert for an opportunity to win points against Britain in the Great Game—provoked local Chinese officials in Sinkiang to protest British maps which showed the Aksai Chin plateau as part of British-held Ladakh. (Interestingly enough, Peking then claimed Aksai Chin as part of Tibet, while in the context of today's Sino-Indian boundary disagreement China inconsistently claims that this high and barren plateau was always part of Sinkiang.) The British did not make an issue out of the protest, fearing that to do so might provoke a Russian invasion of Kashgaria. This would upset the delicate balance of power which required Sinkiang, like Tibet, to remain a nominal vassal of a harmless China.

The Chinese Revolution in 1911 and the subsequent weakening of the Empire held all the ingredients for renewed competition between Britain and Russia in Sinkiang. But General Kuropatkin, Russian Governor General of Russian Turkestan in 1916, had the foresight to point out a more basic fear—one that has become progressively more serious through the decades. He warned:

> The future danger for Russia from this empire [China] of 400,000,000 people is beyond all doubt. The most vulnerable part of the Russian frontier, as 800 years ago, remains that great gateway through which the hordes of Genghiz Khan poured into Europe. So long as Kuldja [in Chinese Sinkiang] rests in the hands of the Chinese, the protection of [Russian] Turkestan from

> China will remain very difficult . . . . A change in our boundary with China is urgently necessary.[2]

But it was not until after World War I and the Russian Revolution that a serious bid for Sinkiang was made by Russia.

A succession of local revolts made for an unmanageable situation and provided the Soviet Union with an excuse to step in to "restore order." Two nationalist revolts—one in 1936 and another in 1937—were suppressed only after much bloodshed by Soviet troops garrisoned in Sinkiang. Moscow's bid for primacy in Sinkiang came during the rule of Sheng Shih-ts'ai, a Chinese warlord who held power through force of arms. In the thirties and forties Sheng encouraged increasing Soviet economic and political penetration of the province with the result that his policies bred frequent clashes with Sinkiang nationalist groups and encouraged competitive intrigues stimulated by China (both Communist and Kuomintang), Japan and Britain. Even the Soviet Union hedged by maintaining contact with rival groups.

A meeting in Moscow between Sheng and Stalin in August 1938 provided a rare glimpse of pre-World War II power competition in Sinkiang. In Sheng's account of his audience with Stalin the latter seemed greatly concerned by revolts in this remote region and the foreign influences behind them. He was inclined to agree with Sheng that at least the 1937 uprising had been a product of "Trotskyite intrigues" aided by "Nazi-Japanese militarists" bent on finding an advance base from which to attack the Soviet Union.[3] As a measure of Moscow's concern with the military dimensions of the problem, Marshal Voroshilov joined the discussion of the defense of Sinkiang against the Japanese.

At a second meeting Sheng pressed Stalin to speed deliveries of goods needed under his country's Three-Year Economic Plan. He recalled arguing along the following lines with the Soviet leader:

> If Sinkiang, the most under-developed province of China, could be improved with the assistance of Soviet advisors, experts and technicians together with Russian-made capital equipment, this would not only affect developments in China's northwest provinces, it would also carry considerable impact in India—thereby allowing 450 million Chinese and 300 million Indians to better understand Communism. It would strengthen their friendship with the Soviet Union. It would prove that the Russians and their

> leader, Stalin, are faithfully carrying out Lenin's will to help the under-developed peoples of Asia.

Sheng then posed the knotty problem of his own relationship with the Chinese Communist insurgents holding Yunan Province. He complained that his application for membership in the Chinese Party had been indefinitely "deferred." Quick to seize advantage of an opportunity, Stalin on the spot extended Sheng an invitation to join the Communist Party of the Soviet Union.[4] As Sheng later reconstructed it, "by enrolling me in the Soviet apparatus Stalin gained an instrument of blackmail, for while my Marxist views were tolerated grudgingly by the Nationalist leaders, being subject to discipline from the Kremlin would lead to outright denunciation as a traitor." The warlord in retrospect complained, "Stalin attempted to keep me subordinate to Moscow thereby preserving Sinkiang as an exclusively Russian sphere to the disadvantage of Yunan."[5]

The Soviet leader warned Sheng to be alert to infiltration by Japanese Fascist spies as well as British Imperialist spies. Stalin volunteered the opinion that it was easier to deal with imperialists than fascists. He then developed for Sheng's benefit the Communist thesis of co-existence: "Ever since the October Revolution human history has moved into an epoch of colonial revolution and proletariat revolution. But because the capitalist, imperialist and fascist countries remain strong the Communists must have a period of 'peaceful co-existence' with at least some of the enemy." With commendable candor Stalin described peaceful co-existence as "an important strategy in the process of proletariat revolution and world revolution led by the Communist International." He added, "Until we are sure the Communist world can destroy the imperialist countries, Communism and capitalism must co-exist peacefully."[6]

Proceeding smoothly from doctrine to practical geopolitics, Stalin advised Sheng:

> During the war against Japan, Sinkiang's position is vital . . . to guard the International communication line for attack. The present war situation is unfavorable to China but Japan will not be able to conquer China alone. If China can get help from allied countries Japanese forces will be ousted. A considerable period of "peaceful co-existence" between the Chinese Communists and Nationalists will follow their victory over Japan. In order to win the war against Japan, to deal with both the Chinese Communists

> and Nationalists during the period of "co-existence," Sinkiang should maintain close contact with both Chiang Kai-shek and Mao Tse-tung. During the war and after the victory the Nationalists will be materially superior to the Communists but victory of the Chinese Communists is ultimately almost a certainty.[7]

By drawing off most of the Soviet Union's energies and resources to the German front, World War II caused a power vacuum in Sinkiang. This enabled Sheng—by then disillusioned with Communism and Moscow's methods—to break with Stalin. It is historically interesting that one issue which brought them to the breaking point was the arrest and eventual execution of Mao Tse-min, brother of Mao Tse-tung and a leading Chinese Communist agent, whom Sheng believed was plotting against him. The Sinkiang warlord recounted how the Soviet Consul General had protested Mao's arrest and had threatened dire consequences for "acting against the brother of Mao Tse-tung, . . . destined to win control of all China."[8] By late 1942 Sheng, taking advantage of Moscow's preoccupation with the war, had demanded the withdrawal of Soviet military and technical personnel from Sinkiang because of what he later described as a "dreary record of plots and uprisings" against him by the Russians.[9]

Having played Stalin's tune for ten years and having killed Mao Tse-tung's brother and another leading Chinese Communist, Sheng had no place to turn but to the Chinese Nationalists. In this way Chiang Kai-shek gained temporary control of the area for the first time since the early thirties and soon was able to replace Sheng with a governor of his own choosing. But with the defeat of Nazi Germany in 1944, the Soviet Union could again turn its attention to the Central Asian problem and Chiang—by this time occupied by his dual struggle against Japan and Chinese Communist forces—could not oppose a reassertion of Soviet influence in Sinkiang's capital.

Soviet domination of Sinkiang inevitably came to an end following the victory of Communist forces in China, although Moscow did seem to make one last attempt to hold the province, according to Allen S. Whiting, General Sheng's collaborator in writing a record of Soviet power politics in Sinkiang during this period. If Whiting's and Sheng's evidence can be accepted as an accurate reflection of Soviet policy, Stalin placed great importance on retaining Sinkiang in the face of Communist victory on the China mainland. As Communist troops approached in 1949 the Soviet Consul in Urumchi—presumably under orders—offered the defending Nationalist General, T'ao Shih-yeh, a proposition in which the USSR would prevent the Chinese Communists from occupying Sinkiang if T'ao would declare the province independent. The province would then be incorporated into a federal republic. Similar to the formula used in Outer Mongolia, this plan would provide a framework permitting the Soviet Union to exercise dominant control.[10] But the Nationalist Chinese, in the Han tradition, refused to relinquish territory considered part of the Empire, even though it would be the Communists who would be the beneficiary of this refusal. Just as in the case of Tibet, it was inconceivable for any Chinese regime, however weak, to deed away the destiny of China.

On September 26, 1949 the Chinese Nationalist Governor, recognizing the strength of the Communist armies and the inevitability of their victory, declared Sinkiang part of the new Communist state of China. Less than a month later Red Chinese army units occupied the province, and China ostensibly began a new era of amity and cooperation there with the Soviet Union by signing an agreement in March 1960 calling for joint exploration of mineral resources. Yet, in fact, the traditional rivalry in the border lands was essentially unchanged.

Soviet experts helped China explore new oil fields, build pipelines and erect refineries. During the next five years a steel plant, a thorium factory and hydroelectric facilities were constructed. A rail line to the Soviet border was also begun and significant new coal discoveries were made. With Soviet assistance, Communist China was well on the way to industrializing the province. Still Peking was distrustful of Moscow's intentions and nervous about continuing Soviet influence in Sinkiang. Like Tibet and all other regions peopled by non-Han nationalities, Sinkiang was vulnerable to anti-Chinese agitation. Through education, propaganda and the importation of Chinese laborers Peking sought to place the Chinese stamp on the region—now called the Sinkiang-Uighur Autonomous Region. The parallel to Tibet is striking in this respect.

There was more concrete evidence of Sino-Soviet tension in Sinkiang by 1955. The Sino-Soviet joint companies, for example, were taken over entirely by the Chinese. The Provincial Secretary of the Communist Party became a Kiangsi Chinese instead of a Sinkiang native, while the bulk of the Party machinery also fell into

Peking's hands. Other efforts at Sinocizing the province stirred up rebellion among the native Uighurs. Serious outbreaks of violence were reported in June 1957 at the time of the "100 Flowers" episode and again in 1958 when Mandarin Chinese replaced the Uighur language in higher schools. Although firm evidence is lacking, there are many indications that the Soviet hand was behind the rebellion or, at least, encouraged ethnic unrest which led to rebellion.

1959 and 1960 brought serious deterioration in Sino-Soviet relations. Beginning in 1959, Moscow had made serious overtures of peaceful co-existence to the United States. Kremlin policy also sought closer relations with both India and Indonesia. These new Soviet directions were viewed with genuine alarm in Peking, which saw total isolation as the only fruit of the "Camp David spirit." Coming on the heels of China's crisis with India over Tibet, Khrushchev's orgy of personal diplomacy in South and Southeast Asia was viewed with anger in Peking. (Particularly galling was the fact that Khrushchev visited India on the tenth anniversary of the signing of the Sino-Soviet Treaty.) Peking fired an ideological salvo at Moscow in a *Red Flag* article in April 1960, entitled "Long Live Leninism," in which Mao openly challenged the Soviet Union as the leader of Communism and the guardian of doctrinal orthodoxy. This led to an escalation of the doctrinal war with added emphasis provided by a withdrawal of a large number of Soviet technicians from China. A massive Chinese purge of pro-Soviet elements in Sinkiang also took place in 1960. Although the Soviet consulates in Urumchi and Kuldja remained open, most of the Soviet technicians were withdrawn that year.

Dr. Satyanarayan Sinha, Indian diplomat, Member of Parliament and outspoken critic of China's Himalayan policy, claimed to have had early information of Soviet-Chinese tensions in Sinkiang. In a book by Sinha entitled *The Chinese Aggression*, a shadowy Kazakh called Askaroff alleges that the Soviet Union foiled Chinese plans to invade India from Tibet in the spring of 1960. Askaroff, who supposedly played a major role for the Soviets in instigating anti-Chinese revolts in the Altai region of Sinkiang in March 1960, told Sinha that Soviet intelligence had come upon the Chinese plan for the invasion of India. According to Askaroff, the Soviets immediately cancelled military shipments to the Chinese in Sinkiang on the basis of this information.[11]

China's actual invasion of India two years later lends some

plausibility to Sinha's story, although it is difficult to understand why the mysterious Askaroff confided in Sinha and it is puzzling that Sinha felt he could publish Askaroff's information—attributing it openly to him—without getting him in serious trouble. Perhaps this was a calculated Soviet leak. If it was, as Sinha hints elsewhere in his book,[12] the question can be fairly asked: Did the Indian government take the warning seriously?

Playing on ethnic abhorrence of Han domination in Sinkiang, a major technique of the Soviets has been to lure across the border into Soviet Kazakhstan as many people as possible. A Kuldja refugee provided details of Soviet agitation in Sinkiang in 1961 in which thousands of Soviet passports were clandestinely distributed to dissident Sinkiangese, enabling them to emigrate to Soviet territory. Some 50,000 escaped Chinese rule in this way until Peking took steps to stop the flow in the spring of 1962. Unable to get out, thousands more demonstrated and rioted in Kuldja toward the end of May 1962, provoking the Chinese in some instances to fire into the mobs with bloody results.[13] The Kazakhstan edition of *Pravda* played the story as a grizzly massacre of innocent people and a conclusive sign that China's nationalities policy had completely failed. This could only have had an inflammatory effect on Peking and must certainly have helped shape China's decision to expel Soviet consular officials believed to be implicated in the riots.

A convincing indication that China was alarmed and greatly influenced by Soviet subversion in Sinkiang during the spring of 1962 was the mention of it in Peking's definitive statement on Sino-Soviet tensions which appeared September 6, 1963. This 20,000-word document, entitled "The Origin and Development of the Differences Between the Leadership of the Communist Party of the Soviet Union and Ourselves," accused the Russians of subverting "tens of thousands of Kazakhs from the Ili region [of Sinkiang] into the Soviet Union," and refusing to return them to China on specious grounds of "legality" and "humanitarianism."[14] Peking complained bitterly that such an "astounding event" is unheard of in relations between socialist countries. Moscow's counteraccusation that more than five thousand Chinese border violations against the Soviet Union occurred in 1962[15] may have been an exaggeration, but it adds to the evidence that the Sino-Soviet borders were no less troubled than those of India.

Events in the borderlands, however, should be viewed in the

context of larger issues of conflict between China and the USSR. These issues created growing tensions during the summer of 1962 and led finally to the October crisis in relationships set off by China's invasion of India and Soviet brinkmanship in Cuba. Despite an outward appearance of relative calm in early 1962, both Peking and Moscow continued to take actions which drove them further apart. Moscow, for example, stepped up efforts to bring Yugoslavia back into the fold, while China continued publicly to support Albania and use it as a front for propaganda attacks against Yugoslavia and the USSR.

Discussions held by Chinese and Soviet representatives made it apparent to both countries that the price for *rapprochement* would be impossibly high. Khrushchev, for example, could not come to terms with Albania and still win back Yugoslavia. Nor could he agree to accept and institutionalize China's separate formula for Communist revolution and repudiate peaceful co-existence as a basis for his relationship with the United States. Similarly, Khrushchev's efforts to reach *rapprochement* with Tito and use Yugoslavia as a center for creating a pro-Soviet "socialist camp" was provocative and totally unacceptable to Peking.

In an August interview with the American columnist Drew Pearson, Tito needled Peking on its India policy, thereby advertising the growing identity of views between Moscow and Belgrade and the hardening of their opposition to Peking's belligerency in the Himalayas. Khrushchev's decision to send Soviet President Brezhnev on a state visit to Belgrade in September was, however, unforgivable. Peking surpassed itself with abuse. But of particular significance was a Chinese-inspired editorial in the Albanian paper *Zëri i Popullit*, which denounced Brezhnev's visit and, for the first time, called publicly for a split in the international Communist movement.[16]

Peking was also seriously concerned by Moscow's promise to equip the Indian air force with jet fighter aircraft. In a two-part article appearing September 19 and 20 *Zëri i Popullit*, again speaking for Peking, attacked Tito as an "imperialist intermediary attached to the revisionist group of Khrushchev." In this same article Moscow was, for the first time, openly criticized for backing India in the border conflict with China and for selling military aircraft to Indian "reactionaries."

Khrushchev's admission that the USSR had responded favorably to the U.S. proposal to deny nuclear knowledge to non-nuclear countries struck China as the culmination of outrages perpetrated by Moscow. Peking replied secretly on September 3 with a strident demand that Moscow refrain from aligning itself with the U.S. on this question.[17] Two days later China withdrew Ambassador Liu Hsiao from Moscow without naming a successor, and on September 25 Peking let it be known that the Soviet Union had been asked to close all its consulates in China.[18] This gesture was probably taken at this time in retaliation for Moscow's nuclear policy, but it is also related to Soviet subversion inside China. A denunciation of Moscow for "scheming activities, provocation, and subversion,"[19] which was aired at a Chinese Central Committee meeting in late September, may have referred back to earlier Soviet adventures in Sinkiang, but it may also have been based on new evidence of Soviet intrigues in the borderlands.

The atmosphere grew more tense as the summer wore on. The gap dividing the two Communist capitals became wider with each salvo of vituperation. Attacks provoked counterattacks, and substantive charges became entwined with doctrinal dispute. The war of editorials waged by Moscow and Peking—either directly or through their respective surrogates, Yugoslavia and Albania—was matched by secret discussions in which more damaging charges were made. One such conversation allegedly took place in Peking on October 8, when the Soviet Ambassador was called in and informed that a "massive" attack on India was imminent and that India's use of Soviet-built fighter planes "was making a bad impression on Chinese frontier guards."[20] According to the Chinese, Khrushchev posed no objections at the time this demarche was made. The Soviet leader was later to deny that he had been forewarned, but if the Chinese account of his acquiescence is in fact true, it is understandable that he was being cautious about his relations with the Chinese on the eve of the Cuban missile crisis.

On October 20 Peking again registered a secret protest, this time against Moscow's intention to sign a nuclear test ban agreement with the West.[21] Simultaneously, as if to show contempt for Moscow's doctrinally impure world of peaceful co-existence, Chinese troops in Tibet attacked India.

CHAPTER 14

A TIME OF RECKONING

We are getting out of touch with realities in a modern world; we are living in our own creation and we have been shaken out of it.

Jawaharlal Nehru

Twenty thousand Red Chinese troops poured into India over snowbound Thagla Ridge at dawn on October 20, 1962. The Dhola outpost, which straddles the ridge three miles high, was the first to fall. The final destruction of India's dream of peace and co-existence thus occurred in a place unknown to most of the world, where India, Bhutan and Tibet come together in a knot of Himalayan peaks.

The nearby outposts of Khinzemane and Tsangle also bore the brunt of China's first wave and were hastily abandoned for more defensible positions five miles to the rear. Khinzemane had been the site of a serious border incident three years earlier and had recently again come under Chinese harassment. But this was no incident nor was it only a "border conflict" as initially described by both the Chinese Communist and Indian governments. It was a full-scale and obviously well-planned attack, launched skillfully across the world's highest mountain range.

The Chinese also struck in Ladakh at the other end of the frontier. This attack was two-pronged. The northernmost strike was aimed at Daulat Beg Oldi, an Indian post guarding the Karakorum approaches from Chinese Sinkiang, and the Chip Chap River valley west of the disputed Aksai Chin bulge. Eleven posts in this sector were simultaneously assaulted during the first few hours of fighting. Four of them were overrun immediately while troops of the remaining posts fell back to less exposed positions in the face of withering Chinese firepower. The southern thrust was in the Pangyong Lake area where five Indian outposts were quickly overwhelmed by Chinese troops fighting with tank support. In this salient the Chinese drove to within seven miles of the important Indian garrison at Chushul.

On the second day of undeclared war China opened a third front, attacking Kibitoo post in the Lohit Valley near the Burmese border. Within twenty-four hours five Indian outposts in this area had fallen to the Chinese. Tanks were used in this salient also, giving some indication of the logistical preparations which must have preceded the Red offensive.

China accused India of preparing a "massive invasion" of Chinese territory. Peking's first official announcement complained: "It is Nehru who orders fighting."[1] Nehru, in angry reply, denounced China as "a powerful and unscrupulous opponent." He addressed the Indian people in somber tones on October 22, saying that "the time has . . . come for us to realize fully this menace that threatens the freedom of our people and the independence of our country. . . ." Yet the time had not come to repudiate a policy with which he had become identified, and Nehru added that "India would not abandon . . . non-alignment."[2]

In India's hours of shock China offered terms. Peking would negotiate peace if both sides withdrew twelve and a half miles from the current "line of control." As the line of control had been pushed deep into Indian territory by four days of steady Chinese advance, the terms were obviously not acceptable to New Delhi. India rejected them and insisted that negotiations could not be held unless China withdrew to positions held before September 8. Despite the mauling which Indian forces had endured, New Delhi looked for help, not terms—especially not terms of capitulation offered by China.

India's leaders, particularly Defense Minister Krishna Menon, had cherished the illusion that friendship with the Soviet Union was insurance against Chinese hostility. According to this reasoning, the Soviet Union would never allow China to make war on India. This was patently a false estimate. Khrushchev wrote Nehru on the very day of China's assault, urging him to enter into negotiations with Peking.[3] The Soviet leader's message was stimulated by earlier incidents along the China-India frontier and, as later revelations proved, was written in ignorance of China's intention to invade India. But the Soviet stand immediately after the invasion—by which time the

Cuban crisis had passed its peak—was clearly in support of Chou En-lai's peace offer and may even have influenced it.

What Krishna Menon could not foresee was the eruption of the Cuban crisis which brought the U.S. and the USSR to the brink of war. Coinciding as it did with the Chinese invasion of India, this critical situation forced the USSR to side initially with China lest it alienate a needed ally in its moment of danger. The Chinese were later to allege that Khrushchev had promised Chou En-lai on October 13, 1962—only a few days before the Chinese invasion—that the USSR would remain neutral in the Sino-Indian dispute. The Soviet leader probably knew by then that he would need Chinese support for the Cuban crisis which loomed and actually broke out only one week later. Similarly Chou needed Soviet support for the crisis he knew would be created by China's imminent invasion of India.

Moscow, caught in an embarrassing dilemma as a result of China-India hostilities, became suddenly ambiguous about an earlier promise to provide India with MIG-21 jet fighter aircraft. At this stage of Sino-Soviet relations the USSR obviously could not rush in with aircraft or arms with which Indians would kill Chinese.

India looked for moral, if not material, support from the non-aligned countries. Only a year earlier the principal uncommitted nations had met in Belgrade and pledged mutual solidarity. But New Delhi found to its dismay that non-alignment could apply to the Sino-Indian hot war as well as to the East-West cold war. Even Tito, long an antagonist of China, reacted to India's suffering with weeks of deafening silence. Ghana's Nkrumah attacked Great Britain for offering aid to India. Sukarno permitted the Indonesian Communist Party to publicize China's cause, and Nasser—although sympathetic to India—was more interested in playing the mediator than in condemning Communist China.

Six days after the invasion Nehru wrote to most of the governments of the world, explaining India's position and asking for sympathy. Later New Delhi sent two missions to plead India's case throughout Africa and Asia. The most useful response came from the West; the United States, Great Britain and Canada promised material aid as well as sympathy. Nehru could honestly report to a delegation of forty-five Congress Party leaders on October 27 that India was making arrangements to match Chinese firepower with arms from abroad. But non-alignment would not be bartered for guns; Nehru promised the delegation that he would make no distinction between East and West in his quest for arms![4]

On the sixth day of battle a state of emergency was declared, and the Indian government assumed extraordinary powers. In the western sector the Chinese had drawn closer to Chushul. The capture of this important post would knock out a vital airstrip and put the Chinese on the road to Ladakh's capital of Leh, one hundred miles to the east. Towang, seventeen miles south of Thagla Ridge on the northeast frontier, had fallen to the Chinese one day before the cutting off of an entire Indian brigade. This placed the Chinese astride a jeepable track leading to the important Assam railhead and military headquarters at Tezpur, just two hundred miles away. It was this very route that the Dalai Lama had traveled in his flight from the Chinese in March 1959.

Ironically, the declaration of national emergency and the disastrous loss of a full brigade coincided with Indian efforts once again to have China admitted to the United Nations. India's chief delegate to the General Assembly, B. N. Chakravarty, asked U.N. members to accept Red China. He reasoned that only by being a member of the world body could China be subjected to its "views and disciplines." India had found disillusioning the slow response of the Afro-Asian nations to its call for support; yet many of these countries must have found such a rationale difficult to understand at this particular moment. If Uganda's Prime Minister Obote could refuse to support China's candidacy until the "shooting stops," why should India—the victim—press for it?

On October 29 the Indian government first announced casualty statistics. The Indian people were appalled to learn that between 2,000 and 2,500 soldiers had been killed during the first week of fighting. Later, more complete statistics made even more grim reading: 1,102 Indians were held prisoner, 291 were wounded, while 5,174 were missing and presumed dead.[6] Now thoroughly shaken by the worsening situation, Nehru formally requested military assistance from the United States on October 29. Particularly needed were troops carrying aircraft, mortars, automatic rifles and mountain artillery. The United States responded immediately with a promise of supplies on a "no strings" basis. Repayment plans were to be worked out later so that delivery could begin almost at once.[7] Nehru admitted with remarkable candor to some of his officials that "we are getting out of touch with realities in a modern world; we are living in our own creation and we have been shaken out of it." Yet the commitment to non-alignment was still strong. New Delhi would not yet expose the unwillingness of the Soviet Union to respond to India's pleas for help. These developments were nevertheless having a profound effect on the Indian government.

The first political casualty was Krishna Menon. Non-alignment was personified in India's controversial Defense Minister who had outraged the Western world by his all too consistent support of Communist bloc policies. It had been Krishna Menon who theorized that the Soviet Union would protect India from Chinese invasion, so it was inevitable that his star must fall when the policy with which he was identified was repudiated by events. Never popular in India, he now became the whipping boy for the Indian public, which felt that incompetence and negligence lay behind the rout of Indian forces. He was arraigned by angry critics on two counts. As Minister of Defense he had neither foreseen nor prepared Indian forces for a major campaign in the Himalayan passes. Some defense factories had been converted to the production of civilian products, which gave rise to wry jokes to the effect that war could not be fought "with Espresso machines." But more fundamentally, Krishna Menon was assailed for being the architect of a national policy which had been proven tragically inadequate, a policy which made military unpreparedness inevitable.

Nehru tried to defend his Defense Minister, but by October 31 the pressure—public and private—was more than even the Prime Minister could resist. Although deprived of the important Defense portfolio, Krishna Menon remained for a few days in the newly created post of Minister of Defense Production, an ironic assignment considering his failure in this field. But soon the Prime Minister's own advisers demanded his removal from the Cabinet altogether.

On November 8 China offered a new cease-fire plan which called for both sides to withdraw their troops twelve and a half miles behind the positions held on November 7, 1959.[8] If carried out, this would put Chinese forces twelve and a half miles behind the McMahon Line which India recognized as the valid boundary in the northeast. But it would still leave China in possession of 15,000 square miles of territory claimed by India in Ladakh, including the road it built clandestinely across the Aksai Chin bulge. Timed to coincide with this announcement was a renewed offensive aimed at Walong in the westernmost corner of Assam. If this heavily defended post were overcome, Chinese troops could romp through the Lohit valley to the vital Digboi oil fields in Assam. Also apparent was an ominous Chinese buildup near Chushul, the key defense post in Ladakh.

Beginning November 3, the United States Air Force began airlifting military supplies to New Delhi. Several giant transport aircraft had been committed to this operation.[9] In the face of the increasingly serious Chinese threat the U.S. government also held discussions with Great Britain and Canada toward reaching a broad and coordinated program of military aid to India.[10] By contrast a Soviet military spokesman announced in Moscow on October 29 that the USSR supported the Chinese territorial claims and would provide no arms to the Indians.[11] On the basis of this, the Indian government could not expect new Soviet military assistance, but for psychological as well as political reasons it was vitally important to India for the USSR at least to make good its earlier commitment to sell the Indian Air Force MIG-21 fighter aircraft. Nehru clung to the hope that some such gesture from the Soviet Union would force the Chinese to halt an alarmingly rapid offensive since no Indian military buildup—regardless of how fast western arms arrived—could be completed in time to stop the Chinese.

These hopes were realized; on November 10 Nehru was able to announce that the Soviet Union had promised to stand by an agreement to sell MIG-21's to India. He reportedly told a parliamentary committee that the USSR, having been brought to "neutrality" from its initial pro-Chinese stand, would meet its promised mid-December 1962 delivery date.[12] The note of relief and triumph struck by Nehru's statement is understandable. The events of October had indeed suggested that China's objective in India was total conquest of the subcontinent.* Assuming the worst, it was logical and realistic for Nehru to conclude that only the Soviet Union could stop China without risking general war. But Nehru's critics—at home and in the Western world—found it inconsistent that he gave only scant public

* It is interesting to note, however, that the Chinese called their invasion troops "frontier guards," and described the fighting as "defensive action."

acknowledgement to dramatic Western military aid while widely publicizing the Soviet Union's shift from unqualified Chinese backing to a posture of ambiguous neutrality.

After nearly one month of fighting the Chinese army broke through on three fronts. The Indian stronghold of Walong fell on November 18, trapping an entire battalion. Those Indian soldiers able to retreat could not find another line to hold for eighty miles. The Chinese simultaneously outflanked the Indian 4th Division on the 14,000-foot Se pass near Jang in a major offensive aimed at Tezpur. The Indian supply base at Bomdi La was captured, which signaled a hasty evacuation of the army headquarters from Tezpur. India's entire defense strategy in the Northeast Frontier area had to be revised since it then looked doubtful if Assam could be held. A third push was made in Ladakh toward Chushul. Nehru stated in New Delhi: "It is no longer a border war between India and China; it is an invasion of India. I do not know how other countries will be affected by it."[13] The latter sentence suggested Nehru's fear of world war—the probable consequences of a Chinese drive to conquer India. Chou En-lai, in fact, had warned twenty Afro-Asian heads of state that U.S. aid to India would enlarge the area of conflict.[14]

But suddenly, in a dramatic and completely surprising move on November 21, the Communists announced a unilateral cease-fire along the entire Indian border and promised to begin pulling back troops on December 1. The statement specified that Chinese troops would withdraw twelve and a half miles behind the lines of actual control of November 7, 1959.[15] This was, to all intents and purposes, the cease-fire proposal offered to and rejected by India two weeks before. If adopted it would leave China in possession of the Aksai Chin area including the strategic road linking Sinkiang and Tibet which China finds so important to the defense and control of Tibet. In return, India would gain only clear title to the McMahon Line in the northeast, which it considered a fixed and legal boundary anyway. The Chinese announcement added that if the Indian government agreed to take corresponding measures, Indian and Chinese officials could meet to discuss troop withdrawal. With monumental relief the world could conclude that, for the time being, China's objectives in India were limited ones.

Nearly co-incident with Chou En-lai's announcement was President Kennedy's statement the day before that the U.S. naval blockade of Cuba had been lifted in response to Khrushchev's pledge that all Soviet offensive missiles and jet bombers in Cuba would be withdrawn within thirty days. Thermonuclear war had not occurred and two serious crises were over. But the momentary relaxation of tensions could not long obscure the far-reaching effects which the Sino-Indian war has had both inside India and in the world at large. The rapidity with which Chinese forces could knife into India over mountains once thought impregnable was frightening. In understanding the enormity of the act, it should be noted that China had succeeded in occupying an area in India equal in size to England. But the act is dwarfed in significance by the changes which it caused and the forces which it set in motion.

The October crisis had an immediate and dramatic impact on the Indian people. Those in the large cities felt an excitement which for the moment lifted them out of the slough of daily routine. Even the great mass of rural dwellers, whose timeless existence is remote from the world beyond their village limits, must have felt some of the tension of the national emergency. Certainly the families of the dead or missing soldiers did.

Indians—divided and subdivided into a maze of mutually antagonistic groups based on caste, color and cultural, communal, linguistic and sectional differences—found common cause during October and November 1962. There existed for this moment in history a sense of national purpose. The immediacy of the Chinese threat evoked a spirit of national sacrifice rarely seen in India. There were stories of Calcutta ricksha coolies volunteering for military duty, New Delhi housewives offering their gold dowry bangles to the government and retired maharajahs contributing jewel collections to finance India's defense effort. But such actions were the phenomena of emotion. They were manifestations of the mass adrenaline flow caused by war's stimulus. Unfortunately, the effect is not lasting. After the initial excitement wears off, a nation begins to feel the real consequences of war and search for a way to accommodate itself to the new world it finds.

But cause is perhaps just as important as consequence. At least cause must be established before consequences can be fully understood and intelligently faced. What were Communist China's motives and what are its long-range intentions toward India and the Himalayan border states?

CHAPTER 15

MARX, MALTHUS AND THE MIDDLE KINGDOM

If the Chinese joined the U.N., we would still not control a majority. Perhaps the world situation might appear to be relaxed a little bit, but in reality the struggle would become more violent.

Bulletin of activities, General Political Department, Chinese People's Liberation Army

International crime, like any crime, usually has a motive. Chinese aggression against India in October 1962 was no exception. If, at first glance, Chinese violation of Indian soil—an act which made a mockery of peaceful co-existence—seemed inconsistent or irrational, it was because it was not judged against the background of Chinese history. The underlying motive for Red China's hostility toward India derived from a national psychology based on an ancient heritage.

The Great Wall of China is a symbol of the Chinese people's struggle against an outer world presumed to be hostile. The "Middle Kingdom" which is bounded by the Wall is, in the egocentric world of the Chinese people, the core of civilization. The guardians of this civilization have alternately been the harassed and the harassers of the "barbarians" beyond the pale. Those neighboring peoples which accepted Chinese suzerainty could enjoy to a limited extent the fruits of its culture. Those which did not were to be conquered if possible or otherwise ignored. During periods of weakness China would be forced to admit its conquerors, but they would eventually be assimilated by a vastly more numerous people and absorbed by the quicksand of a superior culture.

China's history has had a cyclical regularity. The cycle would begin when a strong military leader emerged, unified the country and in so doing created a new ruling dynasty. Inevitably there followed a period of territorial expansion through vigorous military action, then an era of enforced peace. It was during these periods of relative tranquillity that culture flowered. These were eras of prosperity and stability. But in reality these were the ebb tides of dynasty. The conservative policies of a dynasty intent upon preserving the *status quo* discouraged new enterprises and initiative. Population outstripped production; the body lived off its own fat. Inherent in this situation were agrarian depression and discontent. As culture and intellect prospered, military strength and civil administration decayed. Eventually the dynasty would crumble as the "mandate of heaven," which the Chinese believed was responsible for a prosperous regime, was withdrawn. The last phase of the cycle would be the fragmentation of China and sometimes the domination of all or part of it by an alien ruler.

Before the nineteenth century the historical cycles revolved on the same foundation, and the fundamental social order and economy remained unchanged. The flow of empire sent forth military rulers—not settlers. The Chinese people stayed close to the familiar earth of the "Middle Kingdom," whether the tides of conquest were high or receding. But the nineteenth century brought totally new "barbarians" to China's frontiers—Caucasian seaborne invaders from Europe and America. Interested mainly in trade, they brought industry and technology which set in motion changes destined to revolutionize the traditional structure of society.

A new Chinese aristocracy arose, made rich and powerful by its willingness to seek accommodation with Western enterprisers. This aristocracy was a mutation of the traditional, privileged mandarin class. While the new class formed an urban bourgeoisie, the mandarins retained control of the land, clung to the machinery of power and resisted Western influence. Since the old mandarinate could not exert control over the Western traders along the coast, it pushed its influence in the direction of the more familiar "barbarians" beyond the Wall. As the Manchu Dynasty lay dying, wracked by its own corruption and the virus of social change brought by Western imperialism, warlords waged petty campaigns against the non-Chinese peoples of the interior.

Not only was the structure of society changing under the influence of the West, but its physical location was for the first time shifting. The products of Western industry—particularly the railroad—accelerated the dispersal of population and made possible its movement. As China's population outgrew the "Middle Kingdom," it overflowed first into Manchuria. The subsequent population shifts toward Mongolia and Central Asia were on a much smaller scale since these areas were less attractive and access was more difficult. Yet there was some movement of permanent settlers into these areas which had until then seen only Chinese military conquerors.

The present Communist dynasty in China, in the tradition of its predecessors, came to power through strong military leadership and conquest. Like their predecessors, the Communists are dedicated to uniting China and expanding its frontiers to include all irredentist areas; but by the time they had gained control of mainland China there were clearly fixed limits beyond which they could not expand without colliding with the Soviet Union. The power of the United States simultaneously blocked expansion seaward. But there now existed a reason for expansion more compelling than the historical, cyclical urges of a waxing new dynasty; China's exploding population needed new lands.

In November 1954 a Peking announcement revealed that China's mainland population was approximately 583,000,000.*[1] The net annual increase was calculated to be 2.2 percent per year which, when projected into the 1980's, would put Red China's population total over the billion mark.[3] These statistics, reached after a countrywide census conducted by the Communist government in 1953, provided the basis for Peking's economic planning. They caused planners to experiment with birth control as one method of solving the obvious problem of too many mouths and too little production.

Before 1953 the concept of birth control was considered to be a product of capitalist, "neo-Malthusian" thinking, thus doctrinally sinful. According to orthodox Marxism, there can be no such thing as overpopulation in a properly planned socialist society, but in view of the shocking statistics revealed by the 1953 census, Peking flew in the face of doctrine and encouraged birth control. By 1957 there were clinics for this purpose throughout China, and the government

* The total figure given was 602,000,000 persons, but this included 7,600,000 Chinese in Formosa and 11,700,000 overseas Chinese in other areas.[2]

staged massive propaganda campaigns calculated to limit childbirth and encourage late marriages.

In 1958 Communist China began its "great leap forward" toward industrialization. One apparent casualty of the new program was the Malthusian approach to population. Mao Tse-tung announced suddenly that "China's big population is a good thing"; more labor meant faster industrialization.[4] A contributing reason for de-emphasizing birth control was that it simply had not worked. The people had been more irritated than influenced by the blatant birth control propaganda, which in most cases was phrased in overgraphic and offending language.

By 1960 the "great leap" had become a stumble. The second Five-Year Plan was failing, and China faced the possibility of mass starvation. Peking was forced to return again to population control measures. In an effort to play down the inconsistency of this policy with Marxist doctrine, Peking first justified birth control on the grounds that it was in the interest of public health, encouraged better parental care and made possible greater educational opportunity. The fact that a runaway population was outstripping production was glossed over. But the food crisis of 1961 and 1962 was more serious than the outside world imagined. It was a dramatic warning to Chinese planners that there were too many mouths to feed. It proved that there was no shortcut to industrialization and that extreme agrarian regimentation, typified by the dreaded "communes," was not a practical solution. In June 1963 a mass birth control campaign was launched in Shanghai—this time with an emphasis on male sterilization—while somewhat later, China introduced the birth control pill.

Despite the doctrinaire mentality of Chinese leaders, whose faith in their brand of Communism seems boundless, it must be clear that economic planning and population control alone will not achieve a socialist heaven in time to satisfy the demands of a chronically hungry population. If China cannot stem the population growth and if this growth continues to outstrip production, the inevitable results will be accelerated colonization and the development of the more sparsely populated border areas. After that comes expansion beyond China's borders.

Tibet has been viewed by Peking as an area into which Chinese population can expand. Historically, China was prevented from colonizing "Outer Tibet" by lack of easy access, a hostile and independent-minded Tibetan people and Britain's empire, which required Tibet as a neutral buffer protecting India's northern frontier. But Britain's withdrawal from the subcontinent after World War II made colonization possible. Only lacking were roads into Tibet over which settlers as well as military supplies could travel. These were built with the aid of forced Tibetan labor in a remarkably short time—much more quickly than Western observers had thought possible. By 1954 the completion of two motorable roads from China to Lhasa made Chinese immigration into Tibet practical, and Peking officially announced its intention to settle a large number of Chinese farmers. The Dalai Lama himself estimated that 5,000,000 Chinese settlers had arrived in the northeastern and eastern provinces.[5]

In response to Nehru's observation that "a strong China is normally an expansionist China," Peking accused the Prime Minister of wanting China to "remain poor and weak . . . though faced with aggression and the threat of war by U.S. imperialism."[6] This statement suggests an important element of Peking's motivation. Ringed by two hostile powers—the Soviet Union landward and the United States seaward—Communist China views India in terms of the latter's relationships with them. By direct aggression, insurgency or subversion China has fought U.S. influence in the Far East, but South Asia poses security problems of no less importance to Peking. Despite the brief period of *Panch Sheela*, the record shows that Peking has consistently believed India to be but a front for Western "imperialism." This conclusion must be accepted if the motives for Communist China's India policy are to be fully understood. Being accustomed to considering India an imbalanced "neutralist" whose U.N. voting record and sometimes unnecessary judgments on world issues have frequently favored the Communist point of view, it is not easy for an American to see the logic in China's image of India. And only by making allowances for the historical distortions of doctrinaire Communism is there any logic to it.

Peking is convinced that the Indian independence movement fell under the control of the Indian bourgeoisie and landlord class. Both classes—described by Red China as having a "blood relationship with the British bourgeoisie"—compromised the movement in the interest of protecting their economic positions. Gandhi's devotion to non-violence was seen by Peking as part of a bourgeoisie plot to paralyze the "people's struggle." According to China's theoreticians, the result has been a perpetuation of "imperialism" and a retention of the imperialists' economic influence in India.[7]

An analysis of India's economy since 1948, as distorted by Peking, proves that India has not freed itself from bondage. India has simply replaced British "imperialism" with U.S. "imperialism." In documenting this conclusion Peking called attention to a sevenfold increase in U.S. investments in India from 1948 to 1959, as contrasted with only a twofold increase in British investments for the same period. But what seems to have impressed Peking the most is that India's economy has had to rely progressively more on U.S. aid.[8]

The consequence of India's economic "dependency" on the United States is, in China's distorted perspective, New Delhi's alignment with American "imperialist" political policies. China at one time alleged that "Nehru seldom voiced opposition to the major acts of aggression by . . . U.S. imperialism." Specific accusations against Nehru included India's November 1952 United Nations proposal supporting the "forcible retention of North Korean prisoners of war by the U.S., Nehru's malicious slander of the USSR for its role in the 'counter-revolutionary event' in Hungary in 1956, and India's acquiescence in U.S. and British troop landings in Lebanon and Jordan respectively in 1958."[9] Nehru was criticized for expressing his sorrow at the death of King Faisal*—"the common enemy of the Iraqi people"—and for describing the execution of the "traitor" Nagy by the Hungarian people as "contributing to world tensions."[10] Peking also cited India's willingness to supply three thousand troops for Congo U.N. duty as evidence that Indian soldiers were used as "policemen for U.S. imperialism."[11]

Communist China's charges against India have, of course, been intensified since 1959 and can to some extent be discounted as propaganda. But the consistency with which Peking has reviled India as an accomplice of "imperialism" and the media in which these charges have been printed strongly indicates that the Chinese government genuinely believes them. Peking will probably continue to consider India part of the "imperialist" camp regardless of expedient or even strategic collaboration with the USSR, and shape China's policies and actions accordingly. China's leaders reason (not

* King Faisal of Iraq was assassinated on July 14, 1958 by a military junta led by Abdul Karim Qassem.

illogically, considering the assumptions with which they begin) that, in the interest of security and in support of a fundamentalist doctrine which permits no midground between Communism and capitalism, the disguise of non-alignment must be destroyed. By humiliating India—the leading practitioner of non-alignment—the validity of this doctrine is subjected to doubt.

Another basic motive underlying Communist China's actions is the quest for world power. Chou En-lai made it clear that "China's views must be heard in any settlement of any major international issue."[12] China's first objective in the pursuit of its destiny is to become undisputed leader of Asia. This requires the besting and eventual elimination of its prime rivals—the USSR, the U.S.A., and India—as power rivals in Asia. It is not surprising that Khrushchev, Kennedy and Nehru were once publicly branded as China's principal enemies.[13] Because of the obvious power superiority of the USSR, China can best compete against this rival on the ideological battleground by trying to capture Communist leadership among Asian nations. The U.S. can be attacked through its Asian friends and allies. But it is India which represents simultaneously a rival to China of major proportions and a very vulnerable target of opportunity.

India and China stand for two fundamentally opposed systems of government guided by radically different political and economic philosophies. They have sought separate roads to progress and prosperity. Both have been conscious that other newly independent nations of Asia have been watching them closely to determine which has the better system to emulate. Since the Bandung Conference of Afro-Asian nations in 1955, the Indian government has recognized Communist China's ambition to dominate Asia, while Peking has seen in India a competitor for Asia's soul, if not its body. In this spirit the Chinese Communist Party's official organ, *Jen Min Jih Pao*, accused Nehru of trying to control the economies of countries around India and insisting on "absolute obedience from them."[14]

Peking has been conscious that at stake was ideological leadership of international Communism as well as its ability to win the still uncommitted nations of Asia and Africa. India has realized that a failure of its democratic system could not only spell national catastrophe, but would deprive the Asian-African world of a prototype for workable democracy in underdeveloped countries. India had proved by its third general election held in February 1962 that democracy was still a success. Red China, by contrast, was still recovering from the folly of its "great leap" effort to industrialize too rapidly and collectivize too radically. From 1959 to 1962 serious food shortages, which sent thousands of Chinese fleeing to Hong Kong, also gave evidence that Communist planning was far from infallible. A restoration of limited private incentive for farmers in 1960–1961 was proof that pure Communism would not work. Furthermore, the purges of 1958, which followed Mao Tse-tung's shortlived political liberalization, gave testimony that Communism and individual freedom were incompatible.

Finding itself faltering in the race with India and recognizing that there existed much dissatisfaction within China, Peking found it tempting to take action which would both distract the Chinese people and impede India's progress. And recognizing the ideological appeal of co-existence, Peking must also have seen merit in action calculated to discredit the "Pied Piper" of *Panch Sheela.* The invasion of India forced New Delhi to devote a much larger proportion of its already inadequate resources to military defense needs and thus has impeded economic progress. It has also provoked India to seek large-scale military cooperation and assistance, thereby compromising *Panch Sheela.*

Peking's Indian policy, characterized by an attitude of hostility and aggression, is a logical corollary to its Tibet and Himalayan policies. These policies are all strongly motivated by strategic considerations which flow from Peking's assumption that India is fundamentally in the "imperialist" camp, however willing it may be to arrange pacts with the Soviet Union or pretend non-alignment. First, the Tibetan plateau had to be made secure. Efforts by the Dalai Lama in 1956 to seek Indian assistance against China and the Lhasa revolt in 1959 proved to Peking that China could not rule Tibet indirectly through its indigenous theocracy. It had to be controlled through military force and Han-controlled civil administration. By December 1964 even the puppet Panchen Lama was denounced and stripped of power to make way in September 1965 for a purely lay regime under quisling, Ngapo Ngawang Jigme, in a newly created Tibet Autonomous Region of China.

Tibet's culture and religion—both incompatible with Communism and hostile to the Han—had to be eradicated, and an environment had to be created which would encourage large-scale Chinese settlement in the arable parts of the high plateau. This would not only help alleviate population pressures in mainland China but would contribute to making Tibet a more reliable strategic barrier against both the "imperialist" world and the Soviet Union, which Peking believes is edging closer to Western "imperialists."

India, which China accused of aiding Tibetan insurgents, has been made painfully aware of the seriousness with which Peking views its Himalayan security. While the 1959 Tibet revolt precipitated Peking's decision to press more strongly its boundary claims against India, China's determination to reach a settlement on its own terms and thus to fulfill its minimum security requirements has been a constant factor underlying its Tibet and Himalayan policy. To facilitate control, Peking pressed to early completion a road network linking Lhasa and China. From Lhasa roads have been built southward to Yatung near the Sikkim frontier and westward to Gartok and Rudok near the Ladakh frontier. The Gartok road is met by a road leading into western Tibet from Kashgar and Yehcheng in Chinese Sinkiang. It is the latter road—secretly constructed on Indian territory in the Aksai Chin region—which provides the most important strategic reason behind China's boundary dispute with India.

Western Tibet could be made secure only if Chinese military forces and supplies could quickly reach the area by road. Because of the terrain the only feasible western route from China is through Aksai Chin. Therefore, Peking built the since-disputed road and established military outposts along it before agreeing to negotiate the ownership of the area. India was thus presented with a *fait accompli.* China did not want to take the chance that India would interfere with the road's construction; nor would Peking accept agreement with India which denied to China this vital link.

In January 1959—more than two months before the Lhasa uprising—Chou En-lai wrote Nehru on the boundary problem and hinted that China might accept the McMahon Line in return for a clear title to Aksai Chin.[15] Peking continued to suggest this sort of settlement after the March 1959 crisis. In correspondence leading up to Chou En-lai's meeting with Nehru in April 1960, the Chinese left the door open for such an agreement, but India was in no mood to negotiate a compromise. If Peking wanted a settlement, stronger persuasion was clearly necessary, and it is likely that China's invasion of India was intended to provide such persuasion.

Judging by Chinese cease-fire proposals—first on October 24, 1962 when the fighting was at its strongest and again on November 8—Peking was mainly concerned with securing its claim to Aksai Chin, not with pressing its claims south of the McMahon Line. The cease-fire proposal, which China finally carried out unilaterally after its sudden withdrawal on November 21, 1962, called for a no-man's-land twelve and a half miles on each side of what China claimed was the actual line of control on November 7, 1959. The fact that this line runs along the Indian-claimed McMahon Line in the east and along the boundary line which China claims in the Ladakh sector certainly suggests that the latter boundary, including the Aksai Chin road, was China's main concern.

However much Peking may have been and may still be willing to bargain away its claims south of the McMahon Line, it has clearly discernible intentions to project its influence beyond the Himalayan watershed by other means. To protect the Tibetan highlands, China believes it must gain enough control of the border states—Nepal, Sikkim and Bhutan—to eliminate all Indian political influence and create Chinese-controlled buffer zones. Just as Imperial Britain believed that it needed Tibet as a buffer zone for India, China believes it needs the Himalayan border states as buffers for Tibet. For the time being, Peking's techniques will probably be political, diplomatic and subversive, but military action can be mounted at any time if necessary as shown by Peking's threat to attack India border installations in Sikkim in September 1965. China's policies toward the border states to date are clearly aggressive and suggest only too clearly the nature of things to come.

China has excused its acts of hostility toward India on grounds of self-defense; India has consistently been portrayed as the aggressor. Peking, for example, alleges that it was India which attacked China in October 1962 and thus provoked the military action which followed.[16] This is, of course, spurious reasoning since India was seeking to regain what it considered its own territory. But it is likely that Peking was genuinely concerned by India's "forward" policy along the border and could reason that New Delhi would eventually attempt to retake territory which Chinese forces had occupied. The Indian army had, in fact, made several moves in Ladakh to outflank Chinese positions, so Peking was faced with the necessity to defend its newly occupied border outposts one by one. Rather than be forced into a defensive position to protect its posts from piecemeal Indian army operations launched on Indian terms, it made military sense for the Chinese army to mount a general offensive on its own terms along the entire border. Only after decisive defeat would the Indian army abandon its offensive posture along the border and return to a purely defensive stance.

However justified India's actions may have been, it is clear that a mistake had been made in attempting to regain lost boundary positions without adequate military means to do so. But to conclude that India started it all and that Communist China was justified in defending itself is to fall victim to Peking's propaganda. China's October attack was designed to put an end to Indian hopes that it could find a solution to the boundary problem through military action and to force India to negotiate the boundary on China's terms.

At stake in Communist China's ideological war with the Soviet Union is the content of Communist doctrine and the leadership of the Communist world. For that reason China's actions must be analyzed in the context of this struggle. The core of Peking's ideological dispute is the doctrine of "peaceful co-existence." Lenin, who originally formulated the doctrine, said that it is possible for the socialist countries to practice peaceful co-existence with the capitalist countries. Peking has accused Moscow of subordinating the Marxist doctrine of revolution to an unrecognizable exaggeration of Lenin's thesis and treating it "as if it were an all-inclusive mystical book from heaven."*[17] In its policy toward India, and particularly in its hostile actions, China has acted out its contempt for peaceful co-existence.

Peking provided early doctrinal justification for its actions in its December 31, 1962 attack against "revisionism." Although addressed to Comrade Togliatti, Italian Communist leader who had upheld the Soviet position at the 10th Congress of the Italian Communist Party, the attack was of course directed at Khrushchev. Peking criticized the attitude of "some self-styled Marxist-Leninists who invariably make the false charge that China started the clashes on the border." In the attack it was asked, "Is it possible that the only way that China could prove itself 'reasonable' and not 'absurd' was to submit to the unreasonable demands and the armed attacks of

* Peking's reference to "heaven" is curiously un-Marxist. It is tempting to theorize that it reveals the lasting power of the historical concept of the "mandate from heaven" which successful Chinese dynasties were believed to have received.

the Indian reactionary clique?" Peking's theoreticians charged that "the position taken by Comrade Togliatti and certain other comrades [meaning, of course, Khrushchev] on the Sino-Indian boundary question reflects their point of view on peaceful co-existence which is that, in carrying out this policy, the Socialist countries should make one concession after another to the capitalist countries —should not fight even in self-defense when subjected to armed attacks, but should surrender their territorial sovereignty."[18] Peking later asserted that peaceful co-existence can "never be described as the main content of the transition from Capitalism to Socialism," adding that "India is within the imperialist camp and it is doctrinally natural and desirable that China's relationships with India be marked by struggle."[19]

The invasion of India placed the Soviet Union in a position of having to choose between loyalty to its doctrine of peaceful co-existence and solidarity with China. That Moscow chose the former is a measure of the importance which it places on its doctrine and the need to meet rather than avoid the challenge posed by the Chinese. The keynote of the Soviet attitude was enunciated as early as January 15, 1963 by East German Communist leader Walter Ulbricht. Standing next to Khrushchev during the opening ceremony of the East German 6th Party Congress, Ulbricht made the first public disclosure that China invaded India without informing any fraternal Communist government. He castigated Peking for not abiding by the principle of settlement through negotiations which is a basic tenet of peaceful co-existence.

There is one theory that China's attack on India was calculated to force the Soviet Union to repudiate peaceful co-existence and abandon its neutral stance in the Sino-Indian dispute. Whatever merits this theory has, the attack did not accomplish either objective. In fact, Khrushchev pointedly chose the moment when a Chinese delegation, headed by Teng Hsiao-peng, was quitting Moscow in July 1963, following its unsuccessful mission to patch up the ideological split, to say that the Soviet Union and India stood "side by side" on the "problem of securing peace."[20] It is probably not true that China's India action was designed to cause the Soviet Union to abandon peaceful co-existence or its neutral posture on the Sino-Indian boundary dispute; Peking must have known that this was not possible. It is more likely that China pursued this policy disdainful of Soviet opposition and with the intention of pointing up Soviet weakness. By equating Moscow's Indian policy with the withdrawal of Soviet missiles from Cuba, China clearly meant to brand both acts as examples of cowardice in the face of imperialist-capitalist provocation.

China's invasion of India as a means of pressing its territorial claims must also have been intended as a warning to the Soviet Union, with which China also shares a long, disputed frontier. The point that China was willing to go to war in order to retake irredentist land could not have been lost on Moscow. Soviet-provoked uprisings in Sinkiang could have been intended simply to force China to withdraw from India, but they could also have served the defensive purpose of preventing similar Chinese moves into Soviet territory adjacent to Sinkiang.

Peking pursues a belligerent policy because, in the words of its leaders, "there is no historical precedent for peaceful transition from capitalism to socialism—the old government never topples unless it is pushed." China seeks to foment and lead the revolution in the Afro-Asian world. It brands as bourgeois "illusion" the hope that there can be a world without weapons, without armed forces and without wars. Peking seeks not only to pit class against class, the colonized against the colonizer but race against race. The Chinese are dedicated to propagating an ideology of world revolution in which war remains an acceptable instrument. With the power of this ideology, with a nuclear capability and with a vast population which can absorb the mass annihilation of nuclear warfare, Communist China has set forth militantly to dominate the world. Recoiling at the scope and danger of Peking's ambition, the Communist Party of the Soviet Union has stated that it "cannot share the views of the Chinese leadership about the creation of a thousand times higher civilization 'on the corpses of hundreds of millions of people.' "[21] And the Soviet Party—once mentor and idol of the Chinese Party—sees a betrayal of the teachings of Marx and Lenin in China's propagating racist slogans "deprived of class meaning."[22] "The wind from the East prevails over the wind from the West," claims China. This is a strange deviation from "Workers of the world, unite." But it is consistent with the eternal struggle of Han versus "barbarian" which has characterized Chinese history and Chinese psychology. Communist China's foreign policy, an amalgam of Marxist fundamentalism and Han nationalism, is committed to a strategy of "hostile co-existence."

India has already felt the effects of this strategic concept. But, because history has seen fit to make India the battleground for a three-way ideological war between Western Democracy, Soviet Communism—characterized by competitive co-existence—and Mao-Marxist hostile co-existence, India will inevitably find itself continuously involved in a struggle more complex than the East-West cold war which it has so carefully sought to avoid.

CHAPTER 16

PAKISTAN: INDIA'S TROUBLESOME FLANK

In event of war with India, Pakistan would not be alone. Pakistan would be helped by the most powerful nation in Asia. . . .

Pakistan Foreign Minister, Zulfikar Ali Bhutto, in the Pakistan National Assembly, July 17, 1963

The Chronicle of Kings, an early Sanskrit history discovered by Akbar the Great when he invaded Srinagar in 1588, alleged that Kashmir in the beginning was a great lake ringed by towering mountains. This mythological saga credits Kasyapa, grandson of the Hindu God Brahma, with creating the rich valley by trenching Baramulla Pass so that the waters of the lake flowed into the sea. Kasyapa thus provided his descendants with a sanctuary of indescribable splendor. The conquering Moghuls in more recent times also saw the Vale as a place of inspiring beauty and called it *Behesht*, or paradise.

Pandit Jawaharlal Nehru, an eminent descendant of Brahma's chosen people of Kashmir, was once moved to compare his ancestral homeland to "some supremely beautiful woman whose beauty is almost impersonal and above human desire."[1] Unfortunately, Kashmir has not been above human desire. Its tragic history since the partition of the subcontinent has been scarred by the conflicting desires of Indians, Pakistanis and the Kashmiri people themselves. Since the Hindu Maharajah of the predominantly Moslem state hastily joined his realm to India in 1948 rather than see it overrun by Moslem tribesmen from Pakistan, the trials of this paradise on earth have frequently threatened the peace of the subcontinent.

India's defense of Kashmir against Moslem marauders brought on open warfare with Pakistan. The fighting, which the two newly born nations could ill afford, was finally stopped toward the end of 1948 by a cease-fire agreement negotiated through the United Nations. While most of Kashmir, including the coveted Vale and the capital of Srinagar, remained on the Indian side of the cease-fire line, both antagonists accepted a U.N. proposal for a plebiscite to determine the state's permanent status. Since then this troubled state has remained divided, with heavy concentrations of troops on both sides, facing each other in a state of perpetual alert. An uneasy truce, monitored by U.N. observers, has all too often been broken by premeditated fire.

Repeated efforts to bring India and Pakistan to the conference table have brought the Kashmir dispute no closer to solution. India has used the intervening years to solidify its position, while Pakistan has sought unsuccessfully to have the U.N. plebescite resolution fairly implemented. New Delhi's reluctance to hold a plebescite has been based on the fear that the Moslem majority would choose Pakistan. This fear became even more pronounced in February 1954, when Pakistan accepted U.S. military assistance—ostensible, at least, to defend itself against Communist aggression. Recognizing the danger of a strengthened Pakistan astride India's northern passes, New Delhi backed off from its plebescite commitment. Coinciding with Pakistan's acceptance of U.S. military assistance, the Indian-influenced Kashmir Constituent Assembly ratified without reference to Pakistan the state's original accession to India.

China's 1962 invasion of Ladakh in Eastern Kashmir was a dramatic reminder that the India-Pakistan dispute over Kashmir was inexorably connected with the India-China boundary dispute. The situation has been further complicated by Chinese-Soviet tensions, symptoms of which are the opposite positions on Kashmir taken by the two Communist nations.

Moscow's motive at that time in backing India's position on Kashmir is understandable; no less so was Peking's decision to take Pakistan's side. The Soviet initiative was a predictable reaction against Pakistan's affiliation with Western-inspired defense pacts, particularly the Central Treaty Organization, aimed specifically at the USSR. While Red China had been similarly incensed by Pakistan's affiliation with the Southeast Asia Treaty Organization, it became apparent that the threat was more theoretical than real.

Peking in its paranoia found more ominous a bourgeois India which, it was convinced, served as front for Western "imperialism" in Asia.

In the long term it is probably the Soviet Union which China considers its main antagonist. However serious doctrinal differences may be, it is the deep-rooted tensions in the borderlands where these two land giants meet that will most likely ignite conflict one day. China must thus fear linkage between the USSR and India in the Pamirs, as this would dangerously flank both Sinkiang and Tibet. Since China must therefore prevent Soviet-India physical contiguity, it has been in Peking's interest to recognize Pakistan's right to claim and occupy northern Kashmir. Of specific importance is the frontier strip which runs for about two hundred miles in a northwesterly direction from the Karakorum Pass through the principality of Gilgit to the trijunction of Sinkiang, Pakistan and Afghanistan.

Gilgit had been awarded to the Maharajah of Kashmir by the British Indian government shortly before the partition of the subcontinent into independent India and Pakistan. Being part of the Maharajah's domain, Gilgit also became involved in the contest between the two countries for control of Kashmir. While the Hindu Maharajah elected to join India at the time of partition, Moslem Gilgit, seized by local military forces, elected to join Pakistan. The rulers of Hunza and Nagir—two princely states within the Gilgit Agency (to use the British administrative term) near the Sinkiang border—were in no position to protest accession to Pakistan and so also came under Karachi's control. Since then Pakistan has directly administered the former Gilgit Agency area rather than join it to the Azad Kashmir puppet regime created to administer the rest of Pakistan-held Kashmir.

Armed Chinese patrols raided into Hunza as early as 1954, probably to discourage herdsmen from grazing on Chinese-claimed land west of the Shimshal Pass on the ill-defined Sinkiang side of the border. The controversy, which became acute in 1955, was settled for the moment by local negotiations; but these incidents served to remind Karachi that the boundary could be a source of continuing friction with China.

Boundary ambiguity west of the Karakorum Pass became of more concern to the Pakistan government following the 1959 Tibet crisis when China began pressing its territorial claims against India and occupying many of the areas in dispute. Karachi requested the

U.N. Security Council—still officially concerned with the Kashmir problem—to prevent India and Communist China from dividing Kashmir at Pakistan's expense. India's reaction to this was predictably sharp. A spokesman for the External Affairs Ministry in New Delhi expressed astonishment that "Pakistan should use India's border troubles with China to press a claim based on its own aggression in Kashmir."[2]

By 1961 the shoe was on the other foot; it was Pakistan which declared its intention to negotiate a boundary with China in disputed Kashmir. Less than a month after India and China had concluded their unsuccessful border talks, Pakistan Foreign Minister Qadir announced that Peking was willing in principle to have its "border" with Pakistan demarcated. Pakistan was, of course, quick to see the advantages of reaching boundary agreement in Kashmir since this would simultaneously eliminate a source of potential friction with China and, from a political point of view, counterbalance Soviet sympathy with India on the Kashmir issue.

China's underlying concern was a strategic one, but a boundary agreement with Pakistan must also have seemed useful to underscore India's obduracy in not being similarly willing to negotiate. And, insofar as Peking's willingness to negotiate with Pakistan implied rejection of the Indian position on Kashmir, there may have been an element of spite and retaliation in China's action. Still, it was more than a year until actual negotiations began, and it is likely that Peking wanted as much time as possible to exert pressure on India. Only when it was clear that New Delhi would not give in and was in fact building up its military forces in Ladakh, did China proceed to negotiate.

Nehru must have been incensed. He could recall Peking's reluctance to discuss that section of the boundary during the 1960 Sino-Indian boundary discussions. The Chinese representative had then stated that it was not appropriate for the officials of the two countries to discuss the boundary alignment west of the Karakorum Pass. Certainly, if this refusal in 1960 made China seem to prefer Pakistan's side of the Kashmir dispute, Peking's decision to demarcate the boundary with Pakistan removed any doubt about it. But by championing Pakistan, China placed itself in direct opposition to the Soviet Union, which then sided with India in the Kashmir dispute.

From 1948 until 1952 the Soviet Union had abstained from voting on any of the several Kashmir resolutions introduced at the U.N. and had not taken part in the debates. But in January 1952 Soviet United Nations delegate Malik adopted new tactics and launched a scathing attack against the United States and the United Kingdom, accusing both of interfering in the Kashmir settlement and seeking to convert the region into a military base. In 1955 Premier Khrushchev unequivocally enunciated Soviet policy on Kashmir when he stated: "The Kashmir question has already been settled by the people of Kashmir; they regard themselves as being an integral part of the Republic of India. . . . The Soviet Government supports India's policy on the Kashmir question."[3]

A readily apparent explanation of the Soviet switch of position on Kashmir from one of strict neutrality to unequivocal support of India's case can be found in Moscow's reaction to U.S. military aid to Pakistan and all this implied in the context of CENTO. A less obvious but perhaps more important reason behind Moscow's action was Chinese Communist boundary policy, which began to emerge in 1954 with Peking's publication of new maps, the first maps to be issued by the Communist regime. Russia, whose border with China was questioned in these maps, could find common complaint with India.

The 1954 Chinese maps, showing certain areas of Soviet Asia as Chinese territory and describing part of the boundary as still "indefinite," sounded a sour note in Sino-Soviet relations. Just as New Delhi reacted strongly to Peking's maps claiming Indian border territory, so did Moscow complain about Chinese claims against the USSR. In his meeting with Nehru in October 1954, Chou En-lai made passing reference to "errors" on Chinese maps depicting not only India's boundary with China but that of the Soviet Union. He dismissed them as "pre-liberation" maps. But, as subsequent events have shown, Red China was deadly serious in its territorial claims and aspirations and it is unlikely that Khrushchev was put off by Mao as easily as Nehru was.

The offending maps, which first appeared in a new Chinese history book, show China's boundaries as they were claimed by China in 1840. The accompanying text cites nineteen cases of territorial loss by China because of "imperialist conquests." Peking claims, for example, that czarist military action in 1864 culminating in the Treaty of Tarbagatai deprived China of a large area extending up to Lake Balkhash and including the Altai Mountains as well as part of the Pamirs. The 1954 maps incorporate within China parts of Hunza, Gilgit and Ladakh as well as Indian border territory which Peking believes British "imperialist" treaties took away from China. By this reasoning it follows that the Soviet Union is placed by China in precisely the same aggressor category as India and is similarly linked with "forces of imperialism."

Chinese-Pakistan relations had become badly strained during the Suhrawardy government, essentially as a result of Karachi's close ties with Washington. The Pakistan Prime Minister's visit to the United States in 1957 ended on a strong anti-Communist note with a joint communiqué accusing international Communism of posing a "major threat to the security of the free world." This was typical of the Pakistani official attitude, which lasted through the Lhasa uprising and flight of the Dalai Lama in the spring of 1959. President Ayub Khan's proposal of a joint defense policy with India in April 1959 was perhaps the low point in China-Pakistan relations. But the very events which prompted Ayub's offer had set in motion a very basic shift of attitudes in South Asia which would bring Pakistan and China closer to each other.

India's trials with China, which then took the form of more frequent and more serious border clashes, brought a correspondingly closer relationship between the United States and India. This, in turn, excited Pakistani suspicions that U.S. policy in South Asia was veering away from reliance on SEATO to contain the Communist threat to South Asia and turning toward India as a new ally against China. As a result Pakistan began gradually to re-evaluate its policy toward the U.S. and seek closer ties with Peking. Following Secretary of State Dulles' death in the summer of 1959, it was particularly tempting for Pakistanis to leap to the conclusion that SEATO would wither away without the personal patronage of its architect. Certainly the Laotian crisis in 1961 did nothing to reassure the Pakistanis that SEATO would continue to be a vital deterrent to Communist pressures.

On May 3, 1962 it was officially announced in Pakistan that agreement had been reached to begin negotiations toward a demarcation of the border between Chinese Sinkiang and the "contiguous areas, the defense of which is under the actual control of Pakistan."[4] The authoritative Karachi newspaper *Dawn* editorialized pointedly that "China has already concluded border agreements with Burma and Nepal and would, no doubt, have been able to do so with India as well, but the response from the Indian side was anything but friendly." *Dawn* added acidly: "Instead of agreeing to negotiate in the spirit of the so-called *Panch Sheela*, Nehru chose the militant path. By playing up the Chinese bogey, Mr. Nehru may have made sure of a couple of billion dollars in aid, but he has created dangerous tensions."[5] Peking accused India of "wantonly slandering and intimidating" China and "seeking to sow discord in relations between her and Pakistan." A Chinese note asked: "When did the Chinese Government accept without reservation the position that Kashmir is under Indian sovereignty?"[6]

The venom created by the Kashmir dispute could be sensed in October 1962 when large numbers of politically acute Pakistanis applauded China's attack on India. While the government of Pakistan carefully avoided any action which could be considered hostile by India, the average Pakistani was less charitable; there were many voices urging Ayub to exploit India's anguish and settle accounts in Kashmir.

Both countries agreed in late November 1962 to try once again to reach a settlement on Kashmir; but it soon became apparent that the exhortations of the United States and the United Kingdom, rather than recognition of mutual self-interest, was behind the new effort. Something less than a sincere determination to reach accord was shown by the Pakistan government when it permitted Peking to announce the Sinkiang-Azad Kashmir boundary agreement just as Kashmir talks were being held with India. Nehru's dismay turned to fury when Pakistan's Foreign Minister, Zulfikar Ali Bhutto, flew to Peking on March 2 to sign the border agreement and be feted with calculated cordiality.

Pakistan was not interested in finding a compromise solution on Kashmir so long as the U.S. and the U.K. armed India. No amount of logic or reason could convince the Pakistanis that India genuinely needed a greatly increased defense machine to withstand Chinese pressures. Foreign Minister Bhutto, while addressing Parliament on July 17, 1963, stated flatly that India was not augmenting its military strength because of China but because it sought to threaten Pakistan. He cautioned that the Kashmir dispute could be solved only if Western powers made settlement of it a condition for giving arms to India.

In the same speech Bhutto stimulated suspicions that Pakistan had reached some sort of formal defense understanding with Peking when he warned that an attack on Pakistan by India would involve the "largest State in Asia."[7] New Delhi's concern on this score deepened in February 1964, when Chou En-lai said in a speech delivered while visiting Rawalpindi, Pakistan's new capital city: "The continuous development of friendly cooperation between our countries is not only in the interests of the people of China and Pakistan, but also conducive to the defense of peace in Asia and the world."[8] Timed to coincide with Chou's state visit to Pakistan was Peking's endorsement of Rawalpindi's demand that a plebescite be held in Kashmir.[9] Ayub thus succeeded in extracting from Chou, for the first time, unequivocal and explicit support for Pakistan's position on Kashmir. Heretofore, Peking, while clearly sympathetic to Pakistan, had remained technically correct in insisting that the Kashmir problem be mutually settled by India and Pakistan. Chou En-lai, in return, secured Pakistan's support for a second Bandung conference. Pakistan, like China, had been excluded from the Belgrade non-aligned nations meeting in which India and Yugoslavia played the leading roles. Thus, it was not difficult for Ayub to follow Chou's path toward a new Bandung.

In December 1963 a sacred Moslem relic—a single strand of the Prophet Mohammed's hair—was stolen from a mosque in Srinagar. This touched off anti-Indian riots in Kashmir's capital, which soon incited similar communal disturbances in India and Pakistan. New Delhi's deep concern that communal unrest might jeopardize India's hold on Kashmir became obvious in April 1964 when Kashmir's nationalist hero and onetime leader, Sheikh Abdullah, was released from long Indian detention. It was hoped that this gesture would appease the aroused Kashmiri Moslems.

Hopes for a settlement rose slightly when Nehru agreed to meet once again with Ayub Khan. But the Indian Prime Minister's death in May changed the equation. There were many who felt that settlement would be easier with Nehru's passing since it was commonly believed that the Prime Minister's emotional attachment to the land of his ancestors had aggravated the problem. But despite initial optimism, it soon became evident that his successor, Lal Bahadur Shastri, could not control Indian extremists, who forced through several constitutional moves which tied Kashmir all the more closely to India. In December 1964, for example, India proclaimed Kashmir to be an integral part of the Indian state.

Sheikh Abdullah went to Pakistan after his release and predictably appealed publicly for Kashmiri self-determination. Adding to New Delhi's uneasiness was a meeting in March 1965 between Sheikh Abdullah and Chou En-lai in Algiers. The Chinese Premier promised the Kashmir leader his support and invited him to Peking. For his short-lived adventures abroad Sheikh Abdullah was again taken into custody when he returned to Kashmir in May. His detention in South India set off angry demonstrations in Srinagar which served once again to remind India that the feelings of the Kashmiris themselves had to be taken into consideration before a lasting solution could be found. It also provided a cue for Pakistan's Foreign Minister to rattle the saber. On May 9 Bhutto threatened that his country would have to put an end to India's "neo-colonialist usurpation and tyranny."

Bhutto's remark had added significance in view of the serious fighting which had broken out in April between Indian and Pakistani forces in the long-disputed border area known as the Rann of Kutch. This region is a marshy flat on the coast of the Arabian Sea, through which the India-Pakistan border runs. Rawalpindi disputed India's contention that the border line should follow the northern rim of the periodically flooded marshland and believed instead that it should run through the middle. Fighting began when Pakistan tried to fortify Kanjarkot, which India considered to be on its side of the line. Because of the intrinsic unimportance of the Rann, the skirmishes were more a symptom than a cause of tensions. They were symptomatic of the heightened hostility felt by New Delhi since Pakistan and China first began their *rapprochement*.

The Kutch episode, while minor in terms of the military forces committed to it, was of considerable significance to New Delhi. Before the Kutch hostilities India's leaders had been extremely uneasy and bitter about Pakistan's military establishment but had, at least, found some solace in Washington's assurances that U.S.-provided equipment would not be used against India. The Kutch incident, in which India captured U.S. equipment while overrunning Pakistani positions, proved to New Delhi's satisfaction that such guarantees could be difficult to enforce. The more militant faction of the Indian government could and did use the Kutch experience to support its position that Pakistan was an enemy with whom no peaceful accommodation was possible.

As both armies took each other's measure on the salt flats of Kutch, New Delhi and Rawalpindi edged closer to the showdown which somehow had been accepted as one day inevitable. Not until June was a cease-fire possible. By then tempers were raw, and a war psychology had gripped both peoples.

Sometime during the first week of August 1965—most probably August 5, when Indian patrols killed six Azad Kashmiris within Indian lines and found on them what New Delhi considered compromising literature and equipment—India became alert to a new threat from Pakistan. It was apparent that large numbers of armed Kashmiri Moslems from the Pakistan puppet state of Azad Kashmir were infiltrating the Vale. India claimed that they were an organized, irregular force under Pakistan army orders, and were instructed to perform sabotage and other acts of terrorism in Kashmir. Symptomatic of the rage among Indians when news of this development reached New Delhi was a massive demonstration before Parliament by over 200,000 followers of the right-wing Hindu *Jan Sangh* Party. The angry crowd demanded that Shastri take strong action in retaliation against Pakistan. The frustrations and hate of nearly two decades needed venting.

Pakistan's objective was at first ambiguous. Indians saw in the marauding Azad Kashmiris a guerrilla force intent upon harassing Indian authority in the Vale and inciting a Moslem uprising. An announcement by a clandestine radio calling itself the "Voice of Kashmir" described the formation of a Revolutionary Council to fight "Indian imperialism."[10] Recognizing that these broadcasts must come from Azad Kashmir, India found its fears reinforced. It was tempting to compare the new tactics in Kashmir with Mao's doctrine of guerrilla warfare and conclude that direct Peking influence was involved. This was not the case, but the increasingly close consultation between Rawalpindi and Peking must at least be credited with giving Pakistan greater self-confidence.

Pakistan's leaders may also have been influenced in their aggressive attitude by a growing *rapprochement* with the USSR. In April Ayub Khan had negotiated in Moscow three agreements concerning trade, economic cooperation and cultural exchanges. Rawalpindi wanted to regularize relations between the two countries as part of an evolving new policy of non-alignment. Moscow, for its part, wanted more flexibility in the complicated subcontinent situation than its close alignment with India had heretofore permitted. If the Soviet Union could reach an equilibrium in its relations with India and Pakistan, the latter would perhaps be less dependent on Red

China, and the threat of growing Chinese influence to its south could be averted. India realized this and found confirmation in Moscow's refusal to include any mention of Kashmir in the joint communiqué concluding Shastri's state visit to Moscow in May. Conversely, Ayub Khan, whose own visit to Moscow preceeded Shastri's, must have found this omission heartening. *Pravda*'s silence for three weeks on the new Kashmir crisis was interpreted by Rawalpindi as still another encouraging sign which gave rise to hopes that India could be isolated, not only from U.S. military support during the crisis, but from Russian as well.

Pravda's first words on the Kashmir fighting did not appear until August 24. Moscow's voice then struck a note of strict neutrality with an editorial by "Observer" which failed to condemn either side, pleading only for a "war to halt bloodshed."[11] Soon afterward it became clear that Moscow not only would remain neutral but would underscore its neutrality by offering to mediate the dispute in the Russian Central Asia city of Tashkent. This maneuver, calculated to provide Moscow with a stronger position in subcontinent affairs, helps to explain Peking's subsequent effort to keep the conflict alive. China could not afford to see the Soviet Union take honors as peacemaker and emerge as a stronger force in the subcontinent.

But first Peking had to look to its rear in Tibet. This was particularly important because of the continuing rebellion in Tibet. China's announcement on August 23, that Tibet had become an "autonomous region" meant, in fact, that the last vestiges of autonomy had been swept aside. Whatever trappings of home rule were permitted or even encouraged for sake of appearances, Peking would henceforward rule with an iron grip. The Preparatory Committee for the Tibet Autonomous Region, established nine years earlier with the Dalai Lama at its head, would no longer exist. More significantly, the Panchen Lama—long considered Peking's puppet—had been removed in December, marking the end of any pretence of theocratic power. In the future Peking's secular quisling, Ngapo Ngawang Jigme, would function as chairman of the new Tibet Autonomous Region.[12]

In the meantime guerrilla terrorism in Kashmir provoked Indian counteraction. The Cabinet, which began deliberations on August 8, expressed its decision five days later in a grave announcement by Prime Minister Shastri that "force would be met by force." The first

Indian move was to seize two Pakistan outposts near Kargil—the point north of Srinagar where the cease-fire line comes closest to the main route to Leh, capital of Ladakh. This secured the vital route to India's China front along the Ladakh-Tibet border. New Delhi, of course, dreaded the prospect of Chinese action in Ladakh which would draw Indian troops away from the Pakistan front. Even more serious would be a Chinese-Pakistan linkup in the region of the Karakorum Pass, crushing India's Kashmir forces in a pincer.

On August 25 Indian troops captured additional Pakistan posts in the Tithwal area, then probed across the cease-fire line between Uri and Poonch. The next move was Pakistan's; an infantry brigade with tank support struck toward Chhamb near the important city of Jammu on September 1. Pakistan abandoned any pretense that only Azad Kashmir irregulars were engaged and admitted that the Pakistan regular army intended to take Akhnur just north of Jammu and thereby cut India's vital supply line to Srinagar. By this time Pakistan's objective was clear—the military seizure and retention of Kashmir. The war spilled over into the Punjab plain when India launched offensives aimed at Lahore and Sialkot. Aircraft was being used by both sides in support of troops, and scare flights ranged deep into both Indian and Pakistan territory.

The presence of Chinese Foreign Minister Chen Yi in Pakistan at this time gave a third dimension to the drama as seen from New Delhi. Long talks with Pakistan's leaders concluded with a chilling statement by Chen that China supported the "just action" taken to repel "armed Indian aggression."[13] Red China now began to play its hand. On September 7 Peking described Indian action as "naked aggression," which constituted a "grave threat to peace in this part of Asia." The announcement added that "India's aggression against any of its neighbors concerns all of its neighbors," and warned against a "chain of consequences" which could follow. Peking also denounced efforts being made in the United Nations to bring peace, referring to the world forum as "a tool of U.S. imperialism."[14]

A backdrop to China's political maneuvers was a sweeping doctrinal pronouncement issued September 3 by the Chief of Staff of Red China's armed forces. Speaking at a rally celebrating the twentieth anniversary of Japan's surrender, General Lo Jui-ching braced the Chinese people for a possible conflict with the U.S. arising out of hostilities in South Vietnam. Referring again to Southeast Asia, the General said, "U.S. imperialism has recently waved an olive branch but this can only be a deceptive trick."[15] While the fighting in Punjab and Kashmir was not specifically mentioned, General Lo Jui-ching's contempt for U.S. and Soviet peacemaking efforts was pertinent to South as well as Southeast Asia. He denounced "Khrushchev revisionists" for collaborating with the United States and predicted that the Soviet leaders "will be swept like dust from the stage of history by the mighty broom of the revolutionary people."[16]

September 8 brought Peking's next card. India was accused of "military aggression and provocation" along the Chinese-Indian border. While Pakistan's Ambassador to Peking, Mohammed Raza, met with China's President Liu Shao-chi in Peking to discuss "the question of India's aggression against Pakistan," the Chinese government delivered a formal note to India demanding withdrawal of Indian troops from contested posts on the Sikkim border. India was also accused of violating China's borders in July and August in conjunction with "aggression" against Pakistan.

In keeping with its technique of speaking through surrogates, Peking used Indonesia to make more explicit its own motives in entering the India-Pakistan crisis. Following Indonesia's announcement on September 8 that it would send military assistance to Pakistan, D. N. Aidit, Chairman of the Indonesian Communist Party, said that help to Pakistan meant opposition to U.S. "imperialism." He explained: "For two years Peking has sought to draw Pakistan away from its alliances with the Western powers—as the U.S. and Britain have refused to abandon their friendship with India, the Chinese have seen an opportunity in the Kashmir dispute to attain their objective." Aidit added significantly that Peking also hoped to win Pakistan's endorsement of its claim to Aksai Chin in Ladakh. The Communist spokesman then warned, "Chinese Communist troops could easily deal a swift blow to India or at least create enough problems along the border to divert Indian forces from their campaign against Pakistan."[17]

Peking's specific choice of the Sikkim border to protest Indian military installations is not without significance. If China intended an invasion of India in support of Pakistan, an attack at this point would permit Red troops to link up with Pakistan forces in East Pakistan and cut off Assam and the Northeast Frontier Agency from the rest of India. Such a move would also make less tempting an Indian invasion of lightly guarded East Pakistan.

It is difficult to determine the extent to which Peking's bellicosity served to encourage Pakistan at first to respond negatively to the U.N.'s call for a cease-fire agreement. Secretary-General U Thant, who made a flying visit to the subcontinent, received Shastri's promise to order a cease-fire providing Pakistan would also agree. But he was not able to move Ayub Khan, who insisted that a cease-fire be contingent upon a solution to the Kashmir problem by a plebiscite as originally called for by the U.N. in 1948.

The United States viewed Red China's intervention in the South Asian conflict with deep concern. Secretary of State Dean Rusk publicly warned Peking on September 13. An even stronger warning may have been made privately by Ambassador Cabot on September 15, when he met with Chinese Ambassador Wang Kuo-chaun in Warsaw.[18] The Soviet Union too is presumed to have exerted pressure on China to stay out of the affair, although Moscow probably found its common stand with the U.S. on the side of peace an embarrassment in its uneasy relationship with Peking.

China would not easily be deterred from its course, which was obviously calculated to keep South Asian tensions raw. On September 16 Peking delivered an ultimatum to India demanding that certain border posts be dismantled within seventy-two hours on penalty of "grave consequences." Red troops massed at several frontier points, giving substance to the ultimatum. Shastri reported to a worried Parliament that he had no hesitation in agreeing with China's demand that India destroy all its fortifications on Tibetan soil since, in fact, there were none. Hoping that some concession would provide China with a face-saving avenue of diplomatic retreat, he also announced India's agreement to a long-standing Chinese proposal (one, however, not repeated in the ultimatum) for joint inspection of Indian installations along the border.

The need for a cease-fire—now even more urgent because of China's ultimatum—provoked U Thant to propose that the Security Council threaten immediate economic and military reprisals against the combatants. New Delhi simultaneously appealed to the United States, Britain and the Soviet Union for urgent aid against aggression by China. Based on its experience in 1962 when the U.S. rushed to India's assistance in the face of Chinese aggression, New Delhi could hope that Washington would now lift its arms embargo. India may also have hoped that U.S. air power would retaliate against Chinese bases in Tibet if China launched a full-scale invasion.

The introduction of China into the South Asian crisis forced the USSR to edge cautiously away from its neutral stance toward support of India. The Indian Ambassador in Moscow saw both Prime Minister Kosygin and Foreign Minister Gromyko on September 18, and it is reasonable to suppose that the Russian leaders were asked to go beyond the Kremlin's September 13 indirect warning against "those whose inciting statements and policy help fan the conflict."[19] What additional pressure, if any, was exerted by Moscow was not made public, but Peking's shrill cry of protest could be heard loudly. The Chinese *People's Daily* asserted, "If there are people who are adding fuel to the flames of the Indo-Pakistan dispute, they are precisely the Soviet leaders in addition to the U.S. imperialists."[20] Repeating an old theme, Peking's official mouthpiece ranted, "Two of the three founders of Kennedy, Khrushchev and Nehru are dead and the third has fallen from power; their successors are trying hard to keep the failing concern going."[21]

Even as the crisis raced toward a climax there were hopeful signs of relief. Peking extended the deadline of its ultimatum for an additional three days and Pakistan requested a midnight session of the Security Council to hear a statement by Foreign Minister Bhutto, who was hurrying to New York by jet aircraft. Then on September 22 Peking announced that India had satisfactorily compiled with its demands. India had, in fact, taken no action whatsoever, but face was saved. Peking's retreat could only mean that Rawalpindi had already reached the decision to meet U.N. cease-fire terms and did not want a Chinese move against India which, in all likelihood, would provoke large-scale U.S. military assistance to New Delhi.

Pakistan's Foreign Minister announced in a tense pre-dawn session of the Security Council that Pakistan accepted the Council's terms for halting the fighting. President Ayub went on the air to describe the U.N. cease-fire order as "inadequate and unsatisfactory"[22] because it did not include a specific solution for the Kashmir problem; but he announced that in the interests of peace he had accepted it. Another threat to peace was, for the moment, averted; but for how long? The fever of crisis had broken, but the virus was still alive.

Both India and Pakistan had been losers in a senseless war. Men had died and quantities of costly war machinery had been expended for no gain. The acceptance of a cease-fire surely gave Pakistani extremists an excuse to attack Ayub Khan. Shastri too had to face the ire of jingoists who would have had India "fight to the end."

China, however, by its own act of intervention emerged the greatest loser from the September war. Its exhibition of belligerency before an Afro-Asian world tired and afraid of war further tarnished its image and prejudiced certain of its important objectives. China's loss of face was a major reason for its backing out of the "Bandung II" Conference of Afro-Asian Nations which had been rescheduled to take place November 5, 1965. The importance of this should not be minimized in view of earlier indications that Peking had staked much on the Algiers meeting. Peking's pressure on India did not militarily help Pakistan, as presumably it was intended to do. It simply increased tension to a point where both the United States and the Soviet Union redoubled their efforts within the United Nations to negotiate a cease-fire, and provided justification for both to exert the strongest possible pressures to bring this about. This not only led to a cessation of fighting which Peking sought to prolong, but it breathed new life into the United Nations at the very moment Peking was denigrating it as a creature of "imperialists." Peking's precipitous action also presented, at least for the moment, a tableau in which the U.S. and the USSR were revealed in alignment for peace while Communist China, in sharp contrast, beat the drums of battle. While this may have served Peking's purpose of discrediting its Communist rival as a collaborator of the "imperialists," it also reminded the uncommitted, underdeveloped nations whose very existence depends on peace that China's ideology and influence could be dangerous.

The Soviet Union's strong stand against China's entry into the subcontinent crisis brought the tensions between these two Communist antagonists to a new pitch of intensity. Peking could blame the Soviet Union as well as the United States for its diplomatic defeat in South Asia. Peking's bitter denunciation of Moscow on November 10, 1965 for "acting in tacit agreement and close collaboration with Lyndon B. Johnson" in the Vietnam situation must have been influenced by U.S.-Soviet parallel action during the India-Pakistan crisis in September. In China's outburst Moscow's leaders were, in fact, accused of talking with Shastri—a "lackey of the U.S. imperialism"—in their efforts to bring about peace talks in Southeast Asia which would "allow the U.S. to hang on in South Vietnam indefinitely."[23]

The full consequence of China's blunder in inciting Pakistan to press its battle for Kashmir became apparent on January 10, 1966 when the Moscow-sponsored peace conference in Tashkent ended as a victory for Soviet diplomacy. By taking the initiative in bringing India and Pakistan together at the conference table and achieving agreement to withdraw all forces to the original Kashmir cease-fire line, Soviet Premier Aleksei Kosygin committed his country to a policy of preserving peace in South Asia. This was the first occasion in history that the USSR had arbitrated between two non-Communist antagonists and committed its prestige to achieving at least limited settlement. That Kosygin's effort was successful despite opposition from China must have added considerably to Peking's discomfort.

The Tashkent meeting also provided the Soviet Union with a long-sought opportunity to repair its relationship with Pakistan. Ultimately, Rawalpindi may judge the worth of its Soviet relationship by whether Pakistan receives active support for its Kashmir claim, but for the time being Soviet neutrality on this issue is of sufficient benefit to cause Pakistan to welcome it. And implicit in neutrality is a Soviet obligation to deter India from aggression against Pakistan.

With real improvement in the relations between India and Pakistan the latter would become less dependent on Peking, and the Soviet Union would benefit accordingly by reduced Chinese influence on its southern flank. Moscow at the same time would improve its own position in South Asia. But, even immediately, Moscow gained greater flexibility by its more neutral posture in the subcontinent.

By viewing Tashkent in the context of other coordinated acts of Soviet diplomacy which occurred at almost the same time, it again became clear that Moscow's main target in Asia was Peking. The signing of a Soviet-Mongolian friendship and defense treaty and the negotiating of a Soviet-North Vietnam agreement in which Hanoi promised to attend the Soviet Communist Party 23rd Congress must be viewed as two other parts of a Soviet diplomatic offensive against China which gained new momentum at Tashkent. Peking at this time also found significant a new Soviet-Japanese aviation agreement which was signed at this time and must have interpreted it as further evidence that the ring was tightening. Renewed Chinese outbursts accusing the Soviet Union of collusion with the United States gave unmistakable testimony to Peking's ire and concern.

To expect lasting peace between India and Pakistan—much less a mutually acceptable, final solution to the Kashmir problem—demands more optimism than the realities of South Asian politics permit. While the Soviet Union and the West both have important stakes in subcontinent stability and both Indian and Pakistani self-interest demand peace, a heritage of intense communal antagonism cannot be easily eliminated. Extremists in both India and Pakistan cried "sell out" after Tashkent and can be expected to incite hate whenever permitted to do so. Shastri's untimely death at the conclusion of the Tashkent Conference removed a ready scapegoat for Hindu extremists but did not prevent the rightist *Jan Sangh* Party from condemning the Tashkent agreement as "detrimental to the national interests and derogatory to national honor."[24] While the *Jan Sangh* holds only nineteen seats in Parliament, its ability to muster impressive street demonstrations has been proven in the past and will likely be revealed again to embarass Indira Gandhi's new government on the Kashmir issue. Pakistan too has its extremists, who were not permitted in September 1965 to see the severe supply problem facing their army in Kashmir and could not know all the other factors which caused Ayub Khan to sign the Tashkent accord.

But the greatest threat to South Asian peace remains China, which can at any time exercise its option to harass India in the Himalayas, setting in motion the same forces of conflict which have twice already brought the subcontinent perilously close to major war.

Political thrusts at the Himalayan border states and military maneuvers near the frontier may have been intended only as tactical pressures. But they may have deeper significance as indices of future Chinese intentions. The choice of Sikkim, where the border is not in dispute, as pressure point on India during the September 1965 crisis with Pakistan had military logic, but it may also have had sinister political significance when viewed in the context of remarks made at a press conference by Chinese Foreign Minister Chen Yi, questioning India's historical right to speak for Sikkim. Also ominous, at the time of the Tashkent Conference, was Peking's abandonment of its promise to remain twelve miles behind the disputed border—a promise made to the Colombo mediating nations in March 1963. Moreover, Chinese forces then reoccupied Thagla Ridge and Longju, two border passes in the Northeast Frontier Agency which had figured prominently in China's 1962 invasion of India and which had subsequently been neutralized as no-man's-land. India's future in the Himalayas seems anything but auspicious.

CHAPTER 17

ROAD TO REALITY

The world has changed and is changing. We stand at the crest of this change, looking at it, and a tremendous drama is unravelling before our eyes. But we are not mere onlookers. We are actors in this drama.

Jawaharlal Nehru, January 17, 1960, Bangalore, India

Every nation's problems and prospects are significantly determined by history, heritage and its location on the globe. The dream of Nehru's new India was to break out of the limitations imposed by heritage and emerge full-blown from its colonial cocoon as a prototype for independent Asian nations. There are complex reasons why the dream has not been fully realized and may yet be spoiled altogether. But much blame can be fixed on environment since India has no choice but to co-exist along a 2,500-mile border with an aggressive, hostile China.

Communist China has mocked India's political philosophy of peace and non-alignment. It has undermined India's national security, not only directly along its northern border, but indirectly by encouraging tensions with Pakistan and by inciting subversion and separatism within the Indian federation. China, by its harassment, has also placed in jeopardy India's precarious economy.

New Delhi's domestic policies, which are concerned mainly with economic development, internal security and national union, are tragically vulnerable to China's weaponry of subversion and external pressure. Defense policies based on an inherited Himalayan buffer system and a defense establishment adequate to deter Pakistan aggression, have proved deficient because China has not scrupled against invading India or exploiting the tensions between the subcontinent's new nations. Moreover, India's foreign policy, founded in the beginning on ideology and hope, has been rudely wrenched back to reality by its Chinese neighbor, whose own ideology has been linked more effectively with geopolitical reality.

It is perhaps China's assault on new India's ideology which has hurt the most. Peaceful co-existence, non-alignment, Asian solidarity—all related concepts which India reflected in its *Panch Sheela* credo—have been casualties of Peking's aggression against India.

Red China's hostility toward India, more than any other single cause, wrecked the "Bandung spirit" of Afro-Asian solidarity, so hopefully enunciated in April 1955 at the Conference of Asian and African Countries held at Bandung, Indonesia. There was thus something symbolic in the fact that a second "Bandung" meeting, scheduled a decade later in Algiers, was cancelled largely as a result of Chinese pressure. Peking, the principal promoter of the second conference, had originally intended to exploit it as a forum for asserting leadership of the Afro-Asian world. But China's abortive intrusion into the India-Pakistan crisis in September 1965 and the misfired pro-Peking Communist *coup* attempt in Indonesia, which also took place on the eve of the conference, created an atmosphere hardly conducive to achieving Chinese objectives. Moreover, the likelihood that the Soviet Union would be invited and would exploit to the utmost China's misfortunes caused Peking to reverse its position and sabotage the meeting at the eleventh hour.

More basically, Bandung II's failure to take place could be attributed to divisions within the Afro-Asian world which were even more pronounced in 1965 than they had been a decade before. The emerging nations of the former colonial area were caught up in big power competition, including competition between Moscow and Peking. The latter's contempt for peaceful co-existence and its doctrinal break with Moscow on the issue of revolution had confused the meaning of non-alignment. At least to this extent China was succeeding in its objective to prove that non-alignment is a fallacy, that there is no middle way between Communism and capitalism or between violence and peace.

India's first time of acute peril in October/November 1962 exposed those Asian and African leaders who considered non-alignment an instrument, not an ideology. When the leaders of the "non-aligned" countries had met in Belgrade a year earlier to reaffirm solidarity, their failure to condemn the unilateral resumption of nuclear testing by the Soviet Union was a reminder that some uncommitted nations feared to criticize the Soviet Union lest they lose their credentials as neutrals. It was, therefore, not surprising that many of the same nations failed to condemn China for its aggression against India in 1962. Even Yugoslavia's Tito, the host of the 1961 Belgrade conference of non-aligned nations and normally a champion of anti-Chinese sentiment, had been equivocal. As he was in the midst of delicate negotiations to narrow the ideological gap between Yugoslavia and the Soviet Union, it was perhaps understandable that he found it politic to let Moscow take the lead in determining the line to be followed with regard to China's new aggression and did not immediately criticize China for its attack on India. Ghana's Nkrumah, however, not only refrained from expressing sympathy for its Commonwealth brother in 1962 but, by implication, took China's side and condemned Great Britain for rushing arms to India. The third conference of the Afro-Asian Solidarity Organization, held that same year at Moshi, Tanganyika, failed to condemn China; instead, with Chinese prodding it passed a resolution which by implication assumed India to have been no less guilty of hostilities than China. Similarly, when China threatened to attack India again in September 1965, the members of the Afro-Asian world once more reacted on the basis of parochial interest and expediency—not on the basis of the Bandung principles of preserving peace and condemning aggression.

India's experience in two acute crises with China should be proof enough that China does not admit the validity of non-alignment as a policy. Just as Mao Tse-tung originally declared that "neutrality is merely a camouflage," China's National Defense Minister, Lin Piao, in September 1965 stated, in a ringing indictment of peaceful co-existence: "The Socialist countries should regard it their internationalist duty to support the people's revolutionary struggles in Asia, Africa and Latin America." There was clearly no place for non-alignment; the countries of the world must either have gone through the revolutionary stage or endure the hostility of those which had. While defending non-alignment before his death, Nehru argued that China's aggression was the act of an international outlaw forced to live outside the community of nations because its admission to the United Nations had been blocked. Those today who rationalize New Delhi's continued cordiality with Moscow and see it as proof that non-alignment is still a valid basis for India's foreign policy are confusing *Realpolitik* with principle. India's close relationship with the USSR is, to a large extent, a consequence of Chinese hostility, not simply an abstract expression of non-alignment in the East-West cold war sense of the word. New Delhi's policy toward the USSR is also recognition that India's economic and military needs require very large foreign contributions—more than can be provided exclusively by either the democratic consortium, called the "aid-to-India club"* or the Soviet Union. Additionally, the non-alignment label provides entrée to Afro-Asian forums and reassures India's electorate that there has been no backsliding toward colonial subservience. But here again India is guided by practical politics, not abstract principle.

Basically, India's existence as a unified, independent nation depends not on its rigid adherence to principle, but on its ability to deter from aggression those nations—particularly China—which threaten it, and its ability to achieve a rate of economic progress which will satisfy the expectations of an exploding population. The critical questions to which India's leaders are seeking answers are: Can India accomplish these objectives and what kind of policies or attitudes will they require?

New Delhi realizes that India's national security will demand a vastly greater defense effort to back up its diplomatic and political policies. It also recognizes that this will be enormously expensive, particularly if an effort is made to provide a nuclear capability to match China's. For these reasons Indian leaders and planners are concerned that an increased national defense effort will have an adverse effect on the country's already precarious economy.

Considering the staggering costs of maintaining a modern military machine, India may have to conclude that economic reality dictates a defense solution other than complete military self-sufficiency. The defense of the subcontinent against China must depend on the readiness of the West—particularly the United States—or the Soviet Union to intervene if requested to do so. But the events of September 1965 reinforced New Delhi's traditional insistence on maintaining a military establishment, including an

* The aid consortium sometimes known as the "aid-to-India club" consists of the following members: Austria, Belgium, Canada, France, West Germany, Italy, Japan, Netherlands, United Kingdom, United States, the United States Export-Import Bank, the World Bank and the International Development Association.

armament industry, which can at least be effective against Pakistan. The elimination of the Pakistan threat could, of course, be achieved if the Kashmir problem were resolved. Both India's and Pakistan's defense problem would be simplified and some form of a mutual defense plan could be worked out which would relieve both countries of the enormous arms burden they now bear. True peace between India and Pakistan would also eliminate the inhibitions of Western suppliers to provide India with the type and volume of military equipment which it needs for defense against China. But unfortunately, despite the Tashkent agreement, lasting peace in the subcontinent is not assured; the currents of hate still run too fast.

Alarm at increased Western military aid to India following China's 1962 invasion was one factor which drove Pakistan closer to Peking. And because of the lesson learned in September 1965, when the inadequacy of ammunition stocks and spare parts for U.S.-supplied equipment was a factor in causing Rawalpindi to accept a cease-fire, it would be dangerous to assume that Pakistan will refrain from concluding formal defense arrangements with China if the West fails to replenish and supply Pakistan armories. While it was obvious in September 1965 that Peking's threatening posture served only to provoke irresistible U.S. and USSR pressures for a cease-fire and thus became more of an embarrassment than a help, China still appears to Pakistanis to be an important protector to which they can turn should India in the future threaten attack. Most Pakistani leaders genuinely believe that there is basic military and political logic in drawing closer to India's enemy, although there is a considerable range of opinion as to how close.

Rawalpindi is not willing to acknowledge that China represents an ultimate threat to the whole of South Asia, including Pakistan. Peking's aggressive acts against India in October 1962 were dismissed as simply tactical retaliation against Indian army action to clear its borders of the intruding Chinese. Zulfikar Ali Bhutto, in his capacity as Pakistan's Foreign Minister, expressed the view that serious Chinese expansion, if any, would more rationally be directed toward Southeast Asia since it is there where food can be found and there that large overseas Chinese colonies could facilitate aggression. As recently as February 1966 he again denied that China represented a threat to the subcontinent. Blinded by communal tensions with India and the Kashmir dispute, it is not easy for Pakistan to focus on the consequences to South Asia of a China-dominated

Southeast Asia. But Peking's doctrinal espousal of revolution, so eloquently reiterated, cannot indefinitely be ignored by Pakistan's bourgeois leaders, who are ideologically no more acceptable to Chinese Communism than are India's leaders. Lin Piao's September 1965 doctrinal pronouncement, published under the self-explanatory title *Long Live the Victory of People's War*, certainly did not exempt Pakistan when it said, "Revolution must be led by the proletariat and the genuinely revolutionary party armed with Marxism, Leninism and by no other class or party."

One of the greatest dangers to India of continuing friction with Pakistan is a worsening of internal communal tensions. India's large Moslem minority, acutely responsive to co-religionists in Pakistan, teeters dangerously on the brink of violence. Since Nehru's death India can no longer rely on the personal charisma of a unique leader to preserve national unity, and the possibilities of communal explosions are for this reason greater than ever before. While the causes of Moslem dissidence in India are complex and derive from the age of the Moghul rulers, modern tensions between India and Pakistan, dating from partition, seriously aggravate the problem. New Delhi is acutely conscious that there are more than 50 million Moslems within its borders. Were there to be a major communal uprising, India would find itself faced with a frighteningly dangerous security problem.

India's relationship with the Himalayan border state of Nepal is also vital. Nepal's traditional role as buffer became even more important when Tibet was absorbed by China. With considerable geopolitical reality, New Delhi believes that it must maintain a position of paramountcy in Nepal if the latter's buffer role is to be preserved. Yet the Indian government finds itself in a serious dilemma. To abandon its special position in Nepal would be to create a vacuum which could be exploited by the Chinese through infiltration, political intrigue and economic penetration. Yet to insist on a position of primacy which must be maintained by constant pressure, is to alienate the Nepalese and drive them further into the arms of the Chinese.

Aware of India's dilemma, China uses fear, favor and subversion as complementary influences on Nepal with the object of pushing India and Nepal farther apart. Because of India's very limited ability to defend Nepal against Chinese aggression, Kathmandu believes it must reach tolerable accommodation with Peking. Moreover, Nepal is tempted by Red Chinese aid which has been cleverly offered on a no-strings basis. Such aid, given either as grants or loans, is not only helpful to Nepal in its economic development, but serves as pressure on India to be more generous. It also lessens Nepal's dependence on India and thus gratifies a traditionally strong spirit of nationalism in the mountain kingdom.

Perhaps more than any other single factor, overland communication determines the orientation of mountain lands such as Nepal which have traditionally relied on human transportation. With the completion of the road from Kathmandu to Lhasa, Nepal's trade links with China will become progressively stronger. The road also provides China with an invasion route for a modern army.

The Soviet Union's sudden establishment of an embassy in Kathmandu during the 1959 Tibet crisis suggests that Moscow also saw with clarity the implications of Chinese influence in the Himalayan borderlands. Yet it would be unrealistic to expect Moscow to compete with China in Nepal and the other border states. The Soviet Union is and must be primarily concerned with its relationship with India so cannot be too aggressive in the Himalayan states where New Delhi has special interests and responsibilities.

While China may find renewed direct aggression against India difficult, particularly if the Soviet Union makes clear its intention to exert retaliatory pressure in places where China is vulnerable, such as in Sinkiang, or if the West supplies critically needed air support, aggression in Nepal is a very real possibility. Should Peking disguise its actions in Nepal through indigenous subversion or if the legal issues are otherwise clouded, it would be difficult for any country to justify intervention in Kathmandu's defense unless requested to do so. Because of traditional resentment against Indian efforts to dominate it, Nepal would probably be disinclined to seek New Delhi's support against Peking's subversion until too late. And unsolicited Indian initiatives could be misinterpreted or resented by the Nepalese, causing them to draw even closer to the Chinese. All this adds up to the gloomy conclusion that Nepal is extremely vulnerable to Chinese influence and cannot be easily defended by foreign assistance. A Communist-dominated Nepal would put China on the southern slopes of the Himalayas, contiguous with the rich Gangetic plain, with all that implies for Indian security.

The significance of Chinese power in Kathmandu would extend beyond Nepal's boundaries to include Bhutan and Sikkim—two other "fingers" claimed as appendages to the Tibet "palm" described in Chinese Communist propaganda. The concept of a Pan-Himalayan Federation embracing Nepal, Bhutan and Sikkim has articulate advocates in Nepal, who see such a federation as a means of creating a "greater Nepal." The existence of many Nepalese immigrants in Bhutan and Sikkim gives some reality to the scheme. The non-Nepalese people of Sikkim and Bhutan—mainly the "Bhutias" who are closely akin to the Tibetans—do not relish being dominated by Nepalese but are inclined to believe that Nepal would be less overpowering—thus more acceptable—than India. It is no simple coincidence that China threatened India specifically on the Sikkim border during the September 1965 crisis.

It is significant that Communist China favors the Pan-Himalayan concept. Peking may see Nepal as a cat's paw with which to create such a federation and by so doing weaken Sikkim's and Bhutan's treaty ties with India. Indirect aggression of this kind against the mountain principalities would be less likely to invoke foreign backing for Indian military defense of its strategic buffer areas. Yet the assassination of Bhutan's pro-Indian Prime Minister, Jigme Dorje, in April 1964 and the attempted assassination of King Jigme Dorji Wangchuk in July 1965 are ominous events and suggest that a more direct approach to Himalayan conquest by China cannot be ruled out. There certainly exists a body of Bhutanese who are opposed to their country's Indian ties and who may ultimately become powerful enough to challenge the moderate leadership now ruling the country. The seizure of power in Bhutan by an anti-Indian cabal would reverberate in Kathmandu just as Chinese moves in Nepal are felt in Bhutan.

While Communist influence is exerted in the Himalayan border states by subversion and political penetration, it is manifest in India itself through the machinery of the Indian Communist Party—specifically that part of the Party which is responsive to Peking's dictates. The Chinese invasion of India in 1962 accentuated serious factional tensions among Indian Communists which have since been aggravated by the Sino-Soviet doctrinal schism. By early 1963, soon after the Chinese assault, a climax was reached in the long struggle for control between the pro-Soviet faction, which condemned China while staunchly advocating peaceful co-existence, and the pro-Peking faction, which condoned Chinese aggression along the border. In February 1963 the stronger pro-Soviet leadership, whose position was strengthened by the popular reaction against the Chinese border attacks, forced out E. M. S. Namboodripad, the pro-Chinese Secretary-General of the Party. This represented a total victory for the pro-Soviet faction, which at the same time voted unqualified support for Moscow's position on Cuba and backed India in its dispute with China. In the latter connection, pro-Soviet Party chief S. A. Dange spelled out the line: "No communist country should raise a border dispute with its neighbor."

Dange's statement—timed and phrased as it was—appears to have had major significance beyond the Sino-Indian border dispute. It was probably meant to be an indirect warning by Moscow that the USSR would not tolerate Peking's current actions and claims along the Soviet-Chinese border. But it more obviously set the definitive party line that direct Chinese aggression against India was doctrinally inadmissable and made reconciliation between the pro-Soviet and pro-Chinese wings of the party more difficult. In October 1963 a second factional crisis within the party was reached when its pro-Soviet leadership formally censored A. K. Gopalan, leader of the strong Kerala State branch of the Party, for following a Peking line. By April 1964 the Party had broken wide apart and there no longer remained any chance of reconciliation.

The division of the Party into a pro-Moscow faction and a pro-Peking faction is not only a reflection of the Sino-Soviet ideological disagreement but is a significant indicator of the basically different strategy toward India being followed by Moscow and Peking. Soviet policy requires a unified India which Moscow hopes to influence politically, diplomatically and economically through its relations with New Delhi. Conversely, Peking—doctrinally dedicated to bringing about revolution by the masses—is determined to splinter the nation so as to assist the revolutionary objective. Without being untrue to its doctrinal fundamentalism, Communist China cannot have anything but contempt for India's bourgeois central government.

As early as 1946, the eve of independence, the Indian Communist Party campaigned for "national parliaments" for each major language area. Each parliament would have the option either to join the all-India constituent assembly to form a single Indian nation or remain an independent state unconnected with the Union. After independence the regional autonomy thesis found more dynamic expression in insurrection calculated to wrench Telengana State from the Union. This did not work, but of more importance was the death of Stalin and the subsequent shift to parliamentary tactics in Moscow's doctrine. By 1954 Soviet foreign policy, following the dictates of peaceful co-existence, sought accommodation with Nehru. The Indian Communist Party followed, and abandoned insurrection for national front tactics in support of the Prime Minister.

Peking was the inheritor of the militants and hard-liners who refused to abandon insurrection and linguistic separatism. It is understandable that this faction is strongest in the non-Hindi-speaking states of India such as West Bengal, Andhra and Kerala. Encouraged by the strains on Indian unity caused by Chinese aggression, the militants have fought the adoption of Hindi as India's national language and on a variety of other counts have been proponents of total autonomy for India's linguistic groups, even the tribal aborigines. It is here that one can see one of the greatest dangers of China's hostility toward India and another convincing logic of China's actions along the border. That the Indian government recognizes this danger is evidenced by the mass arrests of the top leaders of the pro-Peking wing of the Indian Communist Party which took place in December 1954. Faced then with the likelihood of a pro-Peking Communist regime taking power in Kerala State, New Delhi moved decisively against Peking's agents throughout the country. This is the kind of forceful approach to the internal Communist problem which India probably feels it must continue to pursue if its defenses against Red China are to be effective.

With an appreciation of the causes and consequences of China's actions and recognizing India's vulnerability to communal and linguistic disintegration, New Delhi has to be continually on guard. Chinese aggression and threats have humiliated India and created a defense requirement certain to strain India's economy. Peking's actions have convinced the Himalayan border states, Nepal and Bhutan, that they must respond to the realities of strength—that India, unable to protect itself, cannot protect them. This in turn has deprived India of its traditional northern buffer protection and has provided China with a foothold of influence on the southern slopes of the Himalayas overlooking the Gangetic heartland of Indian strength.

Peking's actions have aggravated India-Pakistan relations, making much more remote any possibility of cooperation between them for the mutual defense of the subcontinent. Tension between these two countries assumes even more significance and provides greater rationale for China's Pakistan policy when viewed in the context of India's huge Moslem minority, which to some extent is responsive to Pakistan and, if incited to major rebellion, could rend beyond repair the fragile fabric of national unity. Peking's aggression brought to a head the schismatic tendencies of the Indian Communist Party and enabled the Pro-Chinese faction to stake out a claim to superior doctrinal purity. While the parliamentary tactics of the pro-Soviet faction may have been more effective when Nehru was alive and politically unassailable, the insurrectionary tactics of the pro-Peking faction could prove superior if the Congress Party monopoly of power is broken and instability plagues the post-Nehru period.

The invasion of India in 1962 and the threatened attack in 1965 were, above all, dramatic demonstrations of China's willingness to use aggression as an instrument of foreign policy in a world which hopes for peace. Viewed now in the context of China's nuclear capability, this has awesome meaning in a world which fears but respects power. The avalanche of publications which pour from Peking's presses preaching violent revolution as the only road to freedom, and aggression as the only solution to disagreement, have been translated from theory into reality in China's relationship with India.

NOTES

CHAPTER 1

1. Filippo De Filippi, (ed.) *I. Desideri, An Account of Tibet* (rev. ed.; London: George Routledge & Sons, Ltd., 1937), p. 119.
2. S. W. Bushell, "The Early History of Tibet from Chinese Sources," *Journal of The Royal Asiatic Society*, XII (1880), 435–541 [a translation of T'ang histories].
3. Sir Charles A. Bell, *Tibet, Past and Present* (Oxford: Oxford University Press, 1924), p. 23.
4. *Ibid.*, pp. 28, 29.
5. De Filippi, *I. Desideri, An Account of Tibet*, pp. 275, 276.
6. *Ibid.*, p. 277.
7. Sven Hedin, *Trans-Himalaya* (London: MacMillan and Co. Ltd., 1913), III, 119.
8. *Ibid.*
9. L. A. Waddel, *Lhasa and Its Mysteries* (London: Methuen & Co., 1905), p. 26.
10. DeFilippi, *I. Desideri, An Account of Tibet*, p. 280.
11. Sir Charles A. Bell, *Portrait of The Dalai Lama* (London: Collins, 1946), pp. 72, 73.
12. De Filippi, (ed.), *I. Desideri, An Account of Tibet*, p. 150.
13. Bell, *Tibet, Past and Present,* p. 39.
14. De Filippi, *I. Desideri, An Account of Tibet*, p. 157.
15. *Ibid.*, p. 280.
16. *Ibid.*, p. 170.
17. *Ibid.*, p. 170.
18. *Ibid.*, p. 280.

CHAPTER 2

1. Philip Woodruff, *The Founders* (London: Jonathan Cape, 1953), p. 24.
2. Samuel Turner, *An Account of an Embassy to the Court of the Teshoo Lama in Tibet* (London: W. Bulmer & Co., 1800), p. xiii.
3. *Ibid.*, p. ix.
4. *Ibid.*, p. xiv.
5. Sir Francis Younghusband, *India and Tibet* (London: John Murray, 1910), p. 9.

6. Schuyler Cammann, *Trade Through the Himalayas*, (Princeton: Princeton University Press, 1951), p. 32.
7. C. B. Markham, *Narrative of the Mission of George Bogle to Tibet* (London: 1876), pp. 135, 138.
8. Younghusband, *India and Tibet*, p. 13.
9. C. B. Markham, *Narrative of the Mission of George Bogle to Tibet.* (London: 1876), p. 135.
10. Younghusband, *India and Tibet*, pp. 16, 17.
11. *Ibid.*, p. 18.
12. *Ibid.*, p. 23.
13. *Ibid.*, p. 24.
14. Cammann, *Trade Through the Himalayas*, pp. 38, 39.
15. Turner, *An Account of an Embassy to the Court of the Teshoo Lama in Tibet*, p. 457–473.
16. D. B. Diskalkar, "Tibetan-Nepalese War, 1788–1793," *Journal of the Bihar and Orissa Research Society*, XIX, No. 12 (1933), 380.
17. Cammann, *Trade Through the Himalayas*, p. 116.

CHAPTER 3

1. George Alexander Lensen (ed.), *Russia's Eastward Expansion* (Englewood Cliffs, N.J.: Prentice Hall, Inc., 1964), Chap. 22, "The Ideology of Russian Expansion," by Andrew Malozemoff, p. 92.
2. *Ibid.*, pp. 92, 93.
3. Samuel Turner, *An Account of an Embassy to the Court of the Teshoo Lama in Tibet* (London: W. Bulmer & Co., 1800), p. 273.
4. Ekai Kawaguchi, *Three Years in Tibet* (Benares: Theosophical Publishing Society, 1909), pp. 497, 498, 499.
5. *Ibid.*, p. 499.
6. Alastair Lamb, *The China-India Border* (London: Oxford University Press, 1964), p. 106.
7. *Ibid.*, p. 107.
8. Sir Francis Younghusband, *India and Tibet* (London: John Murray, 1910), pp. 69, 70.
9. Peter Fleming, *Bayonets to Lhasa* (London: Rupert Hart-Davis, 1961), pp. 43, 44 [footnote].
10. Perceval Landon, *The Opening of Tibet* (New York: Doubleday, Page & Co., 1905), p. 25.
11. Younghusband, *India and Tibet*, p. 73.
12. Landon, *The Opening of Tibet*, pp. 21, 22.
13. Younghusband, *India and Tibet*, pp. 140, 141.
14. *Ibid.*, p. 141.

CHAPTER 4

1. Sir Charles A. Bell, *Portrait of The Dalai Lama* (London: Collins, 1946), p. 75.
2. *Ibid.*, p. 86.

3. Angus Hamilton, *In Abor Jungles* (London: Eveleigh Nash, 1912), p. 43.

4. *Ibid.*, pp. 60, 61, 62.

5. Alastair Lamb, *The China-India Border* (London: Oxford University Press, 1964), pp. 14, 15.

6. *Report of the Officials of the Governments of India and the People's Republic of China on the Boundary Question* (New Delhi: Ministry of External Affairs, Government of India, 1961), p. 112.

7. *The Boundary Question Between China and Tibet* (Peking: 1940), p. 88.

8. *Report of the Officials of the Governments of India and . . . China on the Boundary Question*, p. 112.

9. *Report of the Officials of the Governments of India and . . . China on the Boundary Question*, p. 111.

10. Bell, *Portrait of The Dalai Lama*, p. 350.

11. *Ibid.*, p. 380.

12. *Ibid.*, p. 380.

CHAPTER 5

1. Robert Ford, *Captured in Tibet* (London: George G. Harrap & Co., Ltd., 1957), p. 94.

2. H. E. Richardson, *A Short History of Tibet* (New York: E. P. Dutton and Co., 1962, pp. 183, 184.

3. Girilal Jain, *Panch Sheela and After* (Bombay, London: Asia Publishing House, 1960, pp. 18, 19.

4. Tzu-Yuan, "Historical Relations between the Tibet Region and The Motherland," *Min-tsu Yen-chiu* [Nationalities Research], No. 4 (Peking: April 4, 1959), pp. 1–13.

5. Joseph Stalin, *Marxism and the National Question* (Moscow: 1913).

6. *Jen Min Jih Pao* (Peking), October 2, 1954.

7. C. Brandt and B. Schwartz, *A Documentary History of Chinese Communism* (Cambridge: Harvard University Press, 1952), pp. 223, 224.

8. *Hsi-tang Ta Shih-chi, 1949–59* [Chronology of Events in Tibet, 1949–1959] (Chinese Monograph [Peking: May 1959]).

9. K. M. Panikkar, *In Two Chinas: Memoirs of a Diplomat* (London: 1955), pp. 26, 27.

10. *Indian Views of Sino-Indian Relations*, No. 1, Apx. I-A (Indian Press Digests Monograph Series [Berkeley: University of California, Institute of International Studies, 1956]), pp. ii.

11. *Ibid.*, Apx. I-C.

12. *Ibid.*, Apx. I-D.

13. Panikkar, *In Two Chinas: Memoirs of a Diplomat*, pp. 26, 27.

14. *Indian Views of Sino-Indian Relations*, No. 1, Apx. II-B.

15. "Request by the Delegation of El Salvador for the Inclusion of an Additional Item in the Agenda of the Fifth Session: Note by the Secretary-General", *United Nations Document A/1549*, November 24, 1950

(Official Record of the United Nations General Assembly, Agenda Item 8, Annexes, Fifth Session [New York: 1950]).

16. Chanakaya Sen, *Tibet Disappears* (Bombay: Asian Publishing House, 1960), pp. 89, 90.

17. "Request for the Inclusion of an Additional Item: Invasion of Tibet by Foreign Forces, Item Submitted by the Delegation of El Salvador," *United Nations Document A/1534*, November 24, 1950 (Official Record of the United Nations General Assembly, General Committee, 73rd Meeting, Fifth Session [New York: 1950]).

18. Lowell Thomas, Jr., *The Silent War in Tibet* (Garden City: Doubleday, 1959), pp. 96, 97.

19. *Indian Views of Sino-Indian Relations*, No. 1, Apx. I-E.

20. "Procedures Other Than Questions and Answers," *Parliamentary Debates*, Vol. VI, No. 17, Cols. 1267 and 1384 (Parliament of India Official Report, Pt. II [New Delhi: 1950]).

21. *Jawarharlal Nehru Speeches*, 1949–1953 (New Delhi: Ministry of Information and Broadcasting, Publication Division, Government of India, 1954).

22. *Ibid.*

CHAPTER 6

1. Thubten Jigme Norbu, and Heinrich Harrer, *Tibet Is My Country* (New York: E. P. Dutton and Co., 1961), pp. 230–232.

2. Chanakaya Sen, *Tibet Disappears* (Bombay: Asian Publishing House, 1960), p. 74.

3. Sir Charles A. Bell, *Portrait of The Dalai Lama* (London: Collins, 1946), p. 56.

4. George N. Patterson, *Tibet in Revolt* (London: Faber and Faber, 1960), p. 81.

5. Tzu-yuan, "Historical Relations between the Tibet Region and the Motherland," *Min-tsu Yen-chiu* [Nationalities Research], No. 4 (Peking: April 4, 1959).

6. *Hsi-tang Ta Shih-chi, 1949–59* [Chronology of Events in Tibet, 1949–59] (Chinese Monograph [Peiping: May 1959]).

7. Dalai Lama, *My Land and My People* (New York: McGraw-Hill Book Company, Inc., 1962), pp. 87, 88.

8. Tzu-yuan, "Historical Relations between the Tibet Region and the Motherland," *Min-tsu Yen-chiu*, p. 19.

9. *Hsi-tang Ta Shih-chi, 1949–59*, p. 6.

10. Chanakaya Sen, *Tibet Disappears*, p. 155.

11. *The Question of Tibet and the Rule of Law* (Geneva: The International Commission of Jurists, 1959), p. 139.

12. All quotations from the 17-Point Agreement are from *The Question of Tibet and the Rule of Law*. This publication in turn took its quotations from the *New China News Agency*.

13. George N. Patterson, *Tibet in Revolt* (London: Faber and Faber, 1960), pp. 83, 84, 85.

14. Dalai Lama, *My Land and My People*, p. 90.
15. *Ibid.*, p. 91.
16. *Tibet and the Chinese People's Republic* (Geneva: The International Commission of Jurists, Legal Inquiry Committee on Tibet, 1960), p. 204.
17. Dalai Lama, *My Land and My People*, pp. 97, 98.
18. George Ginsburg and Michael Mathos, "Tibet's Administration in the Transition Period, 1951–1954," *Pacific Affairs*, XXXII, No. 2, (June 1959), pp. 170, 171.
19. Dalai Lama, *My Land and My People*, pp. 97, 98.
20. *Tibet and the Chinese People's Republic*, pp. 3, 4.

CHAPTER 7

1. *Indian Views of Sino-Indian Relations*, No. 1, Apx. I (Indian Press Digests, Monograph Series [Berkeley: University of California, Institute of International Studies, 1956]), p. ix.
2. *Ibid.*, p. xviii.
3. George N. Patterson, *Peking Versus Delhi* (New York: Frederick A. Praeger, 1964), p. 66.
4. Jawaharlal Nehru, *The Discovery of India* (London: Meridian Books, Ltd., 1956), p. 192.
5. *Ibid.*
6. Jawaharlal Nehru, *China, Spain and the War* (Allahabad: 1940), pp. 11–53.
7. Michael Brecher, *Nehru, A Political Biography* (London: Oxford University Press, 1959), p. 593.
8. *China Digest* (Peking), 1949 (column by the "Observer").
9. *New China News Agency* (Peking), December 14, 1952 (cable from Chou En-lai to Lester Pearson, President of the United Nations General Assembly, December 14, 1952—SCMP 473, December 16, 1952).
10. *The Communist* (Bombay), January 1950.
11. *New China News Agency*, October 12, 1952.
12. *Indian Views of Sino-Indian Relations*, No. 1, p. 22.
13. *Indian Views of Sino-Indian Relations*, No. 1, Apx. IV, p. xix.
14. Chanakya Sen, *Tibet Disappears* (London: Asia Publishing House, 1960), p. 122.
15. P. C. Chakravarti, *India's China Policy* (Bloomington: Indiana University Press, 1962), p. 56.
16. The *Times of India* (Bombay), May 6, 1954.
17. *Amrita Bazar Patrika* (Calcutta), June 7, 1954.
18. The *Indian Express* (Madras), May 5, 1954.
19. The *Lucknow Pioneer*, May 1, 1954.
20. *Report of the Officials of the Governments of India and the People's Republic of China on the Boundary Question* (New Delhi: Ministry of External Affairs, Government of India, 1961), pp. 84–87.
21. *Indian Views of Sino-Indian Relations*, No. 1, Apx. IV, p. xx.
22. *Ibid.*

23. *Janata* (Bombay), May 30, 1954.
24. *Indian Views of Sino-Indian Relations*, No. 1, Apx. IV, p. xix.
25. *Report of the Officials of the Governments of India and the People's Republic of China on the Boundary Question*, p. 112.
26. *Vigil* (New Delhi), May 15, 1954.
27. *Ibid.*, May 22, 1954.
28. *Notes, Memoranda and Letters Exchanged and Agreements Signed between the Governments of India and China, 1954–1959 [White Paper]* (New Delhi: Ministry of External Affairs, Government of India, 1959), pp. 1, 2.
29. *Ibid.*, p. 4.

CHAPTER 8

1. *Indian Views of Sino-Indian Relations*, No. 1 (Indian Press Digests Monograph Series [Berkeley: University of California, Institute of International Studies, 1956]), p. 47.
2. The *Lucknow Pioneer*, June 30, 1954.
3. *Indian Views of Sino-Indian Relations*, No. 1, p. 73.
4. *Ibid.*, p. 71.
5. The *Washington Post*, January 3, 1963.
6. The *Statesman* (Calcutta), July 4, 1954.
7. *Notes, Memoranda and Letters Exchanged and Agreements Signed between the Governments of India and China, 1954–1959 [White Paper]* (New Delhi: Ministry of External Affairs, Government of India, 1959), p. 49. (Letter from Prime Minister Nehru of India to Premier Chou En-lai of the People's Republic of China, dated December 14, 1958.)
8. *Report of the Officials of the Governments of India and the People's Republic of China on the Boundary Question [Officials' Report]* (New Delhi: Ministry of External Affairs, Government of India, 1960), p. 87.
9. *Ibid*, p. CR-29, 30.
10. *Indian Views of Sino-Indian Relations*, No. 1, p. 102.
11. *Ibid.*, p. 105.
12. *Ibid.*, p. 121.
13. Michael Brecher, *Nehru, A Political Biography* (London: Oxford University Press, 1959), pp. 111, 112.
14. Jawaharlal Nehru, *India's Foreign Policy* (New Delhi: The Publications Division, Ministry of Information and Broadcasting, Government of India, 1961), p. 277.
15. *Chinese Communist World Outlook* (Bureau of Intelligence and Research, United States Department of State, Publication 7379 [Far Eastern Series 112] [Washington, D.C.: September 1962]), p. 84.
16. *Indian Views of Sino-Indian Relations*, No. 1, p. 138.
17. The *Lucknow Pioneer*, April 26, 1955.
18. Nehru, *India's Foreign Policy*, p. 274.
19. *Janata* (Bombay), May 8, 1955.

20. The *Times of India* (New Delhi), April 28, 1955.
21. "Note of the Chinese Government, 26 December 1959," *Notes, Memoranda and Letters Exchanged between the Governments of India and China, November 1959–March 1960 [White Paper III]* (New Delhi: Ministry of External Affairs, Government of India, 1960), pp. 67, 68.
22. *White Paper*, pp. 11, 17, 18.
23. *Ibid.*, p. 33.
24. *Ibid.*, p. 29.
25. *Ibid.*, pp. 30–33.
26. *Ibid.*, pp. 30–32.
27. *Ibid.*, p. 60.
28. The Dalai Lama, *My Land and My People*, (New York: McGraw-Hill Book Co., Ltd., 1962), pp. 141, 142.
29. *Ibid.*, p. 148.
30. *Ibid.*, p. 151.

CHAPTER 9

1. *Chinese Communist World Outlook* (Washington, D.C.: Bureau of Intelligence and Research, United States Department of State, June 1962), p. 67.
2. The Dalai Lama, *My Land and My People* (New York: McGraw-Hill Book Company, Inc., 1962), p. 164.
3. *The Question of Tibet and the Rule of Law* (Geneva: The International Commission of Jurists, 1959), p. 13.
4. *New China News Agency* (Peking), April 22, 1959. (Morse transmission to Europe and Africa, 2200 GMT, English language broadcast.)
5. The Dalai Lama, *My Land and My People*, pp. 190, 191.
6. *New China News Agency*, April 22, 1959. (Morse release, 2200 GMT, English language broadcast to Europe and Africa.)
7. The Dalai Lama, *My Land and My People*, p. 207.
8. *The Dalai Lama and India* (New Delhi: Institute of National Affairs, 1959), p. 82.
9. *Notes, Memoranda and Letters Exchanged and Agreements Signed between the Governments of India and China, 1954–1959 [White Paper]* (New Delhi: Ministry of External Affairs, Government of India, 1959), p. 67.
10. *New China News Agency*, March 28, 1959. (Domestic and International Radio Services.)
11. The *New York Times*, March 28, 1959.
12. The Dalai Lama, *My Land and My People*, p. 195.
13. *Ibid.*, p. 212.
14. *New China News Agency*, March 28, 1959. (Radio teletype release, 1135 GMT, English language broadcast to Europe and Africa.)
15. *Ibid.*, 1254 GMT.
16. The *Hindusthan Times* (Calcutta), April 28, 1959.
17. The *Hindu* (Madras), May 9, 1959.

18. *New China News Agency*, March 29, 1959. (Hellschriber release, 1731 GMT, English language broadcast to Europe.)
19. The *Statesman* (Calcutta), April 25, 1959.
20. The Dalai Lama, *My Land and My People*, p. 187.

CHAPTER 10

1. *Hindusthan Times* (Calcutta), April 28, 1959. (A Reuter article, datelined Hong Kong, April 27, 1959, quoting Shao Li-tzu, a member of the Standing Committee of the Revolutionary Committee of the Chinese People's Republic.)
2. The *Statesman* (Calcutta), April 6, 1959.
3. *Hindusthan Standard* (Calcutta), April 16, 1959.
4. The *Statesman*, April 15, 1959.
5. *New China News Agency* (Peking), May 15, 1959. (Radio teletype release, 2300 GMT English language broadcast to West and North Europe. Replay of *People's Daily* editorial entitled "Revolution in Tibet and Nehru's Philosophy.")
6. *The Dalai Lama and India* (New Delhi: Institute of National Affairs, Hind Book House, 1959), pp. 78, 79, 84.
7. The *New York Times*, April 2, 1959.
8. *Notes, Memoranda and Letters Exchanged and Agreements Signed between the Governments of India and China, 1954–1959 [White Paper]* (New Delhi: Ministry of External Affairs, Government of India, 1959), p. 86.
9. *Ibid.*, p. 90.
10. *Ibid.*, p. 39.
11. *Ibid.*, p. 26.
12. *Notes, Memoranda and Letters Exchanged and Agreements Signed between the Governments of India and China, September–November 1959 [White Paper II]* (New Delhi: Ministry of External Affairs, Government of India, 1959), p. 27.
13. *White Paper*, pp. 44, 45.
14. *Prime Minister on Sino-Indian Relations*, Vol. I, *In Parliament March 17–September 12, 1959* (New Delhi: Government of India, 1959), p. 91.
15. *Ibid.*, p. 95.
16. *Ibid.*, p. 106.
17. *White Paper II*, pp. 27, 31.
18. *Ibid.*, p. 30.
19. *Prime Minister on Sino-Indian Relations*, Vol. I, *In Parliament*, p. 160.
20. *Ibid.*, p. 146.
21. All references to the Kongka Pass incident are from *Notes, Memoranda and Letters Exchanged between the Governments of India and China*, November 1959–March 1960 [*White Paper III*] (New Delhi: Ministry of External Affairs, Government of India, 1960), pp. 11–19, 25.

CHAPTER 11

1. *All India Radio* (New Delhi), November 2, 1959. (Morse transmission abroad, 1830 GMT, English language.)
2. *Pakistan Radio* (Karachi), October 23, 1959. (Home Service, 1445 GMT, English language.)
3. *All India Radio,* November 5, 1959. (Morse transmission abroad, 1435 GMT, English language.)
4. *All India Radio,* November 5, 1959. (Morse transmission abroad, 1435 GMT, English language.)
5. The *New York Times,* November 9, 1959.
6. *Ibid.,* December 19, 1959.
7. *Press Trust of India* (Bombay), November 28, 1959. (Radio teletype to Tokyo, 1100 GMT, English language.)
8. The *New York Times,* November 24, 1959.
9. *Ibid.,* November 10, 1959 (Reuters, Hong Kong, dated November 9, 1959, quoting NCNA release.)
10. *Notes, Memoranda, and Letters Exchanged between the Governments of India and China, November, 1959–March, 1960 [White Paper III]* (New Delhi: Ministry of External Affairs, Government of India, 1960), p. 49.
11. *Ibid.,* p. 58.
12. The *New York Times,* February 14, 1960.
13. *Ibid.,* February 17, 1960.
14. *Ibid.,* April 23, 1960.
15. *Ibid.,* April 20, 1960.
16. *Ibid.,* April 27, 1960.
17. *Ibid.,* April 26, 1960.
18. *Report of the Officials of the Governments of India and the People's Republic of China on the Boundary Question* (New Delhi: Ministry of External Affairs, Government of India, 1961), p. 11.
19. *Ibid.,* p. 11.
20. *Dawn* (Karachi), May 4, 1962. (Press notice issued by the Ministry of External Affairs, Government of Pakistan, May 3, 1962.)

CHAPTER 12

1. Mao Tse-tung, "The Chinese Revolution and the Chinese Communist Party" (December 15, 1939 version), *Current Background,* No. 135 (Peking).
2. *Indian Views of Sino-Indian Relations,* No. 1 (Indian Press Digests Monograph Series [Berkeley: University of California, Institute of International Studies, 1956]), p. 146.
3. *Ibid.,* pp. 146, 147.
4. Jawaharlal Nehru, "Speech in Parliament given March 17, 1950," *Jawaharlal Nehru Speeches, 1949–1953* (New Delhi: The Publication Division, Ministry of Information and Broadcasting, Government of India, 1954), p. 147.

5. The *Hindu* (Madras), December 7, 1950.
6. Girilal Jain, *India Meets China in Nepal* (Bombay: Asia Publishing House, 1959), p. 111.
7. *Ibid.*, p. 112.
8. *Look Magazine*, 18, No. 22 (November 2, 1954), 31–35.
9. The *Statesman* (New Delhi), January 29, 1957.
10. The *New York Times*, November 28, 1959.
11. The *New York Times*, March 28, 1960.
12. *Ibid.*, June 30, 1960.
13. *Press Trust of India* (Bombay), February 15, 1961. (Morse transmission in English language to Tokyo, 0953 GMT.)

CHAPTER 13

1. T. E. Gordon, *A Varied Life, 1849–1902* (London: John Murray, 1906), p. 97.
2. Richard Pierce, *Russian Central Asia, 1867–1907* (Berkeley: University of California Press, 1960), p. 298.
3. Allen S. Whiting and Sheng Shih-ts'ai, *Sinkiang, Pawn or Pivot?* (East Lansing: Michigan State University Press, 1958), pp. 198, 199.
4. *Ibid.*, pp. 200, 201.
5. *Ibid.*, p. 207.
6. *Ibid.*, pp. 202, 203.
7. *Ibid.*
8. *Ibid.*, p. 243.
9. *Ibid.*, p. 255.
10. *Ibid.*, pp. 117, 118.
11. Satyanarayan Sinha, *The Chinese Aggression* (New Delhi: Rama Krishna and Sons, 1961), pp. 42, 43, 48, 49.
12. *Ibid.*, p. 7.
13. "Sinkiang, Soviet Rustler in China's Wild West," the *Reporter*, June 18, 1964.
14. *Daily Report*, Supplement No. 19, September 6, 1963.
15. *Current Digest*, XV, 3.
16. "A Great Betrayal of Marxism, Leninism," *Zëri i Popullit* (Tirana, Albania), October 17, 1962.
17. *People's Daily* (Peking), August 15, 1963.
18. The *New York Times*, September 26 and November 30, 1962.
19. Edward Crankshaw, *The New Cold War, Moscow V. Peking* (Baltimore: Penguin Books, 1963), p. 143.
20. *People's Daily*, November 2, 1963.
21. *Ibid.*, August 15, 1963.

CHAPTER 14

1. The *New York Times*, October 21, 1962.
2. *Ibid.*, October 23, 1962.

3. *Ibid.*, October 26, 1962.
4. *Ibid.*, October 28, 1962.
5. *Ibid.*, October 27, 1962.
6. The *Evening Star* (Washington, D.C.), December 12, 1962.
7. The *New York Times*, October 30, 1962.
8. The *Washington Post*, November 9, 1962.
9. The *New York Times*, November 3, 1962.
10. *Ibid.*, November 8, 1962.
11. *Ibid.*, November 3, 1962.
12. *Ibid.*, November 11, 1962.
13. The *New York Times*, November 19, 1962.
14. *Ibid.*, November 20, 1962.
15. *Ibid.*, November 21, 1962.

CHAPTER 15

1. *China News Analysis*, November 26, 1954.
2. S. Chandrasekhar, *Communist China Today* (Bombay: Asia Publishing House, 1961), p. 117.
3. "China's Population Problem," *Problems of Communism*, 7 (March April 1958), 36–41.
4. Frederick Nossal, "China's Second Experiment," the *Nation*, 196, No. 23 (June 15, 1963).
5. *The Question of Tibet and the Rule of Law* (Dalai Lama press statement issued in Mussorie, India on June 20, 1959 [Geneva: International Commission of Jurists, 1959]), p. 70.
6. *The Sino-Indian Boundary Question* (Peking: Foreign Language Press, Government of The People's Republic of China, 1962), pp. 103, 104.
7. *Ibid.*, pp. 108, 110.
8. *Ibid.*, p. 111.
9. *Ibid.*, p. 117.
10. *Ibid.*, pp. 117, 118.
11. *Ibid.*, p. 20.
12. A. Doak Barnett, *Communist China and Asia* (New York: Vintage Books, 1960), p. 65.
13. The *New York Times*, July 21, 1963.
14. *Jen Min Jih Pao* (Peking), October 27, 1962.
15. *Notes, Memoranda and Letters Exchanged and Agreements Signed between the Governments of India and the Peoples Republic of China, 1954–1959 [White Paper]* (New Delhi: Ministry of External Affairs, Government of India, 1959), pp. 53, 54.
16. *The Sino-Indian Boundary Question*, p. 26.
17. The *New York Times*, July 5, 1963.
18. *People's Daily*, (Peking) December 31, 1962.
19. The *New York Times*, July 7, 1963.

20. The *New York Times*, July 21, 1963.
21. The *New York Times*, July 15, 1963.
22. *Ibid.*

CHAPTER 16

1. Jawaharlal Nehru, *The Unity of India* (New York: John Day, 1942), p. 223.
2. The *New York Times*, December 4, 1959.
3. Satyanarayan Sinha, *The Chinese Aggression* (New Delhi: Rama Krishna and Sons, 1961), p. 68.
4. *Dawn* (Karachi), May 4, 1962.
5. *Ibid.*
6. The *New York Times*, July 7, 1962.
7. *Ibid.*, July 18, 1963.
8. George Montagno, "Peaceful Co-existence; Pakistan and Red China," *The Western Political Quarterly*, XVIII, No. 2, Pt. I (June 1965), 309.
9. *Ibid.*, p. 316.
10. The *Economist* (London), September 11, 1965.
11. The *Washington Post*, August 25, 1965.
12. *Hsin-hua* (Peking), September 9, 1965.
13. The *New York Times*, September 6, 1965.
14. *Ibid.*, September 8, 1965.
15. The *Washington Post*, September 4, 1965.
16. *Ibid.*
17. The *New York Times*, September 9, 1965.
18. The *Washington Post*, September 16, 1965.
19. *Ibid.*, September 18, 1965.
20. *Ibid.*
21. *Ibid.*
22. *Ibid.*, September 22, 23, 1965.
23. *Ibid.*, November 11, 1965.
24. The *New York Times*, January 17, 1966.

BIBLIOGRAPHY

BOOKS, ARTICLES, AND DOCUMENTS

"A Study of Sino-Tibetan Relations, 1949–56," *United Asia* (special Tibet ed., 1959), Bombay.

Barber, Noel, *The Flight of The Dalai Lama.* London: Hodder and Stoughton, 1960.

Barnett, A. Doak, *Communist China and Asia.* New York: Vintage Books, 1960.

Bell, Sir Charles A., *Portrait of The Dalai Lama.* London: Collins, 1946.

———, *Tibet, Past and Present.* Oxford: Oxford Clarendon Press, 1924.

Bishop, R. N. W., *Unknown Nepal.* London: Luzac & Co., 1952.

Bonvalot, Gabriel, *Across Tibet.* New York: Cassell Publishing Co., 1892.

The Boundary Question Between China and Tibet. ("A valuable record of the tripartite conference between China, Britain, and Tibet held in India, 1913–1914.") Peking: 1940.

Boyd, R. G., *Communist China's Foreign Policy.* New York: Frederick A. Praeger, 1962.

Bull, Geoffrey T., *When Iron Gates Yield.* London: Hodder and Stoughton Ltd., 1955.

Bulletin of the International Commission of Jurists. (No. 8.) Geneva: December 1958.

Brandt, C. and Schwartz, B., *A Documentary History of Chinese Communism.* Cambridge: Harvard University Press, 1952.

Brecher, Michael, *Nehru, A Political Biography.* London: Oxford University Press, 1959.

Cammann, Schuyler, *Trade Through the Himalayas.* Princeton: Princeton University Press, 1951.

Caroe, Sir Olaf, "The Sino-Indian Question," *Royal Central Asian Society Journal* (July/October, 1963), pp. 238–251.

Carrasco, Pedro, *Land and Polity in Tibet.* Seattle: University of Washington Press, 1959.

Chakravarti, P. C., *India's China Policy.* Bloomington: Indiana University Press, 1962.

Chandrasekhar, Sripati, *Red China, An Asian View.* New York: Frederick A. Praeger, 1961.

"China's Population Problem," *Problems of Communism,* 7 (March/April 1958), 36–41.

Chinese Communist World Outlook, Bureau of Intelligence and Research, United States Department of State Publication No. 7379, Far Eastern Series 112 (September 1962).

Clark, Leonard, *The Marching Wind.* New York: Funk & Wagnalls Co., 1954.

Concerning the Question of Tibet. Peking: Foreign Languages Press, 1959.

Crankshaw, Edward, *The New Cold War, Moscow V. Peking.* Baltimore: Penguin Books, 1963.

Curzon, Lord, *Frontiers.* Oxford: Oxford University Press, 1907.

Cutting, Suydam, *The Fire Ox and Other Years.* London: Collins, 1947.

The Dalai Lama, *My Land and My People.* New York: McGraw-Hill Book Co., 1962.

———, (Press Statement issued in Mussorie, India on June 20, 1959.) *The Question of Tibet and the Rule of Law.* Geneva: International Commission of Jurists, 1959.

The Dalai Lama and India. New Delhi: Institute of National Affairs, 1959.

Das, Chandra, *Journey to Lhasa and Central Tibet.* London: John Murray, 1904.

De Filippi, (ed.), *I. Desideri, An Account of Tibet* (rev. ed.); London: George Routledge & Sons, Ltd., 1937.

Documents on the Sino-Indian Boundary Question. Peking: Foreign Languages Press, 1960.

Fisher, M. W., Rose, L. E., and Huttenback, Robert, *Himalayan Battleground, Sino-Indian Rivalry in Ladakh.* New York: Frederick A. Praeger, 1963.

Fleming, Peter, *Bayonets to Lhasa.* London: Rupert Hart-Davis, 1961.

Ford, Robert, *Captured in Tibet.* London: George G. Harrap & Co. Ltd., 1957.

Ghosh, K. R., "Sino-Indian Relations," *Eastern World* (June 1956).

Ginsburg, George and Mathos, Michael, "Tibet's Administration in the Transition Period, 1951–1954," *Pacific Affairs*, XXXII, No. 2 (June 1959).

Gould, B. J., *The Jewel in the Lotus.* London: Chatto & Windus, 1957.

Green, L. C., "Legal Aspects of The Sino-Indian Border Dispute," *China Quarterly*, No. 3 (July/September 1960).

Grenard, F., *Tibet.* London: Hutchinson & Co., 1904.

Griffith, William E., *The Sino-Soviet Rift.* Cambridge: The M.I.T. Press, 1964.

Griswold, A. Whitney, *The Far Eastern Policy of the United States.* New York: Harcourt, Brace and Company, 1938.

Hamilton, Angus, *In Abor Jungles.* London: Eveleigh Nash, 1912.

Harrer, Heinrich, *Seven Years in Tibet.* New York: E. P. Dutton & Co., 1953.

Harrison, Selig S. (ed.), *India and the United States.* New York: The Macmillan Co., 1961.

Markham, Clements, *Narrative of the Mission of George Bogle to Tibet and of the Journey of Thomas Manning to Lhasa.* London: Trübner & Co., 1876.

Masani, Minoo, *The Communist Party of India, A Short History.* London: Derek Verschoyle in Association with the Institute of Pacific Relations, 1954.

McGovern, William, *To Lhasa in Disguise.* New York: The Century Co., 1924.

Moraes, Frank, *The Revolt in Tibet.* New York: The Macmillan Co., 1960.

Nehru, Jawaharlal, *China, Spain and the War.* Allahabad: 1940.

———, *The Discovery of India.* London: Meridian Books Ltd., 1956.

———, *India's Foreign Policy.* New Delhi: Publications Division, Ministry of Information and Broadcasting, Government of India, 1961.

———, *Jawaharlal Nehru Speeches, 1949–53.* New Delhi: Publications Division, Ministry of Information and Broadcasting, Government of India, 1954.

New Development in Friendly Relations Between China and Nepal. Peking: Foreign Languages Press, 1960.

Nossal, Frederick, "China's Second Experiment," *The Nation,* 196, No. 23 (June 15, 1963).

Notes, Memoranda and Letters Exchanged and Agreements Signed between the Governments of India and China, 1954–1959 (White Paper.) New Delhi: Ministry of External Affairs, Government of India, 1959.

Notes, Memoranda and Letters Exchanged and Agreements Signed between the Governments of India and China, September–November, 1959. (White Paper II.) New Delhi: Ministry of External Affairs, Government of India, 1959.

Notes, Memoranda and Letters Exchanged and Agreements Signed between the Governments of India and China, November, 1959–March, 1960. (White Paper III.) New Delhi: Ministry of External Affairs, Government of India, 1960.

Notes, Memoranda and Letters Exchanged and Agreements Signed between the Governments of India and China, March, 1960–November, 1960. (White Paper IV.) New Delhi: Ministry of External Affairs, Government of India, 1960.

Notes, Memoranda and Letters Exchanged and Agreements Signed between the Governments of India and China, November, 1960–November, 1961. (White Paper V.) New Delhi: Ministry of External Affairs, Government of India, 1961.

Norbu, Thubten Jigme and Harrer, Heinrich, *Tibet Is My Country.* New York: E. P. Dutton & Co., 1961.

Official Correspondence between the Central Government of India and the Chinese People's Republic Relevant to the Subject of the Sino-Indian Border. Peking: Foreign Languages Press, 1959.

Overstreet, Gene D. and Windmiller, Marshall, *Communism in India.* Berkeley: University of California Press, 1959.

Hedin, Sven, *A Conquest of Tibet*. New York: E. P. Dutton,
———, *Trans-Himalaya*. 3 vols. London: Macmillan & Co., 1
Hsi-tang Ta Shih-chi, 1949–59 (Chronology of Events in Tib
Peking: May 1959.
Huc, E., *Souvenirs of a Journey Through Tartary, Tibet a*
vols. Peking: Lazarist Press, 1931.
Hudson, G. F., *The Aksai Chin*. London: St. Anthony's Pa
(1963).
———, "The Frontier of China and Assam," *China Quart*
(October/December 1962).
Hudson, G. F., Lowenthal, Richard, and MacFarquhar, Ro
Sino-Soviet Dispute. New York: Frederick A. Praeger, 1
Hutheesing, Raja (ed.), *Tibet Fights for Freedom*. Bom
Longmans for "The Indian Committee for Cultural Free
Indian Views of Sino-Indian Relations. (Monograph Seri
Berkeley: University of California, Institute of Internati
February 1956.
International Commission of Jurists, *Tibet and the Rule of L*
1959.
———, *Tibet and The Chinese People's Republic*. Geneva:
Jackson, W. A. Douglas, *Russo-Chinese Borderlands*. Prince
Nostrand Co. Inc., 1962.
Jain, Girilal, *India Meets China in Nepal*. Bombay: Asia
House, 1959.
———, *Panch Sheela and After*. Bombay: Asia Publishing H
Jenkins, William M., Jr. and Karan, Pradyumna, *The Him*
doms, Bhutan, Sikkim and Nepal. Princeton: D. Van No
Karnik, V. B., *China Invades India*. Bombay: Allied Publish
Kawaguchi, Ekai, *Three Years in Tibet*. Madras: Theosophic
Society, 1909.
Korbel, Josef, *Danger in Kashmir*. Princeton: Princeton Uni
1954.
Kundra, J. C., *Indian Foreign Policy, 1947–1954*. Groni
Wolters, 1955.
Lamb, Alastair, *The China-India Border*. London: Oxfor
Press, 1964.
Landon, Perceval, *Nepal*. 2 vols. London: 1928.
———, *The Opening of Tibet*. New York: Doubleday, Page
Lattimore, Owen, *Inner Asian Frontiers of China*. Boston: I
1962.
Lengyel, Emil, *Krishna Menon*. New York: Walker & Co., 1
Li, Tieh-tseng, *Tibet, Today and Yesterday*. Bookman Ass
Lias, Godfrey, *Kazak Exodus*. London: Evans Brothers Lim
Mao Tse-tung, "The Chinese Revolution and The Chines
Party" (December 15, 1939 version), *Current Backgro*
———, *On People's Democratic Dictatorship* (English la
Peking: New China News Agency, 1949.

Panikkar, K. M., *In Two Chinas: Memoirs of a Diplomat.* London: 1955.

Patterson, George N., *Peking Versus Delhi.* New York: Frederick A. Praeger, 1964.

———, *Tibet in Revolt.* London: Faber & Faber, 1960.

———, *Tragic Destiny.* London: Faber & Faber, 1959.

Prime Minister on Sino-Indian Relations, Vol. I, *In Parliament, March 17–September 12, 1959.* New Delhi: External Publicity Division, Ministry of External Affairs, Government of India, 1959.

Prime Minister On Sino-Indian Relations, Vol. II, *Press Conferences, March 6–September 11, 1959.* New Delhi: External Publicity Division, Ministry of External Affairs, Government of India, 1959.

Parliamentary Debates, Vol. VI, No. 17, Pt. II, "Procedures Other Than Questions and Answers." Cols. 1267, 1384. New Delhi: Parliament of India Official Report, 1950.

The Question of Tibet and the Rule of Law. Geneva: The International Commission of Jurists, 1959.

Report of the Officials of the Governments of India and the Peoples Republic of China on the Boundary Question. New Delhi: Ministry of External Affairs, Government of India, 1961.

de Riencourt, Amaury, *Roof of the World.* New York: Rinehart & Co., 1950.

Richardson, H. E., *A Short History of Tibet.* New York: E. P. Dutton & Co., 1962.

Schwartz, Benjamin I., *Chinese Communism and the Rise of Mao.* Cambridge: Harvard University Press, 1951.

Sen, Chanakya, *Tibet Disappears.* London: Asia Publishing House, 1960.

Shen, Tsung-lien and Shen-chi, Liu, *Tibet and the Tibetans.* Stanford: Stanford University Press, 1953.

Sinha, Satyanarayan, *The Chinese Aggression.* New Delhi: Rama Krishna and Sons, 1961.

The Sino-Indian Boundary Question. Peking: Foreign Languages Press, 1962.

Snow, Edgar, *Red Star over China.* New York: The Modern Library, 1944.

Spain, James W., "Military Assistance For Pakistan," *American Political Science Review* (September 1954).

Stalin, Joseph, *Marxism and the National Question.* Moscow: 1913.

Tang, Peter S. H., *Communist China Today.* New York: Frederick A. Praeger, 1957.

Teichman, E., *Travels of a Consular Official in Eastern Tibet.* Cambridge: 1922.

Thomas, Lowell, Jr., *The Silent War in Tibet.* Garden City: Doubleday, 1959.

Thomas, S. B., *Recent Political and Economic Developments in China.* New York: 1950.

Tibet and the Chinese People's Republic. Geneva: The International Commission of Jurists, 1960.

Tinker, Hugh, *India and Pakistan, A Political Analysis.* New York: Frederick A. Praeger, 1962.

Turner, Samuel, *An Account of an Embassy to the Court of the Teshoo Lama in Tibet.* London: W. Bulmer & Co., 1800.

Tzu-yuan, "Historical Relations Between the Tibet Region and the Motherland," *Nationalities Research*, No. 4 (April 4, 1959).

United Nations Document A/1534, "Request for the Inclusion of an Additional Item of the Fifth Session: Letter, dated November 17, 1950 from the Chairman of the Delegation of El Salvador addressed to the President of the General Assembly," November 17, 1950.

United Nations Document A/1549, "Request of the Delegation of El Salvador for the Inclusion of an Additional Item in the Agenda of the Fifth Session; Note by the Secretary General," November 17, 1950.

Ward, Barbara, *India and the West* (rev. ed.). New York: W. W. Norton & Co., 1964.

Wilcox, Wayne A., *India, Pakistan and the Rise of China.* New York: Walker & Co., 1964.

Wilson, Andrew, *Abode of Snow.* New York: G. P. Putnam's Sons, 1875.

Winnington, Alan, "Statement Of Dalai Lama Is Suspect," *New China News Agency* (Peking), April 22, 1959.

Woodruff, Philip, *The Men Who Ruled India, The Founders.* New York: St. Martin's Press, 1954.

———, *The Men Who Ruled India, The Guardians.* New York: St. Martin's Press, 1954.

Younghusband, Sir Francis, *India and Tibet.* London: John Murray, 1910.

NEWSPAPERS

Amrita Bazar Patrika. Calcutta.

China Digest. Peking.

The *Daily Express.* London.

Dawn. Karachi.

The *Eastern Economist.* Bombay.

The *Economist.* London.

The *Evening Star.* Washington, D.C.

Foreign Broadcast Information Service. Washington, D.C.

The *Hindu.* Madras.

The *Hindusthan Standard.* Calcutta.

The *Hindusthan Times.* New Delhi.

The *Indian Express.* Madras.

Janata. Bombay.

Jen Min Jih Pao. Peking.

The Manchester Guardian. Manchester.

The *National Herald.* Lucknow.

Navbharat Times. Bombay.

New China News Agency. Peking.

The *New York Times.* New York.

The *Pioneer*. Lucknow.
Pravda. Moscow.
Press Trust of India. Bombay.
The *Statesman*. Calcutta.
Swantantar Samachar. Kathmandu.
The *Times of India*. New Delhi.
The *Washington Post*. Washington, D.C.

INDEX

Abor Expedition of 1911, 45
Abor tribe, 42, 43
Acharya, Tanka Prasad, 149, 150, 151
Afghanistan, 37, 134
Afro-Asian solidarity, 150, 151
Afro-Asian Solidarity Organization, 209
Agra, India, 13
"Agreement Between the Republic of India and the People's Republic of China on Trade and Intercourse Between the Tibet Region of China and India"; *see* Sino-Indian Agreement of 1954
"Aid to India Club," 210
Aidit, D.N., Chairman Indonesian Communist Party, 200
Aigun, Treaty of, 26
Aka tribe, 43
Akbar the Great, 188
Akhnur, 199
Aksai Chin area, Ladakh, 30, 52, 102, 125, 129, 137, 141, 157, 166, 171, 172, 182, 200
Albania, 164, 165
Algiers, 196
Ali, Safar, Mir of Hunza, 30, 157
All Indian Congress Committee, 92, 97
Almora, 85
Altai Mountains, 192
Altan Khan, 5
Amban; *see* China, *Ambans* in Tibet
American-Japanese Mutual Security Act, 138
Amrita Bazar Patrika, 84
Amur River, 25, 26
Anglo-Chinese Treaty, 1906, 77
Anglo-Russian Convention of 1907, 37, 39, 41, 45, 47, 77
Anglo-Tibetan Boundary Agreement of 1914, 48, 49
Anglo-Tibetan Convention, 1904, 36, 37, 78
Apo Tribe, 43
Ardagh, Sir John, 29, 30
Asian-African Conference; *see* Bandung Conference
Asian Consultative Committee, 92
Asian solidarity, 91, 92, 95, 96
Askaroff, 162, 163
Assam, 42-44, 46, 48, 52, 74, 172
Assam Rifles, 126
Ayub Khan; *see* Khan, Mohammad Ayub
Ayyangar, N. Gopalaswami, 58
Azad Kashmir, 190, 197, 199

Bahadur, Jang, 145
Balfour, Sir Arthur J., Prime Minister of England, 34, 35, 37
Balkhash, Lake, 192
Baltistan, 3
Bandung, Indonesia, 94
Bandung Conference, 1955, 94-101, 180, 195, 208
Bandung II Conference, 100, 203, 208
Bandung Declaration, 98, 99
Bandung Spirit, 102
Bao Dai, 82
Bara Hoti, 101, 102, 125
Belgrade Conference of Non-aligned States, 1961, 168, 208, 209
Bell, Sir Charles, 64
Bengal, India, 14-16
Bengal Eastern Frontier Regulation of 1873, 43
Bhutan, 18, 38, 39, 42, 74, 77, 121, 127, 128, 142, 144, 151, 153, 166, 173, 183, 213, 214, 216;

see also China, Relations with Bhutan
Bhutan, Raja of, 14, 16
Bhutias, 214
Bhutto, Zulfikar Ali, Pakistan Foreign Minister, 194-96, 202, 211
Bogle, George, 14-18, 20, 21, 38
Bokhara, 26
Bomdi La, 172
Bon religion, Tibet, 4
Bower, Major General Hamilton, 44
Boxer Rebellion, China, 32
Brahmaputra River, 1
Brezhnev, Leonid, 164
Buddha, 3, 28
Buddha Jyanti Celebration, 102
Buddhism, 3, 4, 80
Burhan, 54
Buriat Mongols, 18
Burma, 97, 138, 139

Cabot, Ambassador, United States Ambassador to Poland, 201
Camp David, Maryland, 136, 162
Canada, 171
Carpini, Friar John of Plano, 4
Catherine, Empress of Russia, 18, 27, 28
CENTO (Central Treaty Organization), 189, 192
Ceylon, 98
Chakravarty, B. N., 169
Chamdo, Tibet, 51-53, 84
Chamdo-Lhasa road, 52
Chang Chenmo River, 129, 131
Chang Ching-wu, 70
Chang Han-fu, Vice Foreign Minister, Chinese People's Republic, 85
Chang Kuo-hua, General, 70
Chang Shambhala, 28
Chang Yin-tang, 77
Chao Erh-feng, General, 42-46, 62, 65, 77, 78
Chatso, Kenchung Sonam; *see* Kenchung Sonam Chatso
Chefoo Convention of 1876, 33
Chen, Ivan; *see* Ivan Chen
Chen Yi, Foreign Minister, Chinese People's Republic, 199, 205
Chhamb, 198
Chiang Kai-chek, Generalissimo, President of the National Republic of China, 82, 160
Chibber, Indian Consul General, Lhasa, 109, 112, 124
Ch'ien Lung, Manchu Emperor of China, 15, 19-22
China; *see also* National Republic of China
Agreements:
China-India Agreement of 1954, 85-89, 118, 123, 124, 149
China-India Boundary Discussions, 1960, 139, 141-143
China-Nepal Agreement, 1956, 149, 152
China-Nepal Boundary Agreement, 1960, 152-154
China-Nepal Economic Agreement, 1960, 152, 154
China-Tibet Seventeen Point Agreement, May 23, 1951, 66-74, 103, 105, 107, 114, 120
China-Tibet Talks, 1950, 56, 59
China-Tibet Treaty of 822, 49
Alien Affairs Bureau, Lhasa, Tibet, 124
Ambans in Tibet (High Commissioners), 22, 24, 32, 33, 36, 65, 77, 145
Cartographic claims, 82, 86, 87, 95, 125, 127, 137, 192, 193
Commission of Nationalities Affairs, 66
Commissioner and Administrator of Civil and Military Affairs, Tibet, 70
Cultural Association of Patriotic Youth (Lhasa), 72
Emigration to Tibet, 73, 74
Food crisis 1960-1962, 177, 181
General Tibetan Commercial Corporation, Lhasa, 72
"Great Leap Forward," 177, 180
Middle Kingdom, 39, 72, 174, 175, 176
Military and Administrative Committee, Lhasa, 69, 70
Military Area Headquarters, Tibet, 69
National Assembly, 105
National People's Congress, Peking, 106, 119

China (continued)
Nationalities Doctrine:
Stalin, 54
Burhan, 54
Kiangsi Constitution, 54
Nationalities Affairs Committee, 54
Common Program, 55, 67
People's Political Consultative Conference, 55
Regional Autonomy, 60
Commission of Nationalities Affairs, 66
17 Point Agreement with Tibet, 66-71
New Democratic Youth Federation of China (Lhasa), 72
Notes to India:
October 30, 1950, 57
November 16, 1950, 60
July 7, 1954, 89
March 22, 1959, 109
September 8, 1959, 127, 128
September, 1965, 200
Nuclear capability, 217
People's Bank of China (Lhasa), 72
People's Political Consultative Conference (Lhasa), 55, 72
Population problem, 176-178
Propaganda, 52, 53, 60, 67, 71, 73, 99, 100, 110, 114-124, 130-132, 141, 142, 179, 184
Racism, 186
Relations with Bhutan, 19, 74, 77, 121, 128, 142, 144, 146, 153, 173, 183, 213, 214, 216
Relations with British India regarding Aksai Chin, 30
Relations with Burma, 138, 139, 154, 193
Relations with Nepal, 19, 23, 74, 77, 89, 96, 100, 102, 144, 145, 147-155, 173, 183, 193, 212-214, 216
Relations with Northeast Frontier of India, 74
Relations with Pakistan, 138, 139, 142, 143, 156, 189, 190, 191, 194-205, 211, 212
Relations with Russia, 18, 29
Relations with Sikkim, 19, 74, 121, 127, 128, 142, 144, 173, 182, 183, 200, 205, 213
Relations with The Soviet Union, 83, 84, 93, 95, 101, 134, 136, 138, 139, 153-156, 158-165, 167, 168, 170-172, 176, 178-180, 182, 184-186, 189-192, 201-205, 208-210, 213-215
Revolution of 1911, 45, 157
Road construction, Tibet, 19
Suzerainty over Tibet, 61, 62, 121, 146
Trade Missions in India, 84, 85
Trade Missions in Nepal, 102
Chinese People's Republic; *see* China
Chinese Turkestan; *see* Sinkiang
Ch'ing Dynasty, 32; *see also* Manchu Dynasty
Chip Chap Valley, 166
Chou En-lai, 91, 92, 94-96, 98-100, 103, 105, 110, 119, 125, 127, 133, 139, 140, 148, 150, 151, 152, 172, 180, 182, 192, 195, 196
Chronicle of Kings, 188
Chumbi Valley, Tibet, 36, 50, 64
Chung Ying, General, 42
Chungchen, 71
Chu Teh, 54
Chushul, 167, 169, 171, 172
Colombo Conference, 1954, 85
Colombo Powers, 96
Common Program, Chinese People's Republic, 55, 60, 67
Competitive Co-existence, 83
Congo, 179
Congress of Oppressed Nationalities, 1927, 97
Congress Party, India, 92, 168
Conolly, Arthur, 26
Cooch Behar, Maharajah of, 14, 16
Cornwallis, Lord Charles, 22, 23
Cuban Missile Crisis, 164, 168, 171-173, 186
Cultural Association of Patriotic Youth, Lhasa, 72
Curzon, Lord, 28-31, 33-38, 74, 77

Dafla tribe, 43
Dalai Lama, Tibet,
Third reincarnation, 3, 5
Fourth reincarnation, 5

Fifth reincarnation, 5, 6, 20
Sixth reincarnation, 7
Seventh reincarnation, 8-10
Thirteenth reincarnation, 28, 30, 31, 33, 34, 37, 42, 45, 46, 52, 64, 65, 68, 78
Fourteenth reincarnation, 59, 62-73, 78, 102-108, 111-121, 123, 125, 128, 169, 178, 181, 193, 198
Escape from Lhasa, 111-116
Dalai Lama Vajradhara; *see* Dalai Lama
Dange, S. A., 215
Dam, Tibet, 9
Damzan, 101
Daulat Beg Oldi, 166
Dawn, Karachi, 193, 194
Desideri, Ippolito, 2, 7
De-tsen, Ti-song; *see* Ti-song De-tsen
Digboi Oil Fields, Assam, 171
Dolan, Brooke, 50
Dorje, Jigme, Prime Minister of Bhutan, 214
Dorjiev, Aguan, 28-35, 39, 41, 46, 73
Dras-rin-mo, 2, 3
Drepung Monastery, Tibet, 70
Dulles, John Foster, U. S. Secretary of State, 193
Dundup, Tsering; *see* Tsering Dundup
Dzungar Mongols, 6, 7, 8, 10

East German 6th Party Congress, 185
East Germany, 185
East India Company, 12, 15, 17, 23, 24
East Pakistan, 201
The *Eastern Economist*, 85
Eastern World, 101
Eden, Anthony, British Foreign Minister, 100
Edward VII, King of England, 42
Egypt, 97
Eisenhower, Dwight, President of the United States, 136, 137
El Salvador, Sponsorship of Tibet case in the U. N., 58, 59
Entente Cordiale, British-Russian, 1907, 36, 37; *see also* Anglo-Russian Convention of 1907

Faisal, King of Iraq, 179
Fifth Dalai Lama, 5, 6
Ford, Robert, 51
Formosan Crisis, 1955, 100-102

Gampo, Song-tsen; *see* Song-tsen Gampo
Ganden Monastery, Tibet, 70
Gandhi, Indira, Prime Minister of India, 205
Gandhi, Mahatma, 178
Ganges River, India, 1
Gartok, Tibet, 84, 88, 101, 182
Geda, 53
Gelugpa Sect; *see* Yellow Hat sect, Lamaism
Geneva Conference on Indo-China, 86, 92, 94, 101
Genghiz Khan, 4, 157
Ghana, 168, 209
Ghosh, K. R., 101
Gilgit, 3, 193
Giri, Dr. Tulsi, 138
Gordon, Thomas, 157
Gorwala, A. D., 94
Gosain, Indian traders, 18
Government of India Act of 1858, 44
Grand Lama of Urga, Mongolia; *see* Jebtson Dampa Hutkhtu
Great Britain; *see* United Kingdom
"Great Game," The, 26, 37, 157
Gregorson, Dr., 44
Gurkha, 23
Gurkha Dynasty, Nepal, 145
Gyantse, 35, 71, 84, 88, 124
Gyatso, Sangye; *see* Sangye Gyatso
Gyatso, Sonam; *see* Sonam Gyatso

Hamilton, Alexander, 15, 16
Hardinge, Sir Charles, 28, 29
Hastings, Warren, 14, 16, 18, 20-22, 35
Himachal Pradesh, India, 101, 102, 142
Hostile Co-existence, 186, 187
Hot Springs, 129
Hoti Plain, 90; *see also* Wu-je
Hulumandju, 2
Hungarian Uprising, 1956, 179
Hunza, 29, 30, 190, 193
Hunza, Mir of; *see* Mir of Hunza

India, Boundary dispute with China, 85-90, 93, 95, 96, 119, 125-

India (continued)
128, 135, 137, 139-143, 152, 154, 163, 164, 171, 172, 182, 185, 186, 190, 191, 201
Communalism, 212, 216, 217
Communist Party, 82, 119, 122, 123, 214-216
Consolate General, Lhasa, 76
"expansionism," 117, 118
Invasion by China, October, November 1962, 163-165, 166-174, 194
Threatened invasion by China, 1965, 181, 183, 184, 186, 189, 200-203
Kerala State, 119, 215, 216
Ministry of External Affairs, 126
Neutralism/non-alignment, 80, 82, 91, 131, 133, 134, 167, 168, 169, 170, 178, 180, 207-210
Notes to China:
October 26, 1950, 56
October 30, 1950, 64
August 28, 1959, 126
March 22, 1959, 126
Parliament, 57, 119, 121-123, 127, 128, 133, 138, 139, 146, 147, 151, 162, 171, 201
Relations with Bhutan, 126, 128, 142, 144, 151, 153, 214, 216
Relations with Nepal, 138, 139, 144, 146-151, 154, 155, 212-216
Relations with Pakistan, 134, 138, 139, 142, 143, 156, 188-207, 211, 216
Relations with Sikkim, 127, 128, 142, 144, 151, 212
Relations with The Soviet Union, 138, 139, 156, 162, 164, 167, 168, 170-172, 182, 186, 190-192, 197, 198, 202-205, 209, 210, 213
Soviet arms aid to India, 169, 171, 199-201, 203
Third General Election, 180
Tibet, 53, 56, 58-61, 64, 66, 76, 78-81, 84-87, 103, 111-126
Trade Missions, Tibet, 76, 84, 88, 124
Violations of territory by China, 91, 93, 101, 118, 125-128, 134, 138, 162-174, 181, 183, 184, 186, 193, 215
White Paper I, 89
War with Pakistan in Kashmir and Punjab, 1965, 197-205, 217
India-Tibet Border Force, 129, 130
Indo-China War, 83, 94
Indo-Nepalese Trade Treaty, 149
Indonesia, 97, 100, 162, 168, 200
Indonesian Communist Party, 200
Inner Mongolia, 121
Inner Tibet, 47, 48
Innocent IV, Pope, 4
International Commission of Jurists, 71, 74
International Supervisory Commission, Indo-China, 94
Iran, 98
Iraq, 98
Ivan Chen, 47, 48

Jan Saheb of Nawanagar, 58
Jan Sangh Party, India, 197, 205
Japan, 32, 83, 159
Jebtson Dampa Hutkhtu, High Lama of Mongolia, 27, 28
Jehangir, Emperor of India, 13
Jehol, 20
Jigme Ngapo Ngawang; *see* Ngapo Ngawang Jigme
Johnson, Lyndon B., President of the United States, 203

Kalimpong, India, 85, 88, 123
Kalmuks, 18
K'ang Hsi, Emperor of China, Manchu Dynasty, 6, 7, 9, 10, 25
Kanjarkot, 196
Karakorum Pass, 142, 143, 190, 199
Kargil, 199
Kashgar, Sinkiang, 3, 29, 84, 182
Kashmir, 39, 74, 84, 125, 142, 188-192, 194-196, 198-205
Kashmir Question, 8, 51, 88, 134, 142, 151, 156, 189-192, 194-205, 211
Kasyapa, 188
Kathmandu, 96, 102, 145, 147, 149, 151-153
Kazakhstan, 163
Kebang, Assam, 44, 45

Kenchung Sonam Chatso, 107
Kennedy, President John F., President of the United States, 172, 173, 180, 202
Kham Province, Tibet, 52, 64, 66
Khamba Dzong, 34, 35
Khamba tribal insurgency, Tibet, 102, 105, 106, 108
Khan, Mohammed Ayub, President of Pakistan, 134, 193-195, 197, 201-203, 205
Khapa, Tsong; *see* Tsong Khapa
Khinzemane, 166
Khokand, 26
Khrushchev, Nikita, 134-136, 138, 139, 162, 164, 167, 173, 180, 184, 185, 200, 201, 202
Khurnak Fort, 125
Kiangsi Constitution, 54
Kibitoo Post, 167
Kirkpatrick, William, 23
Koirala, B. P., 151, 152, 154
Koirala, C. P., 148
Koko Nor, Tibet, 5, 20
Kongka Pass, 129, 132, 133, 135
Korean War, 51, 58-60, 82, 83, 179
Kosygin, Aleksei, 202, 204
Kripalani, Acharya, 86, 122
Krishna Menon, Vengalil Krishnan, 60, 80, 82, 94, 100, 133, 167, 168, 170
Kublai Khan, 5
Kuldja, Sinkiang, 157, 163
Kumbun Monastery, Tibet, 63
Kuomintang, 97, 158-161; *see also* National Republic of China
Kuropatkin, General, 157
Kuyuk Khan, 4
Kwangsi, 121
Kyi Chi River, 111

Ladakh, 2, 30, 84, 101, 125, 137, 144, 157, 166, 169-173, 182, 183, 191, 193, 199, 200
Lahore, 199
Lal, Makhan, 129
Lamaism, 1, 4, 5
Lamsdorff, Vladimir, 31, 39
Landon, Perceval, 33
Laotian Crisis, 1961, 193
Lapthal, 102
Latsang Khan, 6-9
Lebanon, 98
Leh, Ladakh, 169
Lenin, 184, 186
Lhasa uprising, 1959, 104-114, 118, 125, 128
Lhuntse Government, Tibet, 112
Li-tang, 7
Li Wei-han, 66
Lin Piao, Minister of Defense, People's Republic of China, 209, 212
Liu Hsiao, Ambassador, 165
Liu Shao-chi, President of the People's Republic of China, 200
Lo Jui-ching, General, 199, 200
Lobsang Paldan Yeshi, the Third Panchen Lama of Tibet, 12, 14-22
Lohit frontier area, 102, 167, 171
Lon-chen Shatra, 47
The "Long March," 53
Longju, 137, 206
Losang Tashi, 65, 71, 72
Lower Tartary; *see* Oelot Mongols
Lucknow Pioneer, 92, 95
Lukhangwa, Prime Minister of Tibet, 65, 71, 72

Macdonald, Brigadier J., 35
Mahendra, King of Nepal (Full name Mahendra Bir Bikram Shah Dev), 148, 154, 155
Malik, 59
Manchu Dynasty, China, 6, 19, 22, 32, 40, 45, 46, 77, 146, 175
Manchuria, 39, 50, 176
Mani Tribe, Assam, 43
Mao Tse-min, 160
"Mao's Panchen"; *see* Panchen Lama (10th)
Mao Tse-tung, 54, 67, 82, 146, 160, 162, 177, 181, 209
Marco Polo, 4
Marxo-Buddhism, 72
Matsu Island, 95
McMahon, Sir Henry, 47, 48, 49, 88
McMahon Line, 41, 86, 87, 112, 113, 137, 170, 172, 183
Meru, 1
Migyitun, 126
Milang, 102
Mir of Hunza, 30, 157
Miri Tribe, Assam, 43
Mishmi Tribe, 42, 43

Moghul Empire, India, 12, 13
Mongolia, 46, 50, 79, 176
Morley, Lord, 38, 78
Mount Everest, 152-154
Mussoorie, India, 59, 112, 115, 120
Mustang, Raja of, 151, 153

Nagir, 190
Namboodripad, E. M. S., 215
Nasser, President Gamal Abdel, President of the United Arab Republic, 97, 99, 168
National Assembly, Tibet, 55, 64
National Republic of China (Taiwan), 59, 117, 136, 158-161
Nationalities Affairs Committee, China, 54
Nawanagar, Jan Saheb of, 58
Nayyar, Suchila, 114
NEFA (Northeast Frontier Agency); *see* Northeast Frontier
Nehru, Jawaharlal, 55-57, 60, 61, 78-82, 84, 86, 88-92, 94-100, 102-104, 109, 110, 114-118, 120-123, 125, 126, 128, 131-139, 146, 147, 151, 152, 167-172, 178-180, 182, 188, 191, 192, 194, 195, 202, 207, 209, 212
Nepal, 18, 22-24, 38, 39, 42, 51, 55, 74, 77, 96, 100, 102, 138, 139, 144-155, 173, 183, 212-214, 216
Nepali Congress Party, 147, 154
Nerchinsk, Treaty of, 25
Ngapo Ngawang Jigme, 52, 66, 68, 72, 106, 107, 181, 198
Nicholas, Crown Prince of Russia, 27
Nicholas II, Czar of Russia, 28, 30, 39, 46
Nighsia, 121
Ninth Panchen Lama; *see* Panchen Lama (9th reincarnation)
Niti Pass, 89
Nkrumah, Kwame, 158, 209
Norbu, Thubten Jigme, 63-65, 70
Norbulingka Palace, Lhasa, 106-109, 111
Northeast Frontier, India, 113, 126, 142, 144, 172, 200, 206
Northwest Frontier, India, 39
Nu, U, 97, 99

Obote, Milton, 169
Oelot Mongols, 5-9
"Outer Line," Northeast frontier, India, 43
Outer Mongolia, 39, 46, 47, 95, 161
Outer Tibet, 47, 48

Padma Sambhava; *see* Urgyen
Pakistan, 51, 83, 95, 98, 138, 139, 142, 143, 188-207, 211, 212, 216
  Chinese arms aid, 195, 199, 201-203
Pamirs, 156, 157, 190, 193
Panch Sheela, 85-89, 91, 92, 94-96, 98, 113, 116, 118, 121, 123, 125, 128, 132, 140, 147, 148, 178, 179, 181
Panchen Lama, 5, 6, 44, 64
  Third reincarnation, 12, 14-16, 18
  Ninth reincarnation, 68
  Tenth reincarnation (recognized by the People's Republic of China but not by the Tibetans), 66, 67, 69, 72, 78, 119, 181, 198
Panggi, 44
Pangyong Lake, 125, 166
Pan Himalaya concept, 214
Panikkar, Sardar K. M., 55-57, 79, 80
Patel, Sardar Vallabhbhai, 80
Patron-priest relationship, 5, 11, 30, 46, 62
Peaceful co-existence, 91-94, 96, 98, 124, 128, 133, 140, 149, 159, 165, 166, 181, 184, 185, 207, 208, 209
  Stalin on: 159
  Lenin on: 184
People's Liberation Army, People's Republic of China
  Duty in Tibet, 52-54, 60, 68-70, 73, 132
  Invasion of India, 166-168, 172, 173, 184, 200
  Proclamation to Tibetans, 110, 111, 114, 115
Persia, 37; *see also* Iran
Plassey, Battle of, 1757, 13
Potala, Lhasa, 6, 35, 41, 42, 107
Poyul, Assam, 42
Praja Socialist Party, India, 87, 89, 101, 110, 122

Prasad, Rajendra, President of India, 149, 150
Preparatory Committee for the Tibet Autonomous Region, 107
Prjevalskii, General M. N., 27
Punjab, India, 142
Purangir, 20-22

Qadir, Foreign Minister, Pakistan, 191
Qosot Mongols, 6-9
Quemoy Island, 95

Rabden, Tse-wang; *see* Tse-wang Rabden
Raghavan, Ambassador, 85
Rajagopalachari, Chakravarti, 80, 133
Rana power, Nepal, 57, 145-147
Rann of Kutch dispute, India-Pakistan, 196
Rawalpindi, 195
Raza, Ali, 129
Red Hat sect, Lamaism; *see* Urgyenist sect, Lamaism
Regmi, Foreign Minister, Nepal, 148
Rhee, Syngman, 82
Rice, Sir Cecil Spring, 31, 32
Rubruck, William of, 4
Rusk, Dean, United States Secretary of State, 201
Russia, Czarist, 18, 25-30, 157, 158
Russo-Mongolian Agreement of October 12, 1912, 46

Sadiya, Assam, 44, 45, 52
St. Petersburg, Treaty of, 26
Sakya Monastery, 4, 5
Sambhava, Padma; *see* Urgyen
Sampo Tsewong-rentzen, 107
Sangchamalla, 102
Sangye Gyatso, 6
Satow, Sir Ernest, British Ambassador to China, 32
Scott, Sir Charles, 31
Se Pass (Se La), 172
SEATO (Southeast Asia Treaty Organization), 95, 99, 188, 193
Sepoy Mutiny, 1857, India, 29
Sera Medical College, 108
Sera Monastery, Tibet, 70, 108
Seventeen Point Agreement, (China-Tibet) 1951, 66-71, 73, 74, 103, 105, 107, 114, 120
Seventh Dalai Lama; *see* Dalai Lama, 7th reincarnation
Shah, Prithvi Narayan, 145
Shastri, Lal Bahadur, Prime Minister of India, 197, 198, 201, 203
Shatra, Lon-chen, 47
Sheikh Abdullah, 195, 196
Sheng, Shih-ts'ai, 158-160
Shigatse, 6, 15, 16, 71
Shillong, 112
Shimshal Pass, 190
Shipki Pass, 101
Shridharani, Dr. Krishnalal, 84
Sialkot, 199
Sikang Province, China, 42
Sikkim, 33, 38, 39, 42, 64, 65, 74, 121, 127, 142, 144, 151, 173, 182, 183, 200, 205, 213, 214
Simla, India, 41, 85
Simla Conference, 41, 47-50
Simla Convention, 1914, 48, 49, 87
Singh, Braj Raj, 126
Singh, Karam, 129, 132
Singh, K. I., 147-151
Sinha, Dr. Satyanarayan, 87, 162, 163
Sinkiang, 6, 26, 29, 30, 32, 39, 73, 77, 84, 101, 121, 156-165, 172, 182, 186, 190, 193
Sinkiang-Uighur Autonomous Region, People's Republic of China, *see* Sinkiang
Sino-Indian Agreement of 1954 (*Panch Sheela* Agreement), 85-89, 118, 123, 124, 149
Sino-Indian boundary discussions, 1960, 87, 130, 95
Sino-Japanese War, 29
Sino-Soviet Agreement on Sinkiang, 1960, 161
Sixth Dalai Lama; *see* Dalai, Lama, 6th reincarnation
Skobeleff, General, 29
Solov'ev, V. P., 27
Sonam Gyatso, 5
Song-tsen Gampo, 2, 3, 20, 28
South Vietnam, 199, 200
Soviet Communist Party, 23rd Congress, 204
Soviet-Japanese Aviation Agreement 1966, 204
Soviet-Mongolian Friendship and Defense Treaty, 1966, 204

Soviet-North Vietnam agreement, January, 1966, 204
Soviet-Pakistan relations, 204, 205
Soviet Union, 208, 209, 210; *see also* China, Relations with The Soviet Union; India, Relations with The Soviet Union; Khrushchev, Nikita; Stalin
Soviet Union, Relations with Tibet, 59, 72, 79, 153
Srinagar, 188, 195, 199
Stalin, Joseph, 54, 83, 158, 159, 160
State Council Order, China, 110, 111, 114
Suhrawardi, Prime Minister of Pakistan, 193
Sukarno, Ahmed, 168
Surat, 12, 13

Tachienlu, 10
Taghdumbash-Pamir area, 30
Tan Kuan-san, General, 108, 114-116
Tang Dynasty, 49
T'ao Shih-yeh, 161
Tarbagatai, Treaty of, 26
Tashi, Losang; *see* Losang Tashi
Tashilhunpo, 6, 16, 22, 23
Tashkent, 26
Tashkent Conference, January 1966, 198, 204, 205, 211
Telengana State, India, 215, 216
Teng Hsiao-peng, 185
Tengyeling Monastery, 65
Tenth Panchen Lama; *see* Panchen Lama, 10th reincarnation
Teshoo Lama; *see* Panchen Lama
Tezpur, 112, 113, 120, 169, 172
Thagla Ridge, 166, 169, 206
Thailand, 98
Thant, U, Secretary General, United Nations, 201
Third Dalai Lama; *see* Dalai Lama, Third reincarnation
Third Panchen Lama (Lobsang Paldan Yeshi); *see* Panchen Lama, Third reincarnation
Thirteenth Dalai Lama; *see* Dalai Lama, Thirteenth reincarnation
Thubten Jigme Norbu; *see* Norbu, Thubten Jigme
Ti-song De-tsen, 3
Tibet, Lhasa uprising, 1959, 181, 182, 190
  National Assembly, 55, 64, 78
  Nepal relations, 145, 146
  Preparatory Committee for the Tibet Autonomous Region, 107
  Proclaimed part of the Chinese People's Republic, 46
  Resistance movement, 73, 102-109, 114, 118, 122, 125, 181, 182, 198
  Roads, 74, 82, 141, 171, 172, 178, 182
  Sinoization, 74, 177, 178, 181
  Tibet Autonomous Region, 198
Tito, Marshal (Josip Broz), President of Yugoslavia, 164, 168, 209
Togliatti, Palmiro, 93, 184, 185
Tolstoy, Ilia, 50
Towang, 43
Towang Monastery, 112
Treaty of Tarbagatai, 192
Tribhuvan, King of Nepal, 147, 148
Tsagan Khan, 27, 28
Tsangle, 166
Tsangpo-Brahmaputra River, 42, 52
Tse-wang Rabden, 8, 9
Tsering Dundup, 8, 9
Tsewong-rentzen, Sampo; *see* Sampo Tsewong-Rentzen
Tsong Khapa, 5
Turkey, 98
Turner, Samuel, 13, 22

U-2 Incident, 134
Uganda, 169
Ukhtomskii, Prince, 27
Ulbricht, Walter, 185
United Arab Republic, 97
United Kingdom, 168, 171, 179, 194, 201, 209; *see also* Britain
United Nations, 56-61, 82, 83, 99, 169, 178, 179, 191, 199, 201, 203, 209
  Charter, 98
  Tibet case, 58-61
United States of America, 55, 97, 100, 101, 117, 136, 150, 154, 162, 164, 165, 169, 171, 172, 176, 178-180, 193-196, 198-201, 204, 205, 211
Upper Tartary; *see* Dzungar Mongols

Urgyen, 3, 4, 9, 10
Urgyenist sect (Red Hat sect) Lamaism, 4, 5
USSR; *see* Soviet Union
Uttar Pradesh, 101, 102, 125, 142

Vasil'ev, V. P., 27
Vietminh, 83
Vietnam, 203
Vladivostock, 26
Voice of Kashmir, 197
Voroshilov, Marshal, 138, 158
Vostochniki, 27

Walong, 171, 172
Wang Kuo-chaun, Chinese Ambassador to Poland, 201
Wangchuk, Jigme Dorje, King of Nepal, 214
Watershed principle, boundary delimitation, 154
Wen-ch'eng, Princess, 2, 3
West Bengal State, 216
White Paper I, Government of India, 127, 123
Whiting, Allen S., 160
Williamson, Noel, 44, 45
Witte, Sergei Y., 27
Wu Hsueh ch'uan, General, 58
Wu-je Area (Bara Hoti), 89, 90

Yamdrok Lake, Tibet, 106
Yatung, 64, 65, 84, 88, 182
Yehcheng, 182
Yellow Hat sect, Lamaism (Gelugpa sect), 5, 7, 8
Yeshi, Lobsang Palden; *see* Lobsang Palden Yeshi, 12
Younger, Kenneth, 58
Younghusband, Francis, 34-36, 39, 41, 44, 47, 121
Yuan Shih-kai, 46
Yugoslavia, 164, 165, 168, 209

Zëri i Popullit, 164

Thesis: "traditional" Indo-Chinese friendship based on existence of an independent Tibet as buffer, but with liberation of Tibet, Sino-Indian conflict became inevitable and permanent.

Feb 1950: India engineered revolution in Nepal to secure against possible influence from China. p. 146-147.

Jan 63, Walter Ulbricht: PRC not consult with SU prior to Oct '62 attack against India. p 185 pamir : 30

Kashmir : SU supports Indian claim, 1953-on
p. 192. As Pakistan moves closer to US.

1965: SU adopts more neutral stance on Kashmir
as it pushes to improve rel. with Pakistan,
thwart ↗ PRC influence, & improve rel. with both
India & Pak. p. 197-198

'65 war, common US-SU objectives : p. 201.

Khrush. mediation effort . p. 138

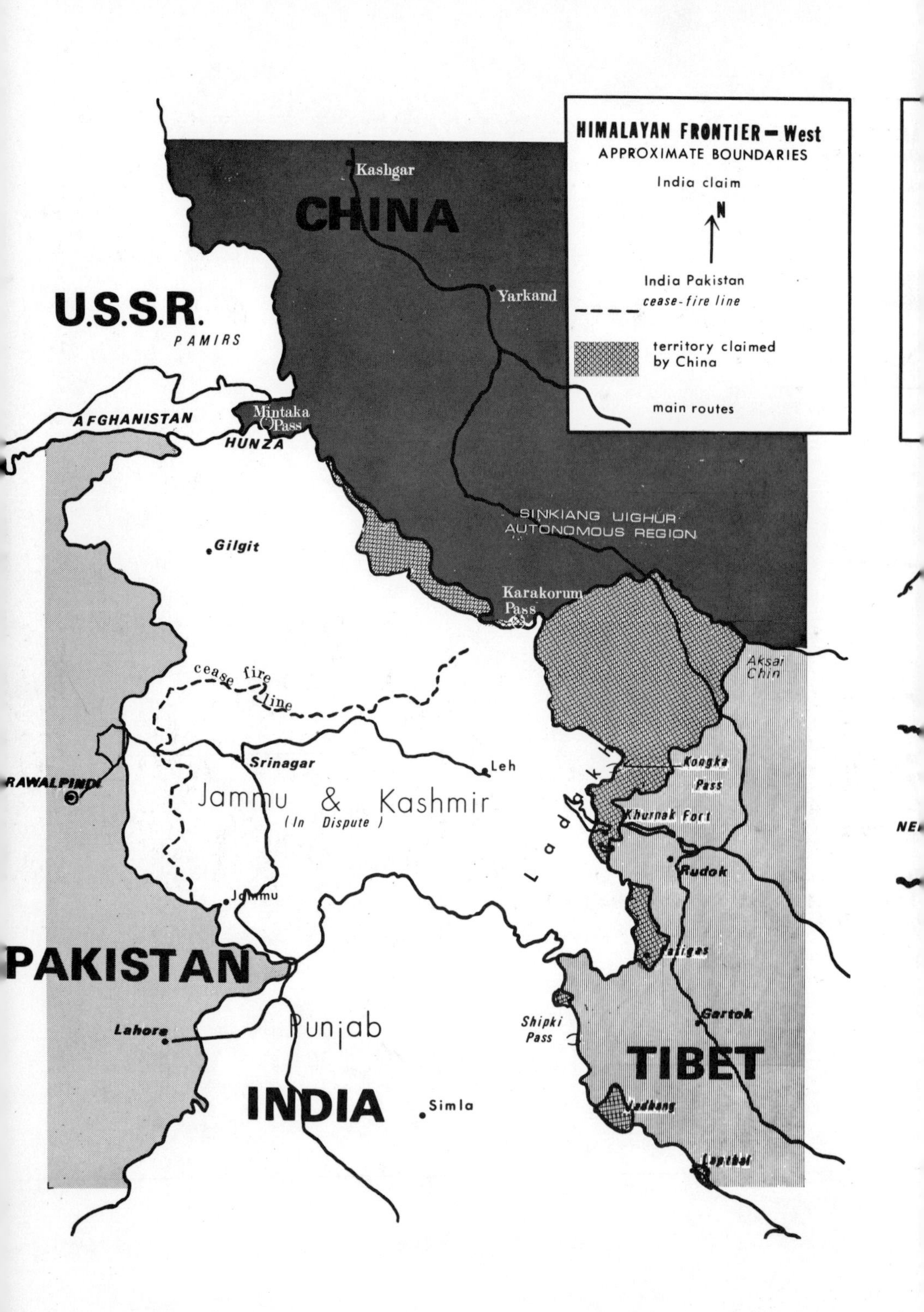
HIMALAYAN FRONTIER — West
APPROXIMATE BOUNDARIES
India claim
N
India Pakistan
cease-fire line
territory claimed by China
main routes
CHINA
Kashgar
Yarkand
U.S.S.R.
PAMIRS
AFGHANISTAN
Mintaka Pass
HUNZA
SINKIANG UIGHUR AUTONOMOUS REGION
Gilgit
Karakorum Pass
Aksai Chin
cease fire line
Srinagar
Leh
RAWALPINDI
Jammu & Kashmir
(In Dispute)
Ladakh
Kongka Pass
Khurnak Fort
Rudok
Jammu
PAKISTAN
Shipki Pass
Gartok
Lahore
Punjab
TIBET
INDIA
Simla